Praise for *Black*

"I treasure this book about a man who was almost famous and the feisty woman who was the love of his life. The story unfolds against a background of rural America as it undergoes decades of important change. The people you'll meet here are extraordinary in their resilience and their passion for each other, their families, and for a life that included enough hard work to have stopped me in my tracks. Brenda Black's writing brings out the adventures, the humor and, best of all, her own palpable affection for Black and Kiddo. Well done."

— **Anne Hillerman**, *New York Times* bestselling author, *Spider Woman's Daughter, Rocks with Wings, Song of the Lion, Cave of Bones*

"This true American saga captures the spirit of the West and makes a music of eternal hope. By the end, Black and Kiddo will feel like kin. A heartening tale thick with humor, honesty, and insight that will deepen your sense of Home."

— **Max Evans**, *The Rounders, The Hi Lo Country*

"Parallel stories of Black and Kiddo merge into a remarkable love story. Love dominates this book—love of land, love of family, love of animals, love of music and art, love of serving others—made even more precious with the sacrifices. Not a religious book by nature, sincere trust in God permeates throughout. Quiet humor, gentle wisdom, life-long passions and dreaming, and an unbelievable strength and courage. 'No tears' was the rule in Kiddo's family but fortunately does not apply to the reader. I sobbed when I read the last line. This book is a treasure."

—**Marilyn H. Collins**, CHS Publishing, *Step-by-Step Writing Guides: Market Yourself, Market Your Book; Memoir Writing Guide*

"The structure is brilliant, the history is fascinating and accurate. The characters are clearly defined and I do love them. Loa is a prize villain. The story flows well, beautifully. And the ending is perfect. Not a dry eye in THIS house!"

—**Linda M. Hasselstrom**, Award-winning South Dakota author, *Gathering from the Grassland, Dakota: Bones, Grass, Sky*

"One of the most human stories I've ever read."

—**Gerald Klingaman, PhD**, University of Arkansas Professor Emeritus, author of *The Civil War Diary of John Klingaman*

BLACK & KIDDO

A True Story of Dust, Determination, and Cowboy Dreams

Brenda Clem Black

Happy Trails!

Brenda Clem Black

et alia
press

For my extraordinary family.

To Russell,
who inherited
his work ethic from both parents,
his mother's verve, and
his father's dreaming.

In memory of my parents,
Lewis and Myrtle Clem,
who understood.

Published in the United States of America by:
Et Alia Press
PO Box 7948
Little Rock, AR 72217
etaliapressbooks@gmail.com
etaliapress.com

CONTENTS

INTRODUCTION

She called him Black. He called her Kiddo.

Keith Leroy Black and Johnnie Dorris McSpadden.

I called them Mom and Pop though they were not my parents. They belonged to my soulmate but treated me as their own. Consummate storytellers, they freely shared their memories, sometimes just for the fun of it but mostly for the lessons learned, to leave those following behind a roadmap to better navigate life's dusty trail.

This compilation is my song to them in gratitude for enriching my life. It is a three-part symphony, composed mostly by me, but the fast-moving allegro comes through Kiddo's spunky writings distilled from forty years of her journals and round-robin letters to her large Scots-Irish family. Black's slice-of-life scrivenings create a calmer adagio. He wrote his childhood memories in longhand on a yellow legal pad when he was in his eighties, focusing each tale on a favorite horse. The stories are here, transcribed as I found them though shortened, labeled "Horses I Have Known," his nod to 1940s author Will James.

I scribed his adult story, writing, among other things, about his stab at Hollywood stardom as a singing cowboy when he "almost" became Roy Rogers. This secret tale Black revealed piecemeal in old age, holding onto a promise he had made to never speak of it. Lacking specific details due to his reluctance, his sojourn is how I imagined this true event happened.

Kiddo interlaced her stories like the yarns she wove into fabric on her antique loom, telling them over and over, until they felt like my own. Her struggle to become a real lady despite dust and deprivation speaks to the long arc of dreams.

Black's and Kiddo's voices speak through me, their words and mine layering to tell the ongoing story of their journey through the twentieth century as they overcome a series of disasters and disappointments. Black and Kiddo didn't dwell on bad times but took life as it came, leaning into love, music, and storytelling to survive the hardships. Isak Dinesen said, "All sorrows can be borne, if you put them into a story."

That is how I have chosen to tell their story, not in 3D, but with rose-colored glasses—much like an old B-Western movie where you are guaranteed a pleasant ride and a happy ending. Songs of the time accompany the reel. If you aren't familiar with the tunes, I hope you'll seek out Roy Rogers, Gene Autry, and others to sing them for you.

If you're lucky, your life can span a century. And if you listen closely to the stories your elders tell, you can absorb parts of another century. Assimilate the stories and you have a sense of the culture that produced someone as unique as yourself. Though you are extraordinary, you are also an ordinary citizen of the specific time and place that you inhabit.

Following America's frontier as it opened, Black's and Kiddo's people had pushed farther west for over two hundred years. The Black (Schwartz) family emigrated from Germany in the mid-1700s, fleeing religious persecution. Stops on their journey west included Pennsylvania, Ohio, Iowa, and Kansas, before they landed in New Mexico shortly after it became a state in 1912.

Before there was a United States of America, Kiddo's ancestral family arrived from County Down in Northern Ireland. The Scots-Irish McSpaddens also pushed west searching for a better life. Their southern route took them from Virginia through the Cumberland Gap and on west to Kentucky, Tennessee, Arkansas, and Texas. During this trek, McSpadden men fought for their freedom and their dreams in the war of their respective generations—Revolutionary, 1812, Mexican-American, Civil, Indian, and eventually the World Wars.

Not all Scots-Irish immigrants stayed in the hills of Appalachia or the Ozarks to become American's hillbillies. Many, like the McSpaddens and Black's mother's family, the Thorntons, moved on with the frontier and populated the West.

By the twentieth century, most of America was settled. In

1890, the director of the U. S. Census Bureau declared that the frontier was closed. The new nation no longer had Frederick Jackson Turner's "safety relief valve" for those individuals seeking freedom and a natural way of life. What do families who have pushed the frontier for 200 years do when it closes?

Cowboy artist Charles M. Russell wrote, "The West is dead,"[1] but there was and still is a lot of West to be experienced. By the time this extraordinary, ordinary couple came into the world around 1920, the cowboy archetype was well engrained in the culture. Black absorbed that ethos as he grew up on the high plains of New Mexico, herding cattle alone amongst majestic buttes and vast grasslands. Kiddo, the daughter of constantly moving West Texas tenant farmers, was imbued with fierce loyalty to family, Texas, and all things "Scotch-Irish."

The Greatest Generation chose to do something, not for recognition or because it was expedient, but because it was the "right thing to do." Coming from survival mode, their dreams were often for their children instead of themselves. Appearance mattered. Hard work was necessary and would be rewarded. Education offered the essential path to "Rise Up." Words like sacrifice, grit, honesty, courage, dignity, and integrity characterized this generation as its members searched for a better life with no distinct frontier left to push toward.

PART I

YELLOW ROSE OF TEXAS

 Folksong from early Colonial Texas. First recorded copy, author unknown, handwritten on plain paper circa 1836, now at University of Texas, Austin. Rewritten and performed by Gene Autry and Jimmy Long, 1933. Performed by Roy Rogers in movie of same name, 1944.

Kiddo
Lubbock, Texas
February, 1940

Dorris McSpadden, spelled with two Rs and two Ds, didn't bother to knock. No one could have heard. Too much noise and too many people. She opened the front door of the prim brick house on 17th Street in the Overton Addition of Lubbock, Texas, and entered. One quick look at the party was enough. She turned right back around and closed the door behind her.

It was a Texas Tech crowd. At twenty-two, she was older than most of them. College was not a consideration. No money. She felt proud and lucky to have graduated Lubbock High when she was twenty, having missed so much school as her family persevered through its *Grapes of Wrath* journey and afterwards, when they lost everything again in the Great Concho River Flood at Ben Ficklin. She was happy to have a decent job clerking at Montgomery Ward. A party was the last thing she needed.

As she turned away and flounced down the porch steps, Dorris admired her new black patent leather pumps, the ones she had chosen to add a bit of height to her short, petite frame. She was tired of people thinking she was still a kid because of her size. The shoes squeezed her feet, but the tiny bow just above the peep toe made up for the pain.

She ran her hand over the bodice of her new dress. The curves of the sweetheart neckline had been hard to sew. Twice she ripped it out and reworked it. She smoothed the gentle gathers at her waist, then touched the soft cotton fabric, the color of bluebonnets, chosen to match her clear Irish eyes. The dress looked perfect when she finished the hem and ironed it yesterday, but tonight it seemed tacky, wrong for this college party, too plain. Some of the college girls wore pants!

Dorris walked briskly down the sidewalk but had second thoughts before she reached the street corner. *Oh, fiddle-de-dee!* She hadn't thanked her cousin Truva for inviting her, even though he'd only done so because some pal asked him to include her. She pivoted on her patent pumps and headed back toward the house, intending to mind the manners her mama had taught her.

"Do you know where Truva is?" she asked a tall blond girl standing in the doorway, her voice screeching its usual high-pitched shrill.

The girl stared at Dorris a little too long before answering, "He's in the kitchen, but I'm not sure you can get through. The living room is jammed. Blackie is about to sing, and everybody's crowding in. You know Blackie?"

"I listen to him on the radio." Dorris smiled, remembering the friend of Truva's, the short kid with the big guitar. She had been in the car with him on several occasions when Truva was hauling them both to different places in his dad's Buick. Blackie was a lot of fun, always smiling, quick with the jokes. A real cowboy, too, roping and trick riding.

"He's going to be in the movies someday. Everybody says so," said the tall blond as she dropped to the floor to sit with her friends. "Sings better than Gene Autry. And he's a whole lot better looking."

Young people draped over the furniture, filled the floor, lined the walls. Dorris sidled along a wall and claimed a leaning spot. Truva appeared from the kitchen, followed by Blackie. The Techies erupted in cheers and applause. Truva cleared someone off the arm of the over-stuffed sofa and motioned Blackie to sit there. The handsome young man sat sideways, one knee raised to cradle his guitar, the other foot on the floor. He looped the wide strap of his Jumbo Gibson Acoustic around his neck, then strummed and hummed and fiddled with the tuning keys until he got the sound just right. He looked up and flashed a relaxed, charming grin to his admirers, who immediately quieted down.

"Think I'll start with 'Tumbling Tumbleweeds.' Feel free to sing along."

No one did. They came to hear him.

Blackie's rich tenor voice filled the room. His fretwork and strumming made it sound like ten guitars working their magic, much better sound than on the radio. Dorris could feel the vibrations of his guitar strings in her bones.

That voice. His voice. Such power it held.

Blackie had changed since she last saw him, more grownup. He was beginning to look like a movie star with that wavy black hair combed back, those piercing eyes, and that grin.

Wow! What a grin! Like he knew some kind of secret.

Dorris pushed her back against the wall and tried to slow her pounding heart. She was mesmerized by the music and by this almost man she almost knew. Would he really be a movie star someday? She told herself to calm down and stop being such a silly goose. She was three years older than him, an old maid compared to these cow-eyed college girls.

Her thoughts briefly drifted to Taylor, the guy she had dated for a year, the good catch. Her sisters thought she was lucky to have such good prospects. Dorris thought they might marry, until Taylor broke it off. Apparently, his family didn't think she was a good catch.

But her heart had never pounded like this for Taylor!

Truva, standing across the room behind Blackie, spied her and waved. She waved back. The motion caused Blackie to glance up from the girls on the floor in front of him and look directly at Dorris, leaning against the wall. She couldn't breathe. It seemed he was looking into her soul. His fathomless dark eyes heated her.

Blackie smiled and gave her a nod, then turned and winked at Truva.

She wished the wink had been hers.

Grinning sideways around the words, he finished the final "*Tum–bl–ing Tummm–ble–weeds.*"

Blackie sang several more songs, the magical sound keeping Dorris pinned to the wall. When he finished, she forced herself to wait for his well-wishers to clear before she moved toward him.

"Hello, Kiddo!" Blackie greeted her.

"Hello, Blackie. Remember me? I'm Dorris, with two Rs, Truva's cousin."

"Of course I remember you, Dorris with two Rs, but I'm gonna call you Kiddo. You look like a Kiddo to me."

Dorris didn't mind the kid reference.

"I reckon that's Kiddo with two Ds, but we're not going to speak of it," Black teased her. "I'm glad you came; I told Truva to invite you."

"Really? That was you?"

"That was me." There was that secret grin again. "And by the way, Kiddo, I'd like you to call me Black."

"I thought everybody called you Blackie."

"You're not everybody."

"Okay, Black."

"Okay, Kiddo. We got ourselves a deal. May I walk you home after the party?"

"Yes, Black." No hesitation.

"What's your favorite song?"

"The Yellow Rose of Texas." Kiddo's face flushed.

"Okay folks, listen up." Black announced in his clear booming voice. "One more song. This one's for Kiddo!"

Black sat on the arm of the overstuffed sofa and sang "The Yellow Rose of Texas," straight into the sparkling eyes of Kiddo, standing beside him in her bluebonnet dress.

There's a yellow rose in Texas that I am going to see

Her eyes are bright as diamonds, They sparkle like the dew

Kiddo
Llano Estacado, Texas
1920s

John McSpadden called his daughters *Little Women* before they were old enough to read the book. There were five girls—Helen, Bernice, Dorris, Dorothy, and Jean—plus two boys. The spunky one smack-dab in the middle was named Johnnie Dorris after her father, but never answered to Johnnie. She was Dorris, spelled with two Rs, long before Black dubbed her Kiddo. Daddy's favorite, she never felt like a left-out middle child.

"Where are my little women?" Daddy John always yelled from the truck when he came home after delivering a load of the sweetest sweet corn, juicy red tomatoes, or luscious watermelons that he had coaxed from the soil. The girls squealed and giggled and raced to be the first to reach him.

"Helen, did the little ones behave? Bernice, did you help Mother?" Daddy started down the list. "Dorothy, Jean, you girls didn't worrit your brothers too much, did you? And where's my feisty Dorris?"

"Here I am, Daddy." She jumped into his arms.

"Oh my, mud pies again? How can such a wee Irish imp get so dirty?"

Big brothers Owen and Cecil didn't have much of a childhood. They worked outside on the truck farm with Dad almost from the time they learned to walk. There was always a field to plow, weeds to pull, vegetables to harvest. They carried the younger girls around on their shoulders and taught them to tie shoes.

The McSpadden children were born all over West Texas, most of them somewhere near Lubbock. Dorris hatched at home, near a tiny town with the silly name of Floydada in Floyd County in 1917. Daddy John didn't own land, so they constantly moved, trying to find a better farm to rent or sharecrop. Sometimes he found a place with enough land to grow cotton or wheat, which brought more money than vegetables. People called them tenant farmers.

Moving wasn't a problem. The family had few belongings. But there was one treasured possession that accompanied them everywhere: Mother's trunk. It held the vestiges of her genteel life in Alabama when she was Ida Berry, before Daddy, before seven children, before the West Texas sun.

Nearly every day, Dorris begged to look in the trunk.

"Not today, honey, too much to do," Mama usually answered. But once in a while, a gentle smile brightened her weather-lined face and she relented.

"You girls wash up first and wait for me to finish my chores. Don't open it until I get there." She didn't have to say that. Dorris and her sisters would never open the lid without her, held back by respect for the wondrous contents of the trunk, remnants of a different life, a life they could only dream of.

"Show us the blue gown first, Mama." Helen loved the smooth satin dress with the full hoop skirt and ruched bodice.

With work-worn hands Mama carefully removed the tissue paper from the folds, then lifted the long gown from the trunk and held it up to her still-slim body. "Who wants to try it on?"

"Me!" "Me!" "Me!" The girls all yelled at once.

"Helen, you're the oldest, you first. Bernice, would you like to try the yellow one? Jean, this green one is shorter. Dorothy, who do you want to be today? Here's a lovely silk blouse with beads."

"Can I try the gloves, Mama?" Dorris impatiently interrupted.

"Yes. Let me help you pull them on."

The long white elbow gloves reached up to Dorris's armpits, transforming her into a queen.

The trunk gave up its treasures: delicate lace shawls, fabric shoes with ribbon ties, hair combs, dance cards, and hats! Each dress had a matching millinery hat with swooping brim and flowing ribbons. Hours passed playing dress-up with Mother's fine things and poring over the pictures of life as a lady, a *real* lady.

By the side of that trunk, wearing long white gloves and a soldier blue hat trimmed with feathers, Dorris resolved she would be a lady someday.

"Tell us again, Mama," she begged, "about how you got to ride on a train and the trunk rode with you."

"The trunk and I rode that big train all the way to Oklahoma Territory from Birmingham, Alabama, a big city in the true South. I lived there with my uncle, the General, when I was a little girl like you."

"Start at the beginning, when you were born in Tennessee," Bernice said.

Ida Berry told her story to her children, over and over again, always beginning with the same sentence:

"My mother was a Cunningham, Sarah Helen Cunningham," she began, "raised on the Cunningham Plantation near Viola, Tennessee, in a big brick house with white columns. Her family farmed acres and acres of land. When she grew up, my mother married Green Jefferson Berry."

The girls giggled. "Did grandpa eat green berries?"

"No, that was just his name. Green Berry sounds funny though, doesn't it? Sarah Helen married Green, my father, against the wishes of her family, who thought she could do better. But she was happy and bore a daughter and four sons, and then . . ."

"You were born," Jean shouted.

"That's right. December 1888. They named me Ida Esta Berry, after two aunts."

Mama quieted her voice for the next part. "One day, my Papa was gone, and the older kids were at school. My mother took me out to the back porch to get water from the hand-dug well. I was wrapped in blankets and put in a basket. She backed away making funny faces and babbling baby sounds. Then she tripped over the casing and fell into the well."

"But she didn't drown," Dorothy helped with the story.

"No, she treaded water and propped herself against the side of the well until Papa came home and got her out. But it was winter. The water was ice cold. She caught pneumonia and became very sick. After a while, she died."

"Were you sad? Did you cry?" Bernice asked.

"I was just a baby, Bernice, but I'm sure I missed her. My Papa was sad. He didn't know what to do. Things were changing all over the South. There was so much loss after the Great War between the States. With no slaves to work the fields, the old plantations were falling on hard times. Besides, the Cunninghams didn't like Papa, so he decided to go way out west to make a new life on the frontier."

"But you were too little," a deep voice chimed in. Long, lanky Cecil stood in the open doorway smelling like sweat and soil. He had unlatched the galluses on one side of his bib overalls and left his muddy work boots on the porch. One of his big toes peeped through a hole in his sock.

"Cecil, I didn't hear you come in. Dinnertime already?" Mama asked.

"We finished the north field early. Dad and Owen are bringing the truck around," Cecil said as he plopped onto the floor beside the girls. "Go ahead with the story, Ma. I haven't heard it in a while. You were too little . . ." he cued her.

"I was just a baby," Mama continued. "Five big kids were enough to take care of and Papa didn't know where he might end up, so he gave me to my mother's oldest sister and her husband who had fought in the Civil War, General Tom Garretson. They had no children and lived in a two-story brick house in Birmingham with a big porch across the front. Good people, monied. My aunt died when I was still young, leaving me motherless again. But the old General raised me as his own. I attended a finishing school for girls where I learned proper manners, how to set a fine table, and how to dress like a lady. I had a coming-out cotillion, a fancy ball where I wore the deep blue dress you love so much, Helen, and the hat with the feather that you always grab, Dorris."

"What kind of feather is it?"

"Probably pheasant." Mama was patient with questions.

"Did you keep your dress and hat in the trunk?"

"No, Dorris, my dresses were hung in a tall chifferobe. The General gave me this big steamer trunk when I came west. Papa and the four boys built a half-dugout on the remote plains in Oklahoma Territory, north of the Texas border, then known as No-Man's Land."

"Why did they call it No Man's Land?" Cecil asked.

"Nobody claimed it. It belonged to no man. Texas and Kansas had already achieved statehood, but neither wanted to be responsible for this big strip of nothing that lay between them, just wild barren plains, a few rolling hills, Indian land. No laws, since it wasn't part of any state, and no one to enforce them. No Man's Land eventually became the Oklahoma Panhandle when they made Oklahoma a state in 1907. When my people lived there, it was wild and rough. My older sister Mary kept house for Papa and the boys for a while, but then she got married. That's when Papa sent for me because he and my brothers needed a cook and housekeeper. So, I packed all my pretty dresses and hats into this big trunk . . ."

"And the book," Dorris interjected, holding the worn copy of *Little Women* high above her head.

"Yes, I put my favorite book in the trunk, too. That was way before I had a passel of little women of my own."

"Read it to us, Mama?"

"Dorris, hush," Cecil said. "Let her finish one tale before you beg her for the next." He pulled his little sister to his lap and wrapped his arms around her. "Go ahead, Ma."

"The General put me and the trunk on the train. I was sixteen years old, 1905. I left my fancy house in the middle of Birmingham and arrived at a small dugout in Indian Territory, near where Texhoma is now though there sure wasn't a town there then, not many people at all. Not many trees, either. The wind never stopped blowing. Dust filled the air. Papa and my brothers were gone for days at a time, leaving me by myself. They were hunting or trading for horses, or who knows what men do? I was lonely. Months passed without my seeing any other women. Sometimes a wagon came by taking a family further west and stopped for water at our well. If they looked friendly, I would go talk to them and offer what help I could.

"Other times, bands of Indians came through. They scared me. Usually they didn't come to the well, but once a large group slowly rode past on their horses, wearing full headdresses and paint on their faces. When I saw them stop at the well, then turn toward the house, I hid in a hole in the bottom of the dugout, under a trap door. Papa had told me to do that if I was frightened, and I used the hidey hole a lot. That day, I lay there shaking, afraid to breathe. I could hear footsteps on the wood boards above my head."

The thought of her mother hiding from Indians was too much for Dorris, and she started to cry.

"No tears," Mama said. "Remember, strong women don't cry. We take things as they come. They didn't find me. I didn't get hurt."

Dorris snuffed it up quick. She didn't want Mama to think she wasn't a strong woman.

About that time, Daddy John's old truck came clanking down the rutted road. Helen ran to the door. "Uh-oh, here come Dad and Owen and we don't have dinner ready."

"Girls, you can't go out in the dirt in those dresses when your father calls. Hide and surprise him."

The truck door slammed and Daddy yelled in his big booming voice, "Where are my little women?"

The girls giggled and hid behind each other and put their hands over their mouths to keep from laughing out loud.

"Little women?" he yelled again. "Where is everybody? I don't smell food." The screen door slapped shut.

"In the bedroom, John," Mama called out, sweet as cane syrup.

Dad stepped through the bedroom door, followed closely by his oldest son, Owen.

Mama had thrown a rose-colored silk shawl gracefully across her bodice and presented her girls with a long, slow swoop of her hand.

"The McSpadden little women," she announced. Six lovely females bowed and curtsied in their elegant attire.

In her white silk blouse with beaded sleeves, prissy Dorothy put her hands on her hips and turned her head sideways in a dramatic pose of attempted elegance. Jean looked like a green pumpkin with emerald *peau de soie* puffed up around her small body. Dorris stood in her flour-sack calico shorts with a pheasant-feathered hat on her head, long white gloves up to her armpits, and red brocade shoes pulled over dirty feet with ribbon ties crisscrossed up to the knees.

"Sir," she said, offering her father the back of an outstretched gloved hand.

His red face mightily fought Mother's No-Tears Rule as he kissed the back of her hand. "This is the finest group of women I've ever seen," he finally muttered.

The little women beamed and ran to hug his tall legs.

"Okay, girls," Mama said, "let's get everything back in the trunk. We have to fix dinner for the men."

"You didn't tell the part about the Good Samaritan yet." Dorris clamored for more.

"John?" Mama asked Daddy for the final word.

"Oh, all right. Finish the story while the girls take these things off and get them back in the trunk. Then we've got to stop all this palaver and get to some serious eating. We got fields to plow."

All nine McSpaddens sat or leaned around the small bedroom, its only furnishings the iron-framed bed, a small chest of drawers and the trunk. Hooks on the wall held Mama's cotton print dresses, Daddy's worn khaki shirts and his old suit that no longer fit, kept for Owen. A drab room getting drabber as the colorful dresses disappeared into the trunk. Dorris snuggled into Cecil, settling down to hear the last part, her favorite part, the part that made them a family.

"One day when I was alone at the dugout," Mama continued, "three young men came to the well. They saw me at the window and hollered to ask if they could get water. They were talking and kidding each other, and I could tell they were good men. I figured I was safe, so I went out to visit with them. They were brothers and lived down south of Fort Worth in Bosque County, Texas, and had come to No Man's Land to buy horses."

"That was Daddy and Uncle Jesse and Uncle Frank," Cecil interjected.

"We know," Helen said. "Daddy was one of seven brothers and had seven sisters. And way back his family came from Ireland, same as Mama's Berrys and Cunninghams."

"Well, my people were in Scotland first, the Isle of Mull," Daddy corrected. "That's where the Mc in McSpadden comes from. Then in the 1600s, the King of England moved our clan to County Down, Ireland, during the Plantation of Ulster. He wanted to thin out the native Catholics, so he took over their land and forced Protestants to move there. That's why we are Scotch-Irish, both. But the McSpaddens have been Americans about as long as anybody has. We followed the frontier west through the Cumberland Gap, through Virginia, Tennessee, and Arkansas to Texas. Always love America, kids. It's the best country there is, but never forget your heritage either. Scotland and Ireland and Texas. Always be proud to be a Texan."

Mama continued her saga. "The boys at the well hadn't eaten in a while, so I heated them some beans and cornbread, and we visited. Then they rode on north looking for horses. A few days later, they stopped back by and I cooked for them again. One of them, the one named John . . ." Mother widened her eyes and raised her eyebrows, ". . . asked the others to step outside."

The girls grinned and kicked their feet because they knew what came next.

"Then John asked me to marry him," Mother smiled and looked at Daddy.

He turned toward her. "She was the prettiest thing I had ever laid eyes on, so refined, and she could cook. I couldn't take any chances one of my brothers would beat me to her."

"John was tall and handsome and had kind eyes, so I said yes."

This was the part Dorris liked best, when her parents looked at each other like that, a look that filled her up.

"But I knew Papa wanted me there with him," Mama went on, "so we made plans to leave before he got back. John's brothers took the horses on to Texas, except for the ones he traded for a wagon. We loaded my trunk onto the buckboard and took off." She patted the top of the big steamer trunk.

"I left a note for Papa. It said: *I am gone to be married, Ida Berry.*"

"But we couldn't find anybody to marry us," Daddy took up the story. "We rode southeast through the panhandle of Texas and over into southwest Oklahoma, trying to find a preacher or justice of the peace. Finally, at the end of the third day, we found a judge in Mangum, Oklahoma, who had authority to marry people, so we went to his house. Your mama opened up that trunk and pulled out one of them fancy dresses."

"The blue one," Mother said. "The judge's wife had to help me with those tiny buttons in the back. She asked me where I got that fine dress. I told her about my mama falling in the well and the General and Papa and the dugout on the plains. She felt sorry for me being motherless and talked to me a long time about the birds and the bees. She insisted we stay with them that night, instead of at the hotel above the saloon. John had money to pay, but she said that place wasn't fit for a proper wedding night. She gave me one of her best nightgowns."

Dorris sneaked a peek at her older sisters, Helen and Bernice, who had already heard the birds and bees talk. She didn't dare look at the boys.

"Next morning, the judge's wife cooked us biscuits and gravy," Mama continued as she reached into the trunk. "She gave me this Bible. She had marked places in it, where it told how to be a good wife and mother. My favorite was Proverbs 31. She told me I would be all right, if I read that and did what the Good Book said."

"She was the Good Samaritan, right Mama?" Jean asked.

"That's what your daddy called her. I think she was an angel." Mama said. "See, I wrote your names and the dates and places you were born in the Bible she gave me."

"Read us where it says virtshush woman and the rubies. What are rubies?"

"Not now, Dorris," Daddy answered. "We'll read scripture some other day. *Virtuous* means really good. Rubies are red jewels worth a lot of money, and your mother is worth more than all the rubies in the world, especially when she cooks. I'm starving. Close the trunk down, girls."

"And that's the end of the story." Dorris stood up, ready for food.

"It was really the beginning of a story," Mama said, "the story of all of you."

RED SHOES

Kiddo
San Angelo, Texas
1920s

"Dorris, it's your turn to get new shoes. You've come out the toes of those. We'll find a nice pair today and have the storekeeper save them back," Mama announced as all nine McSpaddens clambered off the big farm truck onto the streets of San Angelo one Saturday morning. "Mr. Brockmeier is coming to pay for his load of watermelons tomorrow, so we'll have a little money."

"Goody, goody, goody!" Dorris blurted and clapped her hands. She hated the pinching brown clunkers she was wearing. These would be her first new shoes. Hand-me-downs from sisters or used ones selected from the church closet had served her well for her first eleven years.

Most of the merchants trusted John McSpadden and let the family charge goods when he told them he had pay coming. But not the merchant that sold shoes. No money, no merchandise.

"Can I pick them out?" Dorris asked.

"Helen and I will help you," Mama said. "They have to be sturdy so they'll last. We'll get them a size or two up. They'll feel too big at first."

They walked down the wood sidewalk and reached Bennett's General Store. Among the small display of shoes in the window was a pair of bright red espadrilles with cloth ties. Dorris's mouth dropped open.

"I want those, Mama! They look like the ones in your trunk, the red ones with the ribbons!"

"Dorris honey, how can you be so impractical? Those are only for summer. They won't last two months the way you run through mud puddles. Absolutely not. You need solid year-round shoes."

"But they're red. I love red. Can I just try them on, please? Please, Mama?"

Helen shushed her little sister, grabbed her hand, and pulled her into the store. Dorris sat on a small stool, saying nothing as her mother pushed black or brown oxfords onto her feet and mashed the front of the shoe to find her big toe. Finally, Mama settled on the right pair and asked the storekeeper to hold them until they returned on Monday with the cash.

"I won't be here Monday but my wife will," Mr. Bennett said, as he stored the sturdy shoes behind the counter.

"Mama, can I just try the red ones? I know I can't have them but I just want to see them on my feet. Please? Like when we play dress-up with the trunk?" Dorris begged but stopped the tears about to tumble. Those would make her mama mad.

"Oh, all right," she relented, "Helen can help you put them on while I get a few things. But don't get them dirty."

Helen made perfect bows at the front of the ankles with the red ties. Feeling like a real lady, Dorris spun around and around, so fast that the skirt of her feed-sack dress formed a little circle. Then she walked on tip-toes, thrusting her chin into the air, not taking the red shoes off until the very last ounce of Mama's patience wore out.

She thought about those shoes all day Sunday as she fed and watered the chickens and gathered eggs. It was her turn to dry as Bernice washed dishes after supper, but she didn't chatter like a magpie as she normally did. She was thinking. *Thinking*.

Monday morning, Mama gave the exact amount of money to Helen.

"Why can't I carry the money? They're my shoes," Dorris asked.

"Because you're too little and too careless. You'll lose it," Helen said. She wagged her finger. "Money doesn't grow on trees, you know. I'll meet you at lunch and we'll walk to the store."

Dorris's lips puffed out in a big pout, but she knew the order of things.

Owen, her oldest brother, set the magneto, then turned the crank to start the old panel van that served as a school bus. The van belonged to the school but lived at the McSpadden house. Owen fixed it himself when it broke down, which happened often. He didn't have a driver's license, but no one minded. When he got it going, seven McSpaddens climbed in. Then Owen picked up kids from two more large boisterous families, cramming them onto two lengthwise bench seats and in the floor like watermelons in Daddy's farm truck.

Dorris sat quietly all the way to school as the old van rollicked across the rolling west Texas knolls. *Thinking.*

At mid-morning recess, she was done thinking. She told her teacher that she needed to pick up a package. Batting her eyes and flashing a coy grin, she told the storekeeper's wife that her sister Helen was coming on lunch break to bring the money for the red espadrilles Dorris had placed on the counter.

"Pretty shoes. I love red myself," Mrs. Bennett said. "But what shall I do with the brown oxfords my husband saved back?"

Dorris shrugged her shoulders. It was enough of an answer for Mrs. Bennett. She laughed as she tore off a wide sheet of butcher paper and began to package the red espadrilles. "You're going to be in trouble, young lady."

"I know."

Dorris ran behind the row of stores and found a back stoop to sit on. Unwrapping the package, she handled the precious red shoes as if they were glass. She carefully slipped them on her feet after whisking dust from her toes. The fabric ribbons proved difficult, but she tied them into the best bows she could muster.

Leaving the old clunkers and butcher paper on the stoop, she skipped proudly down the dirt road back to school. Townspeople were looking at her, commenting to themselves about how much of a lady she had become, she could just tell. But when she reached the school-yard, big sis Helen stood waiting, a scowl across her face.

The store didn't take back worn shoes. Everybody knew that.

There was a spanking at the end of that day, which Dorris expected. It hurt less than the look of disappointment in her mother's eyes. She thought she detected a slight grin from her daddy but couldn't be sure.

When she wasn't bare-footed, Dorris avoided mud puddles and wore the red shoes until they fell from her feet in tatters. She pranced like a lady with each step, as her mother had pranced in Birmingham, and never regretted her first taste of power.[2]

HORSES I HAVE KNOWN
BY KEITH L. BLACK

Des Moines, New Mexico
1920s

SARCH

How he got that name, I never knew; but he was a real cow horse and one of Dad's all-time favorites. He was a cold blood, out of a mustang mare and sired by a Crosselle Ranch stud. You could read his pedigree just by looking at him: feathery fetlocks, broom tail, long sloping flat rump, and the hind legs of a greyhound. Up front his appearance changed drastically: stout front legs supporting a wide deep chest. He had stamina to spare, along with the intelligence and athletic ability far above the average range horse.

Sarch and Dad, as a team, came to be in demand in handling "rough stock" on the open range of Northeast New Mexico. If someone had a bad mean bull, or a wild unmanageable cow, they usually called in Corwin Black and Sarch.

In the fall of 1917, a man named Jim Fox was buying up cattle around Des Moines. The ranchers and nesters would bring their cattle to the railroad stock pens where they were weighed and bought.

Dad and Fred Caukins had the job of holding the herd as they accumulated on the open country around town. They would pen the cattle at night in the stock yards, move them out next morning to water at the buffalo-waller water holes in the draw north of the pens, then loose-herd them as they grazed throughout the day.

One evening when they brought the herd to the pens, there were three or four Mexican cowboys there. They were telling Mr. Fox that they were short one cow that was so wild and mean, they couldn't get her off Sierra Grande.

Next morning, the herd was just out of the gate when one of those old Mexican cows with horns about four feet wide threw her head up and headed back south through town toward the mountain in a wide-eyed, rattle-hocked run. Dad jumped old Sarch up by her side and continued to run her shoulder, but she wouldn't turn.

When she hit the concrete sidewalk, her feet flew out from under her and down she came, flat on her side. Dad figured she must have cracked her skull because she just lay there, eyes rolled back, trembling and jerking. He climbed down and walked around in front of her and kicked her on the nose. Up she came and took after him, those long sharp horns flashing like new steel in the sun! He made a fast lap around his horse, gaining just enough distance and time to mount ole Sarch.

The cow charged around, threshing the air with her horns, trying to regain her bearings. Then the old critter took off down through the houses and shacks heading southwest through town. Somewhere down near where Joe Marques lived, she spotted a man out by a small adobe house chopping wood and charged him with a full head of steam.

Dad yelled at him to get in the house, even though he thought it was too late, and it would have been if the cow had not become tangled up in a clothesline full of clothes. But she still had her red eyes on that hombre. He raised his axe and swung at her, then dropped the axe and ran. The door to the little adobe house was open and as he ran in, he slammed it shut with a loud bang. The next instant there came a louder BANG as about twelve inches of horn slammed through the door. The other horn sunk into the mud joint between two adobe blocks.

While she was disengaging her horns, Dad had time to get his catch rope down and he started to warp her hide to the extent that the cow decided to run instead of fight. Fred came along with the herd and she joined them willingly.

Dad said he then understood why the vaqueros had left one wild bad cow on the mountain and should have left TWO!

Corwin Black on Sarch, 1917.

BIG PAINT and LITTLE PAINT

The Potts family lived down on the lower Cimarron in a side canyon extending north into Colorado. They ran a sizable herd of horses which Mrs. Potts, part Kiowa Indian, had inherited from the Indian tribe that had once lived in the area.

My cousin Jack Thornton's close friendship with the Potts boys resulted in him being given his choice of the 2-year-old geldings of the herd. He picked a fine, high-spirited black and white pinto, which later turned out to be too high-spirited for Jack. The result was that the horse was turned back in with the herd, where he ran wild for the next two and a half years.

Dad was working at the Baker Ranch at the time, 1925, and Jack asked Dad to bring the horse up to the ranch and break him, with the understanding that Dad use him as his own. Jack never came for the horse, so old Paint became part of the family. He developed into one heck of a cow horse: fast enough for any ranch job, strong enough for heavy rope work, and later, gentle enough to be trusted with kids.

While Dad was looking through the herd of Indian ponies, he

23

noticed a small red and white spotted mare about ten years old. She was already broke to ride and very gentle, so he made a deal for her and returned home with Big Paint and Little Paint.

Dad started me out learning to ride on this little paint mare. I was four years old. He went to great pains to teach me to ride by balance: no saddle, no stirrups, no surcingle. Only a hand full of mane in extreme emergency. I had to learn to shift my weight to accommodate the movement of the horse. Soon I became able to anticipate the movement beforehand. This was invaluable in my keeping a leg on each side and my mind in the middle.

All of this was done slowly, with Dad on the lead shank and moving with the mare just close enough that he could reach me, just in case: first walking, then trotting, then turning. After a few months of this, I was graduated to a saddle. No saddle horn to interfere with my natural balance, and of course covered stirrups which only had room for the fore part of my foot. Thus, in case of a fall, my entire foot could not become ensnared and result in my being dragged. About the only advantage of the saddle was that it made mounting the mare easier, and that's a real consideration for a short-legged kid who was barely over three feet tall.

Little Paint and I developed a real friendship in the months and years that followed. She had the patience of a saint and seemed to have a special sense of responsibility that bailed me out of a lot of tight spots.

Keith Black atop Little Paint.

BIG PAINT

In Northeastern New Mexico, land was not opened up for settlement until about 1910, statehood in 1912. The people who pioneered there filed on government claims of 160 to 320 acres of bare land. No houses, no fences, no wells. Very few scattered small towns. They arrived by covered wagons and drove a few cows. Before that the land was in "open range," used by very large ranches for cattle and sheep raising.

The earliest settlers had already grabbed land that had water, creeks, springs, lakes, etc. So, the now "free" land was just that, land. In the early days as you drove through the country and came upon a campsite, you could tell if they were moving in (scattered tin cans) or moving out (rabbit hides). To qualify for a claim, first you had to locate suitable land not already taken, pay a filing fee, and sign the necessary agreement to:
- Build a house (small shack).
- Plow or "break out" and plant a crop on a required number of acres.
- Mark the boundaries and partially, at least, fence.
- Live on the place a certain number of months per year for a certain number of years.

If you fulfilled these obligations, you filed notice with the land office, with witnesses. Then you were awarded a deed to your land and were on your way to "happily ever after."

That area of New Mexico should never have been plowed up, as we finally learned after it was too late. The high altitude, which limited the variety of crops, as well as the scanty rainfall (14–16 inches annual average), and the short growing season (just over 90 days). If those drawbacks were not enough, then the hard winters with blizzards would finish you off.

At the time I was growing up, life there was still quite primitive. We rented and were living on the Bassett place four miles east of Des Moines in 1929, milking cows and farming enough land to raise most of the feed for the cows. As most other farmers in the area, we depended on the money derived from the sale of cream from these cows to furnish food and clothing for the family, as well as milled feed such as wheat bran for the cows and corn chops for the work horses.

The cream that paid the bills was obtained by the milking of ten to fifteen cows. This was done twice a day. The milk was separated by means of a hand-cranked cream separator, which had to be taken apart and washed after each use. The cream went into a shipping can (five or ten gallons) and the skim milk was carried in buckets, some fed to calves and some to hogs, chickens, etc. When the shipping cans were full, they were loaded in a wagon and driven to the railroad station to be shipped to Denver, Colorado (Gold Coin Creamery). While at the station you gathered up the cream cans from the previous shipments, then on to the post office to get your cream check. Next stop, the general store for groceries, cow feed, kerosene for the lanterns and lamps.

We had a pretty good crop there in 1929 when I was eight years old. The big field ran a quarter of a mile wide and half a mile long, along the top of a ridge up north of the house. The millet was knee high and waved in the breeze. Mother happened to look out the window and saw that the cows were in the field, trampling the millet. It would be useless to try to get them out by running them on foot.

The only horse we had up in the corral was Dad's Big Paint. There was no way I could climb that tall horse without help. I got him bridled. Mother and Sister boosted me up on him. I dug my bare heels into his ribs as he carried me up the lane to where the cows had broken off a fence post and pushed another one over. The barbed wire laid on the ground, but I had no trouble getting Big Paint across it into the field.

Whooping and yelling like a Comanche, I circled the cows, got them in a bunch and headed them for the hole in the fence. They ran out of the field and into the lane without much trouble.

When old Paint came to the wire again, he balked. I thumped him with my heels and coaxed him, but he wouldn't get closer than about six feet from the wire. I circled him and came back: same thing. He wouldn't budge.

I slid down off him, and thought I'd do like I'd seen Dad do at times. Stand on that broken post, hold the wire down, and lead him over. I was walking backwards and tugging on the bridle reins when I felt something cold under my bare feet. Then I heard it. A rattlesnake! I screamed and held onto those reins with a death grip. Big Paint reared backwards as I jumped and jerked me clear of the snake.

Then I went up the side of that big tall horse without any help of any kind.

RABBIT EARS

Kiddo
Clayton, New Mexico
Late 1920s

One summer afternoon when the family was farming near Muleshoe, Texas, a dust cloud on the dirt road foretold a big black car that pulled up to the house. The driver, a man in a suit, asked to speak with John McSpadden. Dorris's mama sent her and her sisters to retrieve their father and brothers from the fields. The men gathered at the kitchen table, girls relegated outside. Hip to hip with her sisters, Dorris peered through the window, watching the confab. Owen got his pencil and Big Chief tablet and started figuring. This man must have a farm he wanted to rent.

After he left, they learned it wasn't a farm the man offered but a bona fide job. He wanted Dad to help him sell land in what he described as an up-and-coming boom town. Dad's reputation as hard-working, honest, and fair was above reproach. The job meant a regular paycheck each month, plus a bonus when he sold property. As an added incentive, the man threw in the use of a two-story house big enough to hold the whole family.

Daddy and Mama called this enterprise a cakewalk compared to truck farming even though it meant leaving Texas, barely. The town was Clayton, New Mexico, about ten miles over the Texas border just northwest of Texline on Highway 87.

"If we stop farming, the kids can go to school every day and get their diplomas," Mama said. Her dream was for her children to be educated.

After the crops were sold in Texas, they loaded the trunk and other belongings onto the farm truck and chased a better life on the high plains of Clayton, New Mexico. The family spread out in the roomy house provided by their daddy's new employer and walked to school that fall. Truck farming days were over.

Some of Mama's Berry family still lived near Texhoma on the border between Texas and Oklahoma. Mama had made peace with them long ago. Family is family, even those with warts, and that means visiting. Closer now, Grandpa Green Berry came often. Trim and short with silver hair, he was a perfect leprechaun. Boy, could he dance the Irish jig, especially when he had nipped poteen from the little jug he carried with him. At the end of a tune, he jumped into the air and clicked his heels together. Dorris thought he was magic. He taught his grandkids old Irish ditties like "When Irish Eyes Are Smiling" and "Too Ra Loo Ra Loo Ral." The tunes looped in their minds long after he went home.

West of Clayton, over forty miles of hard-packed caliche road, sat a small town called Des Moines, New Mexico. A boy of about eight years old lived there. Out on the lonely open range, he sat on his horse and tended grazing cattle, singing hymns and cowboy songs to pass the time while he dreamed his dreams. It would be another decade before Dorris met that boy, in Lubbock, still singing those songs, another decade before he would name her Kiddo.

Daddy John's good looks and honest face helped him sell land. For a while, there was a bit of ease in his lined face. "I'm finally making something of myself" became his mantra. Soon he traded the old farm truck for a car. Dark green, four doors, 1929 Hudson. He practically beat on his chest every time he got in that big car, which was a lot. Sometimes he took the family for a drive to see some land he had sold. Sometimes they drove to nowhere at all, just for the pleasure of being in the car. He demonstrated how easily it accelerated and shifted, how it took the rare curves on the high desert roads.

One day after a big land deal, he put the whole family in the Hudson and drove to the fancy Eklund Hotel and Saloon downtown, though it was plenty close enough to walk. The Eklund had been around for a long time, since cowboy and Indian days, and everyone in Clayton seemed mighty proud of it. The rose-colored crushed velvet seats in the lobby looked like something a lady might have in her parlor. Daddy John treated everyone to ice cream, an Eklund specialty made by their cook. Dorris loved sitting at that round table in the dark dining room, eating her scoops of chocolate out of a frosty footed bowl. Yummy chocolate also for Dorothy and Jean. Strawberry for Mama, Helen, and Bernice. Vanilla for Daddy, Owen, and Cecil.

That was a fine day.

Since moving, Dorris had been captivated by a mountain northwest of Clayton. Dramatically rising over six thousand feet and sporting two peaks, Rabbit Ears was a landmark in the old days for wagon trains on the Cimarron Cutoff of the Santa Fe Trail and for cowboys moving cattle on the Goodnight-Loving Trail.

As she'd begged her mother to try on red shoes, Dorris pestered Daddy John to take her and her sisters there, but he didn't get around to it. One day he gave her, Dot (what Dororthy renamed herself about this time), and Jean a nickel apiece. Dorris instigated a secret plan to buy grape soda pops and take them out to Rabbit Ears for a private picnic.

The girls started the journey after lunch, giving up precious nickels to the filling-station man as he pulled the cold bottles from the icy water and popped the tops. Jean wanted to drink hers right then, but Dorris made her wait. The three girls walked and walked and walked toward that mountain, across the short native grass and malpais in the hot New Mexico sun, dodging red ant hills and razor-edged bear grass. Rabbit Ears didn't get any closer.

Jean tripped and fell, spilled her grape, and began to cry.

"No tears," Dorris was quick to remind her. "We must be strong women. Stop crying and I'll give you half of mine when we get there."

Dot rebelled, "It's too far, Dorris! The grapes aren't even cold anymore."

"Yeah, you're not the boss of us. Let's go back," Jean threw in her two cents.

"Gee fuzz! I'm with a bunch of wimps," Dorris said. "Okay, we'll take a rest."

They sat down on the ground in that vast, wide-open plain, wiped the sweat and Jean's tears with their skirts, and shared two hot grape pops. Then they lay back on the ground and called out animal shapes in the pillowy white clouds drifting through the clear blue sky. Dorris stretched her leg skyward and used her red-shod foot as a pointer.

Before she could say *Jack Rabbit*, she drifted into dreams. When she woke, she found they'd all fallen asleep. The sun had baked their tender faces but was gone from the sky. Only the dusky silhouette of the town could be seen across the plains.

"Run!" Dorris said. They jumped up and ran as fast as they could, stopped to breathe, and ran some more, ignoring the leg-scratches from the bear grass. Clayton disappeared into the darkness.

"Daddy says snakes come out at night," Dot said, the words taking the little breath she had. "I'm scared."

"We'll be okay," Dorris replied, halting and bringing her Daddy's little women to a standstill. "Come here. Let's hold hands so no one gets lost in the dark."

She pulled Dot and Jean to her. A lone coyote's howl echoed across the plains. They held each other tighter. A family rule declared the oldest child in any given group as being the one in charge. Dorris's mantle of responsibility weighed heavy. She had to figure this out. Though Mama's No-Tears Rule echoed in her ears, she couldn't stop the tears from rolling down her cheeks, and soon three young girls were boo-hooing with abandon.

Then bouncing lights appeared on the horizon, getting larger and larger. They heard the roar of an engine and realized it was Daddy John's big Hudson racing across the malpais. Dot and Jean yelled and waved their arms, but Dorris froze. How bad would the punishment be for almost losing her sisters? Whatever it was, she deserved it.

Dad, Owen, and Cecil jumped out of the car and grabbed them up in big hugs. The filling-station guy had overheard them talking about Rabbit Ears. No one was observing Mama's No-Tears Rule and when the family arrived home, Mama broke it herself.

That night the girls got good food, mercurochrome on their leg scratches, and butter on their sunburned faces, but the next day Dorris was scolded and given extra chores to do alone. No sisters for company. Daddy replaced one of the tires sliced on the malpais and booted two of the others.

No one asked again for a trip to Rabbit Ears.

BROTHER, CAN YOU SPARE A DIME?

 Anthem of the Great Depression. 1930. Written by E. Y. Harburg and J. Gorney. 1932 #1 hit for both Bing Crosby and Rudy Vallee. Also recorded by Al Jolsen. Crosby's recording was the best-selling record of the period.

Fortune changed in 1929, when Wall Street crashed. The boom town of Clayton turned to bust as banks closed and the nation fell into the Great Depression. The never-ending winds blew in huge dust storms. Land sales dried up completely as did the sandy soil from drought. John McSpadden's employer was forced to take the big house for his own family.

Dorris's sister Helen, who had been a dear second mother to her siblings, married U. L. Ward that year and moved with him to California. Mama said the family was getting larger with another brother, not smaller with the loss of Helen, but the story didn't ring true. Disappointed that her oldest daughter didn't finish high school, Mama also acknowledged that times were hard. She prayed that Helen would find a job and a better life elsewhere.

In 1930, with no job and nowhere to live, Daddy John stored his beloved Hudson with Grandpa Green Berry in Texhoma, then bought an old flatbed farm truck with wood sideboards. He added tall poles to its bed and tied a grommeted tarpaulin over all. Mama stuffed her precious trunk to overflowing and Owen tied it onto the truck. Dorris watched her father hang giant canvas bags filled with water over the front of the vehicle, to get the family and the truck's radiator through the desert. Then the remaining eight McSpaddens climbed aboard, each with a designated spot. They rode southwest through New Mexico to Albuquerque where they joined the ribbon of vehicles on U.S. Highway 66, flowing toward hope, the promise of jobs in California.

Like almost everyone else, the McSpaddens turned north at Bakersfield, over The Grapevine switchbacks along the dangerous steep canyons and through Tejon Pass. The old truck coughed and sputtered but made it over. Near Visalia, they landed among thousands of other Texans, Arkies, and Okies displaced by drought, dust, and despair.

For a few years, they followed the fruit harvest north and south, through the San Joaquin Valley up to the hops vineyards near the Oregon border and on north as far as Wenatchee, Washington for its "Best Apples on Earth" then back again.

In northern California they came across a town named Dorris, with two Rs! That made Dorris feel right with the world, especially when the other kids made fun of her size and her voice. She grew up but her voice didn't. It stayed high-pitched and squeaky like a small girl's. "Five Feet Two, Eyes of Blue" described her for the rest of her life.

The whole family worked at whatever job could be had on any given day, picking or packing or canning. Dorris's favorite job was pulling hops off the vine. They looked like tiny light-green pine cones. To reach the hops she climbed a tall ladder through long vines which draped all around her. The spicy evergreen scent of the hop meal made her giddy and stayed on her clothes and hair for days. Her least favorite job was swabbing the floors of the canning factories after a run. Fruit and vegetable offal smelled rotten and drew hordes of flies.

Daddy, Owen, and Cecil knew produce and truck farming and sometimes wrangled jobs to use the truck for transport, but they didn't take long-haul overnight jobs. Dad wouldn't leave his little women unprotected. He said bad things happened in the migrant camps and they had strange rules. So, the McSpaddens camped off to themselves or with other trusted families met along the way, usually big Irish ones. Some of them slept in the truck bed, some made pallets on the ground, and occasionally a cabin was rented for a short while.

Near Sacramento was an immaculately painted white house with bright blue trim. Inside lived the first "Oriental" people Dorris had ever seen. Fascinated by their clothing and mannerisms, their shiny coal-black hair, the way their eyes crinkled, she and her sister Dot spied on them often. The children seemed clean and neat and took off their shoes when they entered the house. Then one day when the harvest route cycled back to Sacramento, Dorris and Dot ran to snoop on them again, but the house was empty. The "Orientals" had disappeared. Kids at school said they were spies.

Life wasn't bad. The kids endured better than the grown-ups. People did what they had to do to survive. The McSpadden clan stuck together. No one went off down the river like the Joad boy in Steinbeck's *Grapes of Wrath*, though worry about the future, or even the next day, was a heavy weight for the adults. Parents became very thin. Dorris hoped that her dad could find the quinine he needed for stomach pain that never eased. His retching often shook their nights.

With all that moving, following the harvests, there were very few consistent days of school. Dorris and her siblings fell behind their grade levels even though their parents insisted they attend when classes were available, wanting their offspring to be educated people. Dorris absorbed their dream and studied hard on the scattered days she attended class. On May 20, 1932, she racked up enough school days to graduate eighth grade at Ivanhoe, Tulare County, California. The whole family attended the little ceremony.

By 1933, Daddy had managed to hold back a little money which he constantly hid and re-hid, never trusting banks again. Over and over the radios played a snippet from Franklin Delano Roosevelt's inaugural speech, "The only thing we have to fear is fear itself." Daddy had great respect for Roosevelt and believed "Happy Days Are Here Again." He also wanted his girls away from the hungry migrant boys, so he somehow made a deal to farm a place in the Rio Grande Valley near McAllen, way down in the southern tip of Texas, almost to Mexico.

Once more, the little women packed Mother's trunk. A few hats and the pair of long white gloves remained, but most of the elegant dresses had been plied apart, salvaged to make clothes over the years. In their place were remnants, things saved: a marriage certificate, Mother's worn copy of *Little Women*, a tattered pair of red espadrilles, school papers with As, a few pictures, and the Bible where the judge's wife had long ago marked the words about how to be a good wife and mother. In that same Bible, the best of mothers, Dorris's motherless mother, had carefully written the details of the births of her seven children in her beautiful scroll.

They crammed the trunk, two parents, and six fairly-grown McSpadden youngsters into the tired truck with frayed canvas and missing grommets, then retraced their route over the treacherous Grapevine, hung a left at Bakersfield, and headed home to Texas on Route 66.

HORSES I HAVE KNOWN
BY KEITH L. BLACK

Des Moines, New Mexico
1930s

SPECK

In the early 1930s, Wayne Purvines bought a ranch about six miles north of Des Moines and east of Emery Peak. The ranch horses were part of the deal and among them was Speck, a used-up "flea-bitten" cow horse retired from the range, snow white with tiny red specks.

Even though the ranch had a fairly nice house and out buildings, Wayne was prevailed upon to buy the only brick house in town to accommodate the tastes of his family which consisted of his wife, three girls, and a boy, nine years old. The town property included a barn and corral. This enabled the owner to keep the all-important and necessary milk cow. Since cows require pasture and the little town of Des Moines was growing, the "powers that be" decided that cows, sheep, hogs, horses, and other livestock would no longer be permitted to range at will in town to invade flower beds and gardens, tear down clotheslines, soil clothes, and mess things up in general.

I'll never forget that morning. I had just finished eating breakfast, and someone knocked on the front door. When I opened it, there stood this huge man wearing a wide-brimmed hat, boots, spurs, and chaps, the most complete looking cowboy I had even seen!

He looked me over and said, "I just put my milk cow in your pen and I'd like to hire you to herd her with your cows. Just pick her up ever morning and drop her off in my pen at night. I'll pay you a dollar a month." He stuck his hand in his pocket and handed me the biggest, shiniest silver dollar I'd ever seen in my life, as big as a wagon wheel. He turned and headed for the front yard gate, walking that familiar, bow-legged cowboy walk, to where his son sat mounted, holding the reins of his dad's big brown horse.

As Wayne swung onto his horse, I slammed the door shut. Clutching my big dollar, I ran through the house and out the back door. I was running across the back yard toward the barn calling, "Daddy, Daddy. Come look!" Then from the corner of my eye, I saw Wayne and his son sitting there on their horses with bemused grins on their faces.

I guess they had never seen a poor kid come into instant wealth before.

Wayne looked around and said to my dad, "Corwin, where's your boy's horse?"

Upon learning that my pinto Little Paint had died last winter, Wayne said, "I've got a real good honest horse out at the ranch that I'd be glad to let him use." Late that evening as I came walking in with the cows at milking time, there stood a leggy, trim-built, flea-bitten white horse in the corral. Thus began another great friendship.

Speck was just what the doctor ordered: gentle as a dog, yet able to outmaneuver the oneriest of milk cows. We even won our share of matched races with other boys of the neighborhood.

One morning while driving the herd out to graze, we passed the bean elevator. Mr. Nate Gordon asked me to let the cows graze down the grass and weeds around the buildings between the railroad and the highway. I held them close to the buildings for a couple of hours. Then one old cow decided she would go back home. As she reached the highway, I kicked ole Speck into a lope after her. As he pulled out in front of her, the highway gravel rolled under his feet like ball bearings, and down we came.

Speck scrambled to his feet, but my right foot hung in the stirrup. The old horse, not accustomed to something dragging on his right side, spooked. The stirrup was just high enough off the ground that my head and shoulders bounced on the ground as Speck circled.

I'm told that Nate Gordon, Sam Mitchell, and his dad, Uncle Litt Mitchell, came to my rescue, but I knew nothing of it. They hauled me home and put me to bed, called Dr. Wellman, then stayed with my mother until my dad arrived. The Doctor, after examining me, said he could find nothing broken or badly bruised, so they just sat with me until I regained consciousness about three o'clock in the afternoon. I then realized why my dad had been so insistent and started me riding that crummy old saddle with the covered stirrups.

ROAN

Dad could take an old "dink" and work with it for a while and come out with a decent horse that someone would want. You might say that he had "horse savvy." He loved his horses and they knew it. Never rough or cruel. He knew when they were tired and allowed them to rest before asking for more. He couldn't sit down to eat until his horses had been watered and fed.

We had a team of geldings worth about $60, a black six-year-old and a white seven-year-old. Dad had put them together from other trades—medium size and weight, good dispositions, moved together well. Neither of them excited you much by themselves, but when you put them together as a team under a good set of harness, their contrast in color and shiny soft coats made them look like royalty. Henry Durgelow saw them in town one day and asked Dad about a swap.

Dad said, "I've got to take home a couple of colts I've been breaking for Wylie Hittson next week, so I'll come on by your place."

Tuesday morning, he hitched up the geldings to the wagon, tied the Hittson colts behind, and set off down the long lane east of Sierra Grande. Wylie Hittson was glad to see him and to try out the colts, especially the big brown four-year-old he called Brown Jug. Dad had used Wylie's colts to help move the last of the cattle, about 300 head, from the Baker Ranch on the lower Cimarron to their new owner down in the Mills Country about 96 miles away. By the time this drive was over, both of Wylie's colts were gentle-broke and reining well. Wylie was pleased! Then they went to the house to settle up their deal and eat dinner. In New Mexico, you ate dinner at noon. Evening, you ate supper.

From Hittson's Dad turned the team toward Henry Durgelow's place. Henry drove Dad's team of geldings around the pasture to show Dad his horses. He had a team of light-weight bay mares, showing a little age but still sound. Then there was this big raw-boned strawberry roan horse with heavy mane and feathery fetlocks, powerfully made. But as they got close his head went up, ears pointed forward. You could see his flared nostrils and white-rimmed eyes.

"Now Corwin, I'll tell you about that horse. He'll bite you, kick you, or paw you. When you go to bridle him, he'll stomp and snort and scare the bejeebers outta you. He's a workin' fool, but he's dangerous." Henry Durgelow was one of those old time honest men.

Dad spied an unbroke three-year-old blood-bay gelding with a bald face that wrapped around his head. Must have been from Indian background off the northern range. Again, those feathery fetlocks, long broom tail, and heavy mane. Then there was a two-year-old, well-built, trim-legged blue colt that showed promise of making a good cow horse.

The fact that Henry was horse-poor and short on grass, coupled with his burning interest in Dad's team, seemed to take the usual banter of offer and counteroffer out of this horse trade. In less than an hour, Dad was harnessing the little bay mares and hitching them to his wagon. He then tied the big roan to the back of the wagon, with the bald-faced bay on one side and the blue colt on the other and headed for home. A good day: he'd collected $25 in cash money, $12.50 each for breaking two colts for Hittson, then traded a team of geldings for five other horses!

Next day after dinner, our next order of business must be to get the big roan horse under control. Evidently, he had been abused early in life and when he had tried to rebel, he had been further abused, spoiled to the extent that he now had a lot to unlearn before he could be constructively taught.

When we went back to the corral that afternoon, we carried with us some soft heavy ropes. They were strong enough to withstand far more strain and pressure than an ordinary lariat rope, and of greater diameter and softness that would not cause a cut or rope burn when used on a frantic spoiled horse.

I had never seen a horse throw such a fit as this one. Made you wonder if maybe he'd been on the loco weed. He seemed to know that we wanted to school him in good behavior and he wanted no part of it. He'd trot stiff-legged around the corral, neck arched, snorting like a bugler blowing "charge," a long low guttural snort like distant thunder in a faraway canyon. He'd stop on the far side of the corral, stand and paw or stomp his front feet until Dad came within reach. Then he'd whirl and kick his hind feet sending a storm of dirt and manure, then stop, snort and blow, and shake his heavy mane in defiance.

Dad allowed old Roan to continue with his "bluff and bluster" for about a half hour. Then Dad fashioned a loop in his ketch rope and with one deft movement, threw a hoolihan loop over Roan's head and quickly took a couple of turns around the snubbin' post and tied it off.

He passed the rope a couple of turns around the trailing rope, and then through a neck loop. As he pulled up the slack, old Roan went into orbit again. Every time he kicked, Dad took up the slack until Roan's left hind foot was held about a foot above the ground, the soft rope forming a secure loop around the fetlock. Then he tied it fast.

With Roan in this helpless state, Dad proceeded to trim his fetlocks and hooves. The old outlaw was forced to just lie there helpless and endure the further indignities: tail trimming and shortening. Next came the trimming of his mane which was done using an old pair of hand-operated sheep shears.

Dad was slow and deliberate in his work and occasionally would stop and gently blow a full breath of air through his cupped hands directly into Roan's nostrils. At other times he would reach back to the flank area and pat the underbelly or any other spot where the horse might tend to be touchy. Any reaction on the part of Roan was only to strain at the unforgiving restraining ropes.

"I reckon he's had enough schoolin' for today," Dad said as he started untying the restraining ropes. Roan lay quietly during the untying and remained quiet as the last ropes came off, leaving only the lariat around his neck. Dad placed a half-hitch over Roan's nose, gently lifted and urged him to get up. He got to his feet. Dad led him over to the water tank and let him drink, rubbing and patting him as he drank. Then he removed the lariat from around Roan's neck. He asked me to go to the shop and bring a currycomb and brush. He thoroughly brushed and combed the horse all over until the hair lay smooth and dry.

A W.P.A. highway job requiring the use of wagons, teams and drivers came just at the right time. It was a life saver for a lot of people in the community. There was a graded dirt roadway between Des Moines and Folsom that needed to be hard surfaced. Fortunately, 300 yards from this road lay a kalechi pit. Kalechi is a semi-hard rock substance formed of volcanic ash which hardened over time in large deposits. This substance was to be hauled in false-bottomed team-drawn wagons, holding about a cubic yard of aggregate weighing about 2,700 pounds—a good load for a single team of horses.

Dad got a job for his team and wagon and decided that, since the bay mares were a little small and getting on in years, he would work one mare (Bess) with Roan half a day, and the other mare (Babe) the other half day, thus making an opportunity to gentle down Roan while resting each mare. This arrangement developed into an ideal solution for Dad's problems during the 30s depression. This job paid just enough to buy groceries for the family and some grain for the horses.

Two things contributed to the rehabilitation of a "weedy" horse: steady, reasonable hard work rewarded by a good feeding of grain three times a day. At the end of the job you would hardly have recognized old Roan except for the fact that he still tended to be a little jumpy, a trait that he never quite overcame.

Young cowboy Keith L. Black.

Roan Serenade.

RIVER, STAY 'WAY FROM MY DOOR

Written by Mort Dixon and Harry M. Woods. Recorded by Jimmie Noone & His Orchestra, 1931. Recorded by Guy Lombardo & His Royal Canadians with Kate Smith, 1932, Columbia Record Company. Also recorded by Frank Sinantra on his album, *All The Way*, 1960, Capitol Records.

The McSpadden family's new beginning in McAllen, Texas, quickly turned into an ending. They were forced to split up. The dryland farm they sharecropped was far from town with no school bus. Determined her children be educated, Dorris's mother approached the Methodist Church and found homes in town for her four girls, where they could have room and board and go to school in exchange for housekeeping or other chores. Fifteen years old at the time, Dorris had been well-trained to take care of two small girls in the family she stayed with, just more little women like her sisters.

Owen and Cecil gave up on school. Working to help support the family, they had missed too many classes during the *Grapes of Wrath* sojourn. They shared a job driving a gasoline transport truck from Brownie's Oil Company in McAllen to Pettis Refinery near San Antonio and back again. The roundtrip was almost 300 miles, took ten to eleven hours, and paid $3.85 per roundtrip. They alternated runs with one staying home to help with the truck farm while the other was on the road.

Struggling for a solution, Daddy John wrangled a place with water four hundred miles away back home in West Texas, south of San Angelo in Tom Green County. On the banks of the South Concho River, the area was called Ben Ficklin Crossing. In the spring of 1935

Dad, Mother, and Owen moved ahead to get the crops in the ground. The girls remained in their church placements in McAllen. Cecil kept the job with Brownie's Oil and stayed to look after them, renting a bedroom in a rooming house. One night he fell asleep while smoking in bed. The mattress caught fire. Cecil woke and dragged it across the hall to the bathroom, threw it in the bathtub, and ran water on it. Unbelievably, the landlady allowed him to stay.

After another year, in 1936, Cecil moved himself and the little women—Bernice, Dorris, Dot, and Jean—from McAllen to the farm at Ben Ficklin, though it meant no more school for the girls. Finally, the family was together again, almost. They missed Helen who was making her life in California but were proud that she had found a man and a job. Dad and both boys worked extra hard that year putting in the crops which included two big fields of tomatoes. Maybe things would get better.

In mid-September, the skies opened and dropped buckets of rain on the droughty land for several days. Forced inside, Dorris made pies with her sisters and everyone played cards to pass the time. Dad's foot was injured from a fall a few days earlier. He was going stir crazy, being down with his foot, so he was happy to have company in the house. Late afternoon one day, they all piled into the beds for warmth and talk, falling asleep despite the sound of pounding rain hitting the tin roof and plunking into pails set around to catch the leaks.

After a while, Dorris woke and swung her feet to the floor. She landed in murky water almost up to her knees.

"Oh, good gosh! Water's coming in the house! Wake up everybody!" she yelled.

Owen ran to the door and opened it. Everyone peered out at a lake surrounding and inundating their house. The South Concho River had flooded the farm. Through the rain, they could see a small patch of land at the top of the slope above the house.

"We have to get to that high ground. Right now!" Dad said.

"This water is still rising."

No one could swim. They discussed the safest way to cross the rising current. Dad asked his tall sons if they thought they could safely walk it with a person on their back. Both said yes.

"Take the little girls first," Dad said. "Dorothy, get on Owen's back. Jean, climb on Cecil. You two are the lightest. That will let us see how it goes. Boys, take small steps. Feel as you go. Slide your feet, stay centered. Follow the road, don't try to go over the fences. They'll trip you up. And everybody, hang on to each other. Don't let go, no matter what. Even if you fall, don't let go."

Dorothy and Jean protested but climbed on the backs of their brothers. Dorris anxiously watched from the doorway as Cecil and Owen heroically deposited each of her sisters on the hillside and returned drenched, gliding in waist-high water.

"Hard to see where we're going." Owen said.

"Dorris, Bernice, climb on. Fast now." Dad ordered.

"What about your foot, Daddy?" Dorris asked. "You can't carry Mama."

"No, I can't. The boys will come back for us."

"No, take Mama first," she cried.

"Dorris, I will be right behind you," Mama said. "Everything will be all right. Keep your head. No tears. No sass. Get up there, right now." She nudged her strong-willed daughter.

Dorris climbed on Cecil's back. Bernice was already on Owen's. They were both bawling like babies, but fear soon stopped the tears.

"Girls, do not move," Dad cautioned. "Watch your arms, don't choke your brothers. Do not look back. Just tuck your head down and stay still." The rain pelted as the brothers walked slow and steady across the swirling water. They rolled Dorris and Bernice off their backs onto the hillside and didn't waste a second turning around and walking back into that cold, murky water strewn with debris.

For what seemed like an eternity, Dorris shivered and huddled close with her sisters and peered through the falling rain trying to make out forms. Finally, Owen appeared carrying his petite mother clamped to his chest. Once he delivered her, he fell exhausted onto the soaked ground.

No Cecil. No Dad.

They waited. They wailed.

Finally, a figure appeared through the downpour. One. Fear seized Dorris's heart. But as the form came closer, they saw four arms and realized a second head bobbed directly behind the first. Every muscle in Cecil's body strained. Buckets of sweat mingled with rain and river water. Finally, they reached the hillside, and both collapsed. The girls dithered over them until their breathing returned to normal.

A tree limb dislodged by the roaring overflow had plowed into them and knocked Daddy off Cecil's back. But Cecil didn't let go. They both went under several times while struggling to gain balance in the chest-high water. With brute strength Cecil planted his legs as wide apart as possible and pulled his father in with one arm. Daddy draped over his back and Cecil slowly walked.

All eight McSpaddens hugged and thanked God and cried, even Mama. There are times when the No-Tears Rule doesn't apply.

The family was marooned on the hill for several hours, even after the rain stopped. They watched as the swollen river stole their year's income: the fields of staked tomatoes, soil eaten away from the roots. Debris of all sorts swirled past: trees, furniture, pieces of houses, boards, tin, even animals. Dogs, cats, sheep and cattle were in the water, mostly drowned but some struggling to keep heads up. One sheep was bleating, as if cursing the high heavens.

No thought was given to the house or the old shed beside it until Cecil said, "Uh-oh. That big tree is headed right for the shed." Sure enough, a whole tree was sailing down the river trunk first, the leaves protesting. It smacked the side of the shed dead-on and all four walls gave up at the same time. The shed split apart. The river took the roof and the lumber downstream, along with Daddy's rakes, shovels, and wheelbarrow.

Then they saw it.

"What's that bobbing in the water?" Dorris squinted, as if trying to make it out, afraid to say the words.

"That's my trunk, Dorris," Mama said matter-of-factly. "It was in the shed."

No one cried. No one wailed. They stood in silence, holding each other, as the monstrous floodwater smashed Mother's trunk and stole the few treasures entrusted to it: the one dress still intact, the soldier blue with tiny buttons that Mama and Helen had been married in, a pair of long white gloves stained by small hands, moldy red shoes with frazzled ties, a marriage certificate, family pictures, keepsakes from California, a tattered copy of *Little Women*, and the old *King James Bible* with the names of all seven McSpadden children and dates of their births written between the Old and New Testaments.

Dorris and her sopping wet sisters huddled around their mother. "They are just things, girls," Mama said. "We loved them, but they don't really matter. Look at your big brothers. Look at yourselves. We are strong women. We have each other, all safe and sound. There will be people who aren't safe. People who have lost family today. We should be thankful. I am thankful."

"Me, too," said Daddy. "Thank God that Owen and Cecil were home today. They saved our lives. I couldn't have gotten across that water with my bum foot. Let's say a real prayer."

They held hands and gave thanks. No tears, well, none anyone would admit to. The family stood strong. Together.

Neighbors took the family to San Angelo where they slept in a school with strangers. Later they returned to the house. It was still standing, the floor covered with a foot of silt, a difficult, depressing cleanup. They salvaged what they could—clothing and kitchen stuff that hadn't been ruined or washed away through the door and broken windows. Owen and Cecil tinkered with the waterlogged farm truck and got it running again. They found tomato vines stuck in the barbed wire fences and hanging from trees. Friends showed them a low spot farther down the river where green tomatoes, ripped from the vines, had collected. Dorris giggled when she saw them piled up like a giant's helping of English peas. Dead animals were the worst with their carcasses stuck in trees or rotting in the fields. The smell of decay was horrendous, but not as bad as the smell of burning animal flesh when the bonfires began.

San Angelo Morning Times, September 18, 1936: ─────

An insane burst of brown waters wrapped round the dust of a prolonged drought leaped the channels of the Concho rivers here yesterday, hurled to destruction an approximate of 300 houses in all parts of town and left an uninsured flood damage of about $1,500,000, the worst water damage in the history of this 68-year-old city. It is the major catastrophe of all time for San Angelo.

More than 100 persons were rescued from drowning on the streets or from flooded houses, while many hundreds more were removed under conditions less dangerous. There was an estimated 300 homeless families last night, who were sleeping in the schoolhouses and in other public buildings, in stores, while hotels were filled. Numerous buildings not destroyed were flooded and filled with silt.

The North Concho River, chief troublemaker of the day, charged drunkenly into the Negro and Mexican section, threw houses and shacks against the Sixth Street bridge now under construction, spread wanton piles of other wrecked houses here and there. Then it moved into the elite residential district, climbed a 40 ft. cliff to run a stream knee deep in the home of Preston Rothrup. It tore the C. R. Hallmark home from its foundations, raced it over the Santa Fe Golf Course, and cracked it into matchwood at the submerged Millspaugh bridge. ─────

GANDY DANCERS BALL

Written by Paul Mason Howard and Paul Weston. Recorded by Frankie Laine, 1951, Columbia Record Company. Refers to railroad workers.

Again, the family had to split up, this time for good. Helen and her husband, U. L. Ward, drove to Texas and took Bernice back to California with them. Bernice planned to finish high school, but instead found a job and sent money home.

Owen and Cecil roamed west Texas looking for work, any work they could find that would bring a few dollars into the family. They slept in the truck or stayed with relatives, mainly Daddy John's McSpadden brothers, when they could.

Dad's stomach trouble surfaced again. He ate little and became very thin but soldiered on. By the end of the year he found a kind man who agreed to let him sharecrop a few acres of his land at Christoval, so the family moved their meager things. No trunk to haul this time. They shared a small house with another family, the Donovans, in space just big enough for Dorris, her mama, and her two younger sisters. Dad joined the boys looking for odd jobs and staying with his brothers, coming home when he could, waiting until it was time to put in the crops. Dorris, Dorothy, and Jean enrolled in Christoval High School.

Eventually, with a dire money situation and no jobs in west Texas, Dad asked Owen and Cecil if they would be willing to go to California and hunt for work. They could stay with Helen, U. L., and Bernice. He helped them find a ride in a produce truck that belonged to his friend who owned Walker-Smith Wholesale Grocery Company. Dad had earned a lot of respect from the wholesale grocers he had sold vegetables to. They knew his crops and his character. The boys made the journey in the back of a produce van with only a two-foot opening for light and air, but it beat thumbing it.

Every day they hitch-hiked from Helen's home in Glendale to Market Square in downtown Los Angeles and tried to find work. Every day they hitch-hiked back, exhausted and depressed, talking about what it was like to stand in Market Square next to thousands of men trying to find jobs, any jobs. They described a high-mounted chalkboard with listings of jobs that could be bought: office worker for $150, concrete finisher for $75, ditch digger for $50. Owen and Cecil had no money to buy a job, and even if they had, the wage for ditch-digging was only thirty cents an hour.

Weeks and weeks passed with only a day job now and then. One day while the boys were separated in their search, a new friend named Red Berryquist whispered to Cecil about the possibility of a steel gang job with a railroad. Cecil frantically looked for Owen but couldn't find him. Conflicted about going out into the unknown without his brother, he decided he couldn't let the opportunity pass. He thumbed it to Glendale for his bedroll, left a note, then met up with Red back in Los Angeles. The two of them stole a ride on an open trailer being pulled by a car when it stopped at a traffic light. Thirty miles later they jumped off as the car rolled along. They landed in Pomona where a Union Pacific work train waited on the siding. Two hundred eighty-seven men stood in line, hoping.

Cecil and Red were hired as "gandy-dancers" and spent the next seven months digging out old iron rails and replacing them with new steel—grueling work. They were paid thirty-seven cents an hour and charged $1.01 per day for room and board on the work train. They rebuilt the railroad across California near Death Valley in 115-degree heat, through Nevada, Utah, and into Wyoming. Cheyenne was the end of the line.

Union Pacific provided Cecil a paid rail ticket from Cheyenne to Denver where his first stop was to purchase cowboy boots for himself and his three youngest sisters. The train on to Lubbock was expensive. Wanting to take as much money as possible home to his family, he arranged a cheaper ride with a travel bureau that matched automobiles going to a certain destination with travelers who needed a ride. He folded his tall frame into a small automobile cramped with four others and endured the six hundred miles which took him home.

Owen had also returned to Texas when he couldn't find work in California, so he was in Christoval with the rest to welcome Cecil home. Dorris was overjoyed that her brother had made this trek into the larger world and returned home safe and sound. The reunion was the happiest highpoint of the year.[3]

And the boots? Well, those boots!

(L to R) Dorris, Jean, Cecil, and Dorothy
McSpadden. Christoval, Texas, 1937.

HORSES I HAVE KNOWN
BY KEITH L. BLACK

Des Moines, New Mexico
1930s

TRIXIE AND QUEEN

It was the Fourth of July, 1930, and there was to be a big celebration at Des Moines out on the flats north of the stockyards. Horse races, goat roping, bronc riding, trick riding, etc. An old-fashioned country Wild West show. The railroad shipping pens were used to hold the wild stock for the various events, which took place inside an enclosed strip made up of farm wagons, Model-A Fords and early Chevys, as well as quite a few people on horseback. Everyone was looking forward to a rip-roaring Fourth.

But we didn't get to go! I was thoroughly disappointed. Heck no, I was disgusted. Mama had raised holy Ned with Dad about the foolishness of the whole thing. She had heard that some of those wild cowboys were liable to be drinking white mule (bootleg whiskey)!

"That just isn't the place for decent people to be. Fourth of July or not."

I could sense that Dad's heart just wasn't in it as we harnessed up the teams that morning, but he said nothing as we took off up the turn row to the fields. At the edge of the bean field, he tied his team to the fence and went with me to get hooked up to the four-section spike-toothed harrow that I would be using to pull down the lister ridges in the corn. I had run the harrow the day before, but he re-instructed me as to how to handle the team and especially turning them at the end of the row.

"Turn them in a long sweeping half-circle, don't turn too short, give the rig plenty of room. Stay about three feet back of the harrow. Then go back on the next four rows." After I got started Dad walked back to his own team, hooked them to the cultivator, and started plowing the weeds from between the bean rows.

My team was a pair of gentle grey Percheron mares. Queen, the taller of the two, was calm and steady and tended to make up for the fact that Trixie, more dappled, was a little nervous and excitable. Dad told me to stop about every two rounds and let the team blow, because that four-section harrow was quite a load for two horses in that soft plowed ground. Keeping up with the horses was also a load for me, a nine-year-old, short-legged boy.

That old sun was beaming down, not a cloud in sight, and it was getting HOT! The dust boiled up behind the harrow into my face as the morning wore on. I squinted at the sun, figured it was a little past eleven o'clock. As I looked up, the salty sweat trickled out from under my straw hat and ran into my eyes, burning. This reminded me of just how badly I felt sorry for myself.

No rodeo, just chores.

Partially blinded by all this frustration, I realized we were coming to the end of the rows. Time to turn. I drew back on the right-hand line to turn the team. The right-hand section of the harrow dropped into a furrow and lodged behind the lister ridge. As Trixie and Queen swung around, the end section burrowed into the loose dirt, causing the opposite end to rise up. The mares continued pulling and before I knew it, the whole thing was standing on end. Straight up in the air! The double tree and single trees were lifted as high as my head, which in turn skewed the harness on the team.

In desperation, I dropped the lines, releasing the pressure on the mares. They straightened their course resulting in a more gradual turn, and the whole rig fell back to the ground with a WHACK and rattle of the metal harness. The team bolted forward.

I ran to catch them, but the lines were hung under the harrow with only six inches of the ends sticking out. I frantically grabbed for the lines a few times. Then I stumbled and fell forward hard, striking my face on the harrow's lever handle which punctured my cheek and came back out as the end of the lever hit my lower jaw. I jumped up and continued running after the team, spitting blood and slobbers, wiping my eyes and nose as I ran.

Dad had seen the dust cloud as it rose behind the running horses. He tied his horses and ran to the turn row. Trixie and Queen reached the end and turned toward him and home. Dad waved his hat in an effort to slow or stop them, but on they came. The harrow being so wide, twelve feet, clipped about every third fence post as they came. The mares spread, one on the right, one on the left, as they reached Dad. As he grabbed the cheeks of their bridles, the force of the running team swept him off his feet. He dragged them to a stop, tied them to a fence and came running toward me.

I came stumbling along, whimpering like a whipped dog. Dad did his best to console me and assured me it would be alright. We unhooked my team, went on down and unhooked his team and headed to the house for dinner. As we went in to wash up, Mama pitched another hissy about me doing team work. But when she saw the pretty little half-moon-shaped hole through my right cheek, she felt bad and said, "I've got something special for you. Mincemeat pie!"

Mincemeat pie had always been my favorite, so she cut me a piece. As I started to eat it, some of it came out that half-moon hole and fell into my lap. I laid my fork down and moved back from the table.

It had been a bad day all around, but the first hurt was far worse than the last.

BALDY

Baldy was a three-year-old blood-bay with long black mane and tail, even black stockings fading out at the knees and hocks. His bald face was overdone to the extent that the white almost wrapped around the lower jaw. He had a naturally gentle disposition, which with careful but firm handling caused him to be easy to break to the saddle. Dad only rode him four or five times before turning him over to me.

It had always been Dad's theory that riding a green colt down the road was not the best way to break him to the saddle. Better still was to ride him to drive cattle because this gives the colt something to think about as you ride him. He can't help but be concerned about the movement of the cattle in front of him. At the same time, this was invaluable in teaching him to rein.

I was only ten years old at the time but had already been riding very gentle and trust-worthy horses for several years, so when this un-usually docile colt came to us, Dad felt comfortable to let me take him. I felt that I had made a big step up in the world when I graduated to the status of helping to train a green colt. By the time school started in the fall, Baldy and I had become great friends. So when some ranchers needed help gathering cattle, we were ready.

After Grandpa Thornton died, my grandmother's cows were sold to Mr. Haggard whose farm was located about 18 miles away, southwest of Sierra Grande Mountain. Baldy and I were volunteered for the job of delivering the cattle. The route started at Des Moines and ran west toward Capulin Volcano, between the state highway (a gravel road) and the branch line of the Santa Fe Railroad.

About eight miles out we came to a section line road run-ning south through Sierra Grande Valley. This was a fenced lane with barbed wire fences on either side. Each time we came to a farm house, the cows would try to turn in. The thirsty cows could smell the water at the stock tanks as we passed. This really tested the ability and endur-ance of Baldy and me, as we had to protect the gardens and front yards of the farm houses.

As the morning wore on, I noticed a black cloud gathering in the southwest. We had passed the Lanier place when a thunderstorm erupted. The lightening was fierce and steady as the storm intensified. There was an ear-shattering explosion about 30 yards up ahead, and a ball of fire came rolling toward us, riding on top of the fence line. I felt a peculiar sensation throughout my body as Baldy dropped to his knees, then scrambled to regain his footing. I don't know which of us was shaken the most. The air all around had an acrid, burnt brimstone smell. The end of Baldy's nose was smeared with mud from the fall. After rubbing the mud off his nose with the sleeve of my jacket and reassuring him, I climbed back up on him and continued on.

About 2:30 pm we arrived at the Haggard place. I left the cows in the corral and rode on up to the house. Mrs. Haggard asked me to come in for something to eat, but I told her that I had carried my lunch on my saddle and had already eaten. I needed to start back as it would be dark long before I got home.

A few evenings later Dad got a phone call from Mr. Bob Gleason who lived at the mouth of Toll Gate Canyon down on the Cimarron. He had seen me riding Baldy as I brought the cows in one evening. He liked the calm steady way the colt handled as he reacted to the movements of the cattle and asked Dad how much he would take for the bay colt.

The next morning we saddled Little Blue and put a halter and lead rope on Baldy. I rode Little Blue and led Baldy to Mr. Gleason's place. Rather than going around to Folsom on the main road, I took a cutoff across Doherty's pasture, entering at a gate about two miles east of Folsom, then going north to where the track crossed Pinabete Creek. At Mr. Gleason's I said good-bye to my friend Baldy, hard for a ten-year-old boy, and rode Little Blue back home.

GINGER

In the early 1930s there began to be an exodus from the small farms
of northeastern New Mexico. As people left the country, quite a few
farmhouses were left standing empty. It was not uncommon for some
family that had starved-out elsewhere to take up residence temporarily
before moving on.

One such family moved onto a 160-acre place about two miles
west of us. They were a pretty scroungy-looking outfit, as they only
had an old high-wheeled wagon pulled by two old broomtail horses. A
man and wife sat in the wagon, and with them about enough furniture
to make a fair camping outfit. Behind the wagon a girl and boy rode
bareback on a little strawberry roan mare with flaxen mane and tail,
blazed face, and stocking feet.

Dad always had extra horses around to trade. When this man
said he needed a work horse to relieve the strain on his team, Dad
swapped him a big ole slow, puddin'-footed sorrel mare for this little
roan. It didn't take long to figure out why this guy had wanted to let
this pretty mare go. She didn't lead worth a hoot and wouldn't stand
tied. When you walked in front of her, she would run backwards and
if tied, break the bridle or reins. She had been badly abused by jerking
the reins to the point that she would always be tender-mouthed. If you
raised your hand in front of her, she would throw her head up and fly
backward.

Dad said that we'd have to work very slowly with her and use a
hackamore instead of a bridle with a bit. As time went by, she regained
confidence in the human race, and she and I became good friends. I
named her Ginger. Since I used her to herd the cows, we retired old
Speck back to Purvines Ranch.

Ginger remained my friend and companion for several years
and we got into various tight spots and close shaves as is common for
an over-ambitious kid and a smarter horse.

One such incident happened out west of town, as I herded the cows on a wide grassy strip between the Raton highway and the Santa Fe Railroad. Herding cows is a lonely and often monotonous endeavor for a growing boy of ten or eleven years. You can play marbles or mumbley-peg with your pocket knife for just so long, so you are always looking for something with a little more action.

I heard a noise in the distance on the highway. It slowly increased until I could make out a Model-A truck as it clattered and labored up the road. It was Newt Click and his son Orville with a load of hogs, headed for the railroad stock pens. I could hear the hogs squealing as they drew closer. I jumped up on Ginger bareback and held her until they were even with us. Then I let out a war whoop and turned Ginger loose. I figured we could beat that truck to the Starkey's Cafe sign on down the road about 200 yards.

We were flying along, staying neck and neck with the truck when Ginger stepped into a badger hole and down she went, throwing me end over appetite ahead of her. I landed on my head and the back of my neck. The impact caused me to fold in the middle, knocking all of today's air and part of tomorrow's out of my body. Next thing I knew, Newt and Orville were kneeling over me, fanning me with their hats and grinning.

In those days of drought and depression, entertainment was scarce, and the price could be high!

Black trick riding on Ginger.

DON'T FENCE ME IN

 Music by Cole Porter. Lyrics by Robert Fletcher and Cole Porter. 1934. Made popular ten years later 1944 when sung by Roy Rogers in the movie *Hollywood Canteen*. Recorded by Roy Rogers, Bing Crosby and the Andrews Sisters, and Ella Fitzgerald, all in 1944.

Black
Des Moines, New Mexico
1936

Keith Black ran out the door and across the yard to the barn. He grabbed his saddle from the tack room, dropped it outside on the dirt, and went back for his bedroll and rifle.

"Where are you going, Bud?" His father caught up with him and stopped in the open doorway of the barn, hands on his hips.

Keith didn't answer but brushed past Corwin and headed for the corral. Ginger was already at the gate, apparently sensing the excitement. He slid the latch to let her out and she followed him back to the barn. He saddled her quickly, jerking the cinch tight, then tied down the bedroll and shoved the .30-30 into its scabbard.

"I asked you a question, Bud. Where are you going?"

Keith didn't want to answer. He couldn't even look at his father. But he didn't want to be followed, either.

"To the timber, the batchin' cabin. I'll be back in a couple of days."

Corwin grabbed his arm. "Don't go. Not when you're mad. Wait till you calm down."

Keith looked directly at his father. "I'm not gonna calm down.

I'm planning on staying mad. And when else would I go, Dad? When? You're selling out—the ranch, the horses. You're moving us to Lubbock, for Pete's sake. Nobody asked me nothin'."

The screen door banged and both men looked toward the house where the long white curtains were blowing outward from open windows. Loa, Keith's mother, stood leaning against a porch post, arms folded across her chest. A thin woman with prematurely gray hair, she appeared so slight she might disappear in a gust of hot, dry wind.

"What's wrong with Sonny Boy?" she asked, her voice syrupy.

No one answered. The three of them stood in silence for several minutes, staring at the hard-baked dirt or the horses or the Sangre de Cristo Mountains on the horizon.

Loa abruptly turned and went back into the house. The screen door banged again.

Corwin turned to his son. "You're just fifteen years old, Keith. This is grown-up business. We have to do what we think is best for all of us. We're about to starve-out here."

"We have plenty of venison and vegetables from the garden. You're not fooling me. You're doing this for Joyce, so she can go to Texas Tech. Whatever Sissy needs . . ."

"Your mother and I want both of you to go to Tech, and that's not going to happen if we stay here. I need to find a job with a regular paycheck. This horse trading just goes so far. There's things I can do in Lubbock and get paid cash money for it. Dub Flowers said they're hiring at the Cotton Compress." Corwin put his hand on Keith's shoulder. "It's what we've figured out to do. We want you to have a better life than this."

"There's not a better life than this, Dad. You taught me that. Being free, being your own man. You're gonna hate living in a town. No cows. No horses. And me, what am I gonna do without Ginger? I can't believe you sold my horse. You know how long it took to train her. I can't do trick riding without her." Ginger's ears pricked as Keith softly rubbed her neck. "And what about Hollywood? Uncle Norval told me to bring her with me when I come."

Corwin stiffened. "It's a done deal, Keith. Wayne Purvines had his eye on Ginger for a while and he offered top dollar. We need all the money we can get. There's always another horse, son. If you need a few days to come to grips with it, go ahead and ride off, but be back in time for church Sunday. The Purvines' hands are coming for Ginger Tuesday. Dispersal sale is Saturday next. And if there's anything of ours at the batchin' cabin, bring it down when you come." He pushed his hat back and set his jaw. "That's the end of it, no more."

The conversation was over for Corwin, but Keith couldn't let go. He softened his voice and tried again, "Dad, can I go to Hollywood then, instead of Lubbock? Uncle Norval said he could get me on with the Western talkies. They're always looking for guys who can ride and rope. I know I could get a job, even without Ginger. I can send money back. You can stay here."

"Keith, you heard your mother. You know she won't let you go to Hollywood. That moving picture business is sinful. It's a den of iniquity out there. You're too young to go off someplace like that with all those temptations. It would ruin you. She's always been afraid you're gonna wind up a rounder, like your Uncle Jim. She will never let you go."

"But what about you, Dad? You're the cowboy. You're always saying those drugstore cowboys are fake, that somebody should show them what a real cowboy is. I could do that."

Corwin scuffed the dirt. Little dust clouds formed off the toes of his boots. "I can't go against her, Son. You know that. She's too fractious. I'm not gonna buck her." He turned and headed back toward the house. "You can be a cowboy in Texas. They have cowboys there, too."

Keith watched him walk away. His tall, lean, sun-baked father was the toughest man he knew, yet often brought to his knees by his love for a strong-willed, yet fragile woman.

Furious that his eyes had betrayed him with tears (his mother's weapon of choice), Keith quickly mounted Ginger and dug his heels into her side. She bolted into a run, down the dirt lane, then across Dunchee Hill. They skirted Briggs Canyon and headed for the ridges of Emery Peak. Finally, he slowed her to a walk, then pulled her to a stop. Her sides heaved with each breath. He patted her withers and scratched between her ears.

"Sorry, girl. Shouldn't have pushed you so hard. I got you lathered up." He climbed down and dropped the reins. "Rest a bit, then we'll take it slow and easy to the creek and get us both a drink. Take as much time as you need."

The sun bore down from a clear sky. Keith looked across the dramatic panorama of northeastern New Mexico's high plains. He could see almost to Clayton. The jagged outline of Rabbit Ears Butte in the east, the gentle slopes of Sierra Grande in the south, the round cinder cone of Capulin Volcano in the west and, on the far western horizon, snow-topped Wheeler Peak capping the Sangre de Cristo range. Familiar, comforting landmarks in this majestic expanse. Steam puffed from a Santa Fe Railroad locomotive churning up the slow grade toward Folsom, trailed by its mile-long line of coal cars. A farm truck crawled along the highway to Raton, then disappeared beyond Johnson Mesa. Near the town of Des Moines, herds of cattle grazed the open range, each tended by a lone cowboy, probably a young boy. Further from town, scattered pronghorn shared the deep-rooted native grama grass.

Keith spotted his Grandpa Black's ranch by the tall wooden windmill and near it, the trees shading the small cemetery where his other grandpa, Wilson Valentine Thornton, lay buried. Though only nine years old when his grandpa died, Keith had carved "W. V. Thornton, 1849–1930" into a sandstone rock with his pocket knife and placed it at the burial site. He wanted something permanent to mark his grandfather's walk in this spiritual land, and there had been no money for a proper tombstone.

The Blacks and the Thorntons were among the first Anglo people to set roots in this wide-open country. He remembered stories his father and mother told of coming to the Territory in covered wagons as children. The Thorntons had homesteaded in half-dugouts on claims in Corrumpa country east of Des Moines until their land patents were proved up. In 1909, the wagon carrying his grandmother, Nancy Angeline Cope Thornton, and her youngest daughter Loa (the eleven-year-old girl who would become Keith's mother) had lost its way in a blizzard and halted. Next morning the father and brothers found the wheels had stopped mere inches from a sheer drop into Palo Dura Canyon in Texas. There were perils in coming west, trying to find a better life.

Always a search for a better life.

"What's wrong with this life?" he asked Ginger, stroking her neck. "This is where I belong. I feel it in my bones. This land is mine, even if I don't own any of it. Someday I'll come back and buy a big ranch. I'll find you again."

Keith pulled the crisp dry air deep into his lungs, then mounted Ginger and turned her down the back slope, toward the deep ravine of Pinabete Creek.

"Better keep moving, girl. It's still a-ways to the cabin. Let's hope Doherty's boys left some canned beans. I don't want to hunt 'til tomorrow."

T IS FOR TEXAS

 Blue Yodel No. 1. Recorded by Jimmie Rodgers in 1927 at Trinity Baptist Church, Camden, New Jersey, for Victor Talking Machine Company.

Lubbock High was quite a change from the rural school in Des Moines, New Mexico, where Keith Black had known every one of his nine classmates and all their family members. He had grown up among a mix of white and brown students of Indian-Spanish-Mexican descent. The faces were almost all white in the new multistory Lubbock High building on 19th Street, built in Spanish colonial style with graceful arches and a red tile roof. Keith changed rooms for each class, shared a locker for his books, and walked long hallways and stairs filled with hundreds of kids his own age.

His initial anger about moving to Lubbock had cooled. Keith had made his peace with the world during long days alone on the plains, herding cattle, singing hymns, talking to the clouds. His cowboy ways, the slow enigmatic grin and easy everybody's-equal manner, endeared him to new faces in this place he considered a temporary holding pen until he could get back to the land. When Lubbock friends learned that music flowed through his veins and that he could pick out any song on a guitar or piano and perform the tunes they heard on the radio, the deal was sealed.

Keith liked the agriculture courses best. There he met Truva McSpadden, a kindred soul and instant sidekick. Never at a loss for words, Truva could talk to a fence post. Keith didn't use many words, only necessary ones. In awe of Keith's singing ability, Truva appointed himself Keith's promoter and dubbed him "Blackie."

Keith's parents bought a two-bedroom white house on 26th Street with a separate storage building at the back of the lot. His older sister Joyce claimed the second bedroom, so Keith convinced his mother to let him make the little building out back his own. It gave him the same sense of freedom he had felt in New Mexico where he slept summer nights in the barn. There was fancy indoor plumbing in the house, the first they had, but he still liked to pee in the grass when his mother wasn't around. At bedtime, he often heard the back door squeak and knew his father had sneaked outside for a last piss off the stoop. Another little preservation of freedom.

Corwin worked long hours at the Cotton Compress. Keith missed the daily camaraderie with his father, tending crops and cattle, riding horses. As much as possible, he stayed away from the hen party in the house with his mother and Joyce, glad to have his private quarters.

One day Corwin brought home an old bent bicycle someone had thrown out. The two of them straightened the frame, found patched tubes for the tires, and Keith became mobile again. Not a horse, but he could ride it to school and in downtown Lubbock where a horse couldn't go. He fashioned a basket from wire over the rear tire to hold his books. That gave him an idea. He rummaged another basket and wired it over the front tire, then biked over to the Mark Halsey Drug Store on Broadway and Avenue L. He had seen boys on bicycles delivering for Mr. Halsey, mostly prescriptions and household goods. But the fastest pedallers screamed through the streets delivering malts and ice cream, hopefully before they melted.

There were two drug stores in Lubbock, Mark Halsey Drug and John Halsey Drug, both downtown on Broadway. Two friendly brothers carrying on their father's business, separately. It was Mark Halsey's store that pulled the young crowd. He had installed twenty booths and the longest fountain counter in Texas. Smooth marble, it ran from the front of the store almost to the back. In a place where the old west never completely disappeared, the soda jerks slid malts and sodas down that long marble counter in the same manner beers journeyed down slick wooden saloon counters to thirsty cowhands.

Keith asked Mark Halsey for a delivery job. Mr. Halsey required a demonstration in the street beside his store. When he saw that Keith could handle the bike as well as a horse, including controlling its direction with no hands on the handlebars, he hired him on the spot.

"What's your name, boy? Who're your folks?"

"My name is Keith Leroy Black, but everybody calls me Blackie. My dad is Corwin Black. He works at the Compress now but, really, he's the best horse trainer there is. Ask anybody."

"He teach you to train horses?"

"Yeah, but I'm not as good as him, yet. Someday I'm gonna have a big horse ranch in New Mexico. He says I gotta go to college first, and that's gonna take some money, so I need a job. I know how to work, sir."

"I believe you. Well, you got a job, Blackie. Be on time and don't mess around flirting with the girls. Anything else you know how to do?"

"I can rope and trick ride. I can sing. I lead the singing at church every Sunday. Church of Christ. And I can play the guitar. Course I don't play it at church."

"Don't imagine any of that will do you any good here, but you can sure ride that bike. Let's give it a try."

Keith took his first paying job seriously. Every day after school he biked to Mark Halsey's Drug: "Right on the corner, Right on the price, and Right on your way home." He delivered pills and pillows and notebooks and malts while learning the streets and short-cut alleyways of wide, spread-out Lubbock. If there were no deliveries, he helped Mr. Halsey stock the shelves or sweep the floor, whatever needed to be done. Sometimes he watched the soda jerk entertain the customers and soon learned to mix sodas and malts.

After several months of pedaling through the brick streets, Keith's calf muscles were bulging—not that anyone noticed under his jeans, which he wore with his signature long-sleeved western shirts.

Then the hot-shot soda jerk made the mistake of being late one time too many. Mr. Halsey asked Keith if he wanted to step up.

Mark Halsey's fountain business increased as friends piled in to watch Blackie's shenanigans as the showman worked levers to mix sodas and malts. He threw the upper part of the metal tumbler in the air, caught it in the lower half, added ice cream and malt powder and milk in exaggerated up and down gyrations, then mixed them with the high whirr of the malt machine. He poured half the mixture into a tall, footed glass and served both the glass and the remains in the frosty can to his waiting customers. He slid the cans down the long marble counter. Sometimes he took their nine cents, but usually Mark Halsey's daughter Joyce acted as cashier. She kept a pile of pennies to give as change for a dime. The nine-cent malt was a Halsey specialty.[4]

One afternoon, a pretty brunette from school ordered a double-chocolate malt. "Blackie, do you know that Jimmie Rodger's song with the yodeling?"

"You mean, 'T is for Texas'?"

"Yep, that's it. Sing it for us. Can you yodel like him?"

"Well, I can, but I'm busy here, working, making your malt."

"Haven't you heard of singing while you work? I'll ask Mr. Halsey if it's okay." The brunette spun out of the red vinyl booth on her way toward the owner at the drug counter. She was back in a heartbeat. "He said he wants to hear what you got. I'm not the first one to bring it up."

"Okay, but all of you have to join in on the chorus to back me, 'cause I can't play a guitar at the same time I'm jerking sodas."

Blackie's strong, rich voice carried the lyrics a capella, then boomed above the others when they joined in on parts they knew. A few of the boys tried the yodeling but soon gave it up. Everyone was laughing and singing and having a good time. Some folks came in off the street to see what all the commotion was about. They stayed and bought sodas and malts.

"Well, I'll be," said Mark Halsey who could recognize a draw when he heard it. "Looks like we better make this an everyday deal."

Blackie packed them in day after day, especially on Saturdays. His friend Truva became part of the show by running a de facto taxi service for young people. He drove his dad's boaty Buick and picked up kids all over Lubbock, hauled them to Mark Halsey's and dropped them home again, earning free malts as his pay. He started hanging around the radio station KFYO (the only station in the region), bragging about his friend, the singing soda-jerk. He soon offered to drive the manager down to Mark Halsey's to hear Blackie sing.

Singing cowboys had made a big splash when the talkies came, adding sound to the action. The station manager recognized talent when he heard it, especially when accompanied by the siren call of opportunity. He struck a deal with Mark Halsey to sponsor a weekly show broadcast straight from the drug store featuring Blackie singing and playing his guitar and reading advertisements about Mark Halsey Drug. No extra pay besides his soda jerk money for Blackie, just a chance to be heard by more people.

His mother threw a small tirade, mentioning the devil and sin several times, but finally relented when Keith promised to sing at least one hymn during each broadcast. With radio stations now strung across the nation, America was trying to find its own sound, mixing blues and hymns and folk songs and jazz. Some people called this new sound hillbilly music. Others called it western or cowboy or country. The hymns were familiar and comfortable for listeners. They grounded an audience turning knobs on a box, learning to appreciate this new sound of music, whatever it was called. Blackie worked in his hymns and endeared himself to many listeners. "Amazing Grace" was familiar to everyone, no matter the denomination, so Blackie ended his performances with it until the station manager decided to make "America the Beautiful" the sign-off song.

It didn't matter to Blackie. Both songs touched his heart. He could rarely get through either without tears falling or voice cracking in reverence. *'Tis grace hath brought me safe thus far, And grace will lead me home.* No amount of practice or repetition could strip his feelings from his songs. So many emotions were tied to the hymns he had learned at his mother's knee and honed to perfection during long hours alone on his horse, singing them directly to God's ear. He intimately knew the *spacious skies, amber waves of grain* and *purple mountain majesties* of a beautiful New Mexico, the land he loved best in America.

With the money he earned, Keith contributed to the family coffers, but he tucked back the amount he was allowed to keep. A guitar in the window of the Broadway Music Store just down from Halsey's had caught his eye. Larger than his mother's, the one she had taught him to play and the one he still used, this new one was a Gibson Jumbo Acoustic L-OO, almost 15" wide with 14 frets clear. Mahogany sides and back. Spruce top with sprayed-on yellow sunburst, sporting a fire-striped tortoise pick board. The store owner had allowed him to strum a few chords. Incredible resonance. Man, what a guy could do with a guitar like that! $30! Could he ever get hold of that much? He used a Lord Clinton cigar box from Halsey's as a hope chest and hid it far from his mother's eyes in the little house out back. Slowly, the money accumulated.

After he finished tenth grade, his first year at Lubbock High, Keith Black approached his parents about going back to New Mexico to look for summer work. He waited until supper was almost done. His mother had just served raisin pie.

"Pie's really good, Ma. Thanks."

"You're welcome, Sonny Boy. I was out of mincemeat, thought the raisin would do fine."

"It's larrupin'." After a few more bites, he got up his courage.

"Mother, Dad, I want to go home for the summer. Mr. Purvines likes me. He always has horses that need to be broke. Or the haying or something else I can do. I can stay at the home place with Grandpa and Aunt Jo and Wop and Razz. Truva McSpadden said he would go with me."

"Truva McSpadden? That drives around in that big car?" Keith's mother asked. "His daddy gonna let him drive you up there?"

"No, Ma. It's their family car. His dad lets Truva drive it when he's not using it. I thought we would thumb it. It's not that far. I'm sure we can hitch a ride."

"Who is that little girl with the strange voice staying with Jesse and Vivian McSpadden?" his mother asked. "She was at church with them on Sunday."

"Her name is Dorris. She's Truva's cousin from down around San Angelo. But she's not a little girl, she's older than Truva."

"Why is she living with them? Finishing school?"

"Yep. Her folks are truck farmers. They move around a lot and she missed some grades and got behind. Then they got wiped out in that big flood on the Concho River last year, had to split up the family. She came up here to live with her dad's folks." Keith wasn't comfortable talking about this, but if it softened his mother for his real purpose, he would keep it up. "Seems bent on getting her high-school diploma. Nobody else in her family got one."

"She's a pretty little girl. Church-going girl. A good size for you."

"It ain't like that, Ma. She's close to twenty, a lot older than me and Truva, and way more serious. Besides, some guy named Hollis is trying to get with her. His folks have money. It would be a good deal for her."

"I was just saying, she is a nice size and all, not tall like girls are getting these days. You need somebody like that. You're gonna be short, Sonny Boy, like my Thorntons, not tall like the Blacks. Your sister Joyce took after them."

"Truva don't know anything about horses, Keith," his father finally rescued him. "What's he gonna do if you find work? And that's a pretty big IF. Work that pays is hard to come by in that country. There's men with families, mouths to feed, who need that money more than you. You got work here at Mark Halsey's. Best just stay here and keep what you got."

"Truva can ride. He knows enough. Mr. Halsey said he would hold my job, that I can come back any time. I really miss the ranch, Dad. Please let me go. If I can't find anything, I'll come back in a few weeks and work at Halsey's all summer." Keith was jittery. He had never lied to his parents before.

They mistook his nervousness for emotional attachment to the open plains of New Mexico and fear of being refused. After two days of mulling and a discussion with Truva's parents, Coleman and Rilla McSpadden, they agreed to allow him this adventure that seemed to mean so much to him.

"Keith, we've decided to let you go," his father began, "but there's no money to send with you. You need to figure this out as you go, make your own way. There's no one to help except when you're close to the home place. They can feed you and give you some jerky to take, but you're gonna get hungry. Have to just work through it."

"I've got a little money, Dad. Saved it out of my pay for a deal, but that can wait. I'll be okay."

"Sonny Boy," his mother interjected. "Truva's not as tough as you, and that's hard country. The Bible tells us to look out for those less fortunate. That's Truva. He doesn't have your savvy. You watch out for him, hear?"

"Yes, ma'am, I will."

CALIFORNIA, HERE I COME

 Written in 1921 by Buddy DeSylva and Joseph Meyer for the Broadway musical *Bombo*, starring Al Jolson. Recorded in 1924 by Al Jolson.

The next day, when his mother and sister Joyce left the house to buy groceries, Keith dug through the catch-all drawer in the kitchen and found the small notebook where his mother kept important addresses. He copied "Norval Clum, 2587 Santa Monica Blvd, Hollywood, California" and the phone number on a small slip of paper which he tucked into his shirt pocket.

Later at Mark Halsey Drug, Keith dialed the number and shoved coins into the pay phone. A woman answered after several rings.

"Hi, Aunt Gertie? It's Keith. Is Uncle Norval there?"

Gertrude Clum was Keith's great-aunt, his grandfather Albert Black's younger sister. After losing her first husband and children to the influenza epidemic of 1918, she had married prosperous Norval Clum. Seeking a better life, they had left the Kansas Dust Bowl and moved to Hollywood where Norval opened a furniture store. During visits to the Black Family Ranch in New Mexico, they had become entranced with Keith's singing voice and cowboy skills.

"Keith Black, is that you? Lord a mercy!" Gertrude answered. "What's wrong? Who died?"

"Nothing's wrong, Aunt Gertie. Nobody died. I just want to talk to Uncle Norval. He's been writing letters to me, sending them to the place I work. You know about that?"

"Yes, and I don't like it. Your mother would have a conniption if she found out."

"Can I talk to him? Not much time left." Keith was mindful of the three minutes he had paid for. He didn't have more coins with him.

"Norval's not here, honey. He's at the studio. You want me to tell him something, or can you call back tonight?"

"I don't know if I can call again. Just tell him I'm coming. In a week or so, soon as we can get there. My friend Truva and I are going to hitch out."

"You're coming here? To California?" Gertrude sounded anxious.

"Yep, we're gonna loop through New Mexico first, so it'll be a while. Don't write and tell any of the family we're coming out there. They'll think we're still in New Mexico. Nobody knows about California and it has to stay that way."

The operator interrupted. "Your time is up. Please deposit ten cents for an additional minute."

"Bye, Aunt Gertie. See you in a few days." Keith hung up the phone and glanced around to be sure no one had overheard him.

PUTTIN' ON THE RITZ

Written by Irving Berlin, 1927, revised lyrics in 1946. Sung by Henry Richman and chorus in musical of same name, 1930. First song in film to be sung by an interracial ensemble. Recorded by Fred Astaire, 1930, Columbia Record Company. Performed by Astaire in the film *Blue Skies* in 1946.

Dorris McSpadden was almost twenty and still in school. Her grades were good, so her family decided that she would go to the big city, finish high school, and get a diploma that would help her find a job. Lubbock was the mecca for anyone from west Texas who wanted to better themselves with education. She stayed with Daddy John's brother, Jesse McSpadden, his wife Vivian, and their children Douglas and Verlene. It wasn't a gimme. She had to cook and clean and run errands in exchange for room and board.

Another of her dad's brothers also lived in Lubbock, Coleman McSpadden and his wife Rilla. Their son Truva, her cousin, became a dear friend, though several years younger. He had access to the family car and drove Dorris anywhere she wanted to go. That is, after he got back from his big adventure! His friend Blackie had talked him into going hitch-hiking to New Mexico that summer.

There were things to buy in Lubbock and Dorris got into trouble. Handling money was new to her. Aunt Vivian and Uncle Jesse gave her what she needed for school supplies and other necessities, but they kept a strict record and needed to be repaid. Thinking about money made her nervous. She wrote home asking if there was any way to pay them back.

Her Daddy replied from Christoval:

Hello Dorris, This Sunday morning and the weather is fine. Owen and I are going to wash about 1000 lbs. turnips we gathered yesterday. Sold them to Mr. Butler, the truck farmer. We get .80 if delivered here and $1.00 per hundred if we take them to town. Cecil gets $45 and eats driving the truck for Uncle Frank. He stays with Frank and family.

The Rat and the Horses fit and Slick sure looks good and we will try to sell them for enough to pay Whitaker Bros if we can do that we will have a few dollars left when we get Strong payed. Balance due on our Crop lone yesterday $200.

As to your Uncle Jess you must remember his work is plenty tough and all he kneeds is a little petting. If you will just do him all the little favors it is the little things that count for us all.

We are going to send you some money, so you can pay Jess and Vivian all you owe them. Tell Jess to please be patient and we well take care of all expenses as soon as we can.

Now Dorris Just a little pollicy and common sense is all there is to it after all and we No you are there when it comes to show. Don't Kid yourself and don't let anybody else do that either. Love, Johnnie McS.

Even though Dorris couldn't pay her expenses right then, she used a little "pollicy and common sense" to find enough money to buy a birthday present for her dear brother Owen. It was a different kind of pencil, not wood, with lead that came out when the barrel was twisted. She mailed it to him.

Owen honey, I hope you like this little "do-thang" and will use it. I started to send you sox's or something, but I thought that you might like a little something different for a change. I saw this down at the drug store and it was so cute and different I just bought it.

Now listen sonny if you don't write me with this pencil, I'll know you don't like or appericate it—so you'd better take my hint and write—or beware!

Love and best wish (have luck), Your sister, Johnnie Dorris

A few days later, Owen wrote back:

Hi sappie, A norther blowed up about noon today. We all went out to the tomatoe patch late this afternoon and picked about five bushels that were under the vines and didn't get frosted Wednesday nite.

Say Dor, you ought to see our new car, new to us anyhow. We sold the old standby to Jennings Wrecking Co. and bought an old Buick. Sure runs good. We like it fine, starts a lot better than the Hudson did.

I am riteing with the pencil. Sure does rite good or would if I could rite. Sure is a nice gift. Many thanks.

Bernice sent me a box of candy that she made, part of it was fudge and part was fudge covered marshmellows, was awfully good. Mom made me a big chocolate cake with lots of pecans. You ought to see Mom, the dog, the pig and the calf all in a mix up at milking time. The dog and pig follow her into the house and then what a chase.

See you turkey day, Owen

After Thanksgiving in Christoval, Dad sent a postcard:

Dor, Judge Vickers told me to come to see him this fall said he would figure on fixing a place for us with pump. His office over Bank North of Square. Tell Truva he must take you. I had the flue last nite. Better tonight. We can't find James. Did you take him? Dad, Jno McSpadden[5]

Dad's words always made her feel better. But Dorris knew his "flue" was probably his stomach again. And yes, she had taken James to Lubbock after Thanksgiving. She needed a cat to love on. Her cousins Douglas and Verlene helped hide him.

Life in Lubbock wasn't hard, just doing chores she was used to. Work never bothered Dorris. *Doing necessary things without resentment is one of the secrets to being happy.* Her dear little mother taught her that. Besides, she loved to cook and became really good at it in Aunt Vivian's kitchen. The cook stove was gas. Just light a match and pouf, a flame appeared. Instant heat. Much easier and faster than coaxing heat from a wood stove. Their house had electricity that always worked. All one had to do was flip a switch or pull a string. But the best was the bathroom inside the house! No snakes to look for, no flies or wasps to battle, no bottom feeling vulnerable to the wind, and no crinkled noses or holding your breath from the horrid stench. Just flush the handle and whoosh, smell and all was gone. *Goody-goody!*

Dorris liked school and made friends even though she was older than most of her classmates. Many girls (well okay, women) were married with babies at that age. In Domestic Science class she learned to sew and make her own clothes, alongside her new friend Edith Ausmus. Mother was happy because she had tried to teach her to sew, but Dorris had been too fidgety and wouldn't stay put long enough to learn. She wrote her mother about progress on her first dress:

I almost have my dress finished, everything done but putting in the hem and fixing the placket. It's so pretty and sweet, but I'm afraid the skirt is going to stretch and swag. It's kinda stretchy material and so heavy. We have to have them finished by this coming Wed. and it will take me until that time to put in the hem. Hollis said "How in the world did you do all this crinkled stuff around here?" (meaning the shirring).

Hollis. Boyfriend. They double-dated with Edith and Harry, often going to midnight movies because they were cheaper. Dorris shared her city-life activities with Mama, Dot, and Jean:

Last night Edith and Harry came by and asked me if Hollis and I would like to go someplace with them and I said sure (cause it sure was cold and I dreaded to walk). So, they went over and got Hollis and then came back by for me. I wasn't ready, and I got so nervous having them set out there and wait for me. Anyway, we went riding all over this country for about 10 miles every direction from Lubbock. Harry has a new V8 and it has a heater in it—boy we really had a swell time.

We got back in Lubbock about 11:30. Edith and Harry went home, and Hollis and I went to the preview to see Wells Fargo. Oh, but that is the most wonderful picture I've ever seen. It was sad all the way through and so pretty (if that's any way to describe a story). I enjoyed every minute of it.

So did Hollis. Bob Burns is so good in it. It is a very different type picture. It seemed so real and true to life.

Dorris missed her family and got homesick at times but also liked being on her own, becoming who she was supposed to be. She wasn't exactly independent but somewhat free to work hard toward being a grown-up, the goal of becoming a real lady always in her mind.

THIS LAND IS YOUR LAND

American Folk Song. Written by Woody Guthrie in 1940 as a back-lash to Irving Berlin's war song "God Bless America." Recorded with changed lyrics by Woody Guthrie in 1944.

Dawn, two days after the phone call to Aunt Gertie in California, Keith and Truva caught a ride to Amarillo with a friend of Truva's dad. The man bought them blue plate specials at Coyote Café, then set them out on Highway 87, north of where it intersects with Route 66. Carrying bedrolls, a haversack and Truva's small valise, they walked through the outskirts of town before turning to walk backwards and throw their thumbs in the air at the sound of coming vehicles. Keith's old cowboy hat shaded his face. The long sleeves of his western shirt kept the searing sun off his arms. Truva couldn't pass for a local, with his new Stetson set too far back on his head to help his nose. The short-sleeved shirt and loafers with no socks didn't do much for his status either.

Within an hour, a farmer in an old Dodge truck with side-rails pulled over ahead of them. "Where you boys headed?" The farmer yelled out the open window when the running pair caught up with him.

"Des Moines, New Mexico." Keith yelled back to be heard over the clanking engine.

"I can take you as far as Dalhart if you want to ride in the back. Just sold a load of pigs. Swept the bed, but it ain't been washed down yet. Smell's not too good, but there's a tarp you can pull over the rails for shade."

"Much obliged, mister," said Keith as he climbed on the bumper and over the tailgate before he realized Truva wasn't following him.

"I ain't riding in no pig truck, Blackie. Can't you smell that?" Truva curled his nose.

"Smell won't hurt you none. We can sit on the bed next to the cab. Wind will blow that smell out the back. Tarp's a good deal, you'll be glad to have some shade." When his friend kicked the gravel, he tried again, "Get in here. This is backcountry. There's not gonna be a Cadillac come along and offer you the front seat."

Truva didn't budge.

"Listen, Truva. We can part ways right here. Nobody said it would be easy." Keith offered his hand. "Are you coming with me or not? Driver's not gonna wait forever."

"How'd I ever let you talk me into this?" Truva grumbled, as he took his friend's hand and clambered onto the truck.

Luck favored them. Their thumbs caught another truck ride from Dalhart, Texas, to Clayton, New Mexico. That one had a clean bed. As they rode along, Truva dozed with his head on his bedroll, covering his face with his Stetson. No way could Keith close his eyes.

Rays shot from the bright yellow ball in the west looking much like the stylized sunrays on the New Mexico state flag. Keith appreciated the sacredness of the flag's Zia symbol: the four rays symbolizing four directions, the four times of day, the four stages of life and the four seasons with the Circle of Life in the center binding all four paradigms together.

He studied the fluffy cotton clouds floating through the wide azure sky and let the openness of the land seep in. The clean smell of the hot, dry air was exhilarating. Something familiar blew with the wind. Aunt Maybel would say the spirits were coming to greet him and bring him home. Peace settled under his skin as he remembered Maybel Word, the Choctaw woman who had married his uncle, Oscar David "Dee" Thornton, his mother's brother. She had delivered her own baby, a girl named Hazel, a few weeks before Keith's difficult birth.

While his mother struggled to survive the traumatic birth of a ten-pound baby and the operations that followed, Aunt Maybel lovingly took Keith to her breast, nursed him along with Hazel, and cared for him during his first year of life. More than milk had flowed through the Choctaw mother to baby boy Black. The spirit of proud people who venerate their land permeated his being as well.

That evening, when the truck rolled to a stop in Clayton, Keith jumped down and kissed the ground. "Wahoo! New Mexico. Home at last."

"Looks like a desert to me," Truva observed.

"Just wait till tomorrow when we get to the home place. Look over there, that mountain with two peaks is called Rabbit Ears. When you see that, you're in God's country."

"Yeah, well, sun's going down on God's country. What do we do now?"

"Sleep on the ground. Why do you think we brought the bed-rolls? We'll get going real early. I know a fella we can catch a ride with to Des Moines. He hauls cream over there to the train every morning about dawn."

Two miles west of the Clayton city limits sign, off the road a bit, they spread out their bedrolls. That close to Rabbit Ears, there was a lot of rough malpais, but they found a dense patch of short grama grass to soften their night. Keith shared the fruitcake and biscuits spread with peanut butter that his mother had wrapped in bandanas.

After they finished, Truva reached into his shirt pocket. "I've been saving this all day," he said, fishing out a Hershey bar. It folded over his fingers.

"Yep, you've been wearing it all day, too. Is there anything left that didn't melt?"

The two of them took turns licking chocolate off the Hersey wrapper.

"Hand me the canteen," Truva said. "Gall dang heat. We've

been in hell all day. Why did you make me bring a blanket anyway?"

"Wait an hour or two. You'll be glad you got it."

The inky night enveloped them. Keith lay back on his bedroll and absorbed the heavens. A sliver of moon hovered above the western horizon, curved upward like a cup waiting to be filled. "Just look at that moon and those stars," he said. "Millions of 'em. Have you ever seen so many stars? There's the Milky Way and the Big Dipper."

"We got the same stars in Texas."

"Not this bright and clear. You can't see a light in any direction except those stars."

"What about snakes, Blackie? Coyotes? Bears?"

"They won't bother us, Truva. Real cowboys don't taste good."

Next morning, the Clayton dairyman dropped them off in the middle of Des Moines, New Mexico, population 153. Paint was peeling from the tired clapboard buildings holding limp hands down one side of the wide highway. It hadn't changed during the year Keith had spent in Lubbock. Heck, except to accommodate cars and trucks, it hadn't changed much since it was founded thirty years ago when the railroad came through. The population had boomed to 800 before the droughts and dust bowls of the '20s and '30s drove over 600 of them away.

"This is it?" Truva asked. "This is where you come from, what all this hoo-ha is about? Not much here, Blackie."

"Not the town, dumbbell. The place. Look around. See that volcano? That's Capulin Mountain, a perfect cinder cone. On a clear day, you can see five states from the top of the rim, over 8,000 feet high. When settlers first came here, they wanted it all for themselves, so when they saw a new wagon train coming, they would build a giant fire in that crater with the dead chokecherry wood and tell people the volcano was about to erupt. That big mountain in the south, that's Sierra Grande, a shield volcano. Takes three days on horseback to ride all the way around the base. Did it once. And that peak in the northwest, that's Emery. I got a secret spot up there."

Truva rubbed his stomach. "Tummy's growling. I need food. Why don't you play tour guide later? How do we get breakfast?"

"We'll have to hoof it on home, about two miles." They started walking the dirt road that led north past the Des Moines Cemetery to the Black home place. Keith cautioned Truva again to not tell anyone their plans. "Don't even mention the word California."

Just past the railroad tracks, near the buffalo wallows, a blob of dust whirled toward them. "That's Razz's old truck. Stand out in the middle of the road, so he has to stop. Otherwise he'll blow right past us. Norm or Wop would stop out of curiosity, but not Razz."

Razz, real name Russell Black, was Keith's uncle though he was only five years older and seemed more like a brother. Runt of the litter, short as Keith but scrawnier, he sat low in the truck. When he saw that the strangers weren't moving, he stood on the brakes and waited for the dust to clear. A sideways slow grin crossed his weathered face. "That can't be Keith Black. No horse. No guitar. Unless you shrunk them and stuck them in that sissy valise."

"It's me alright, Razz. Figured I would ride your horse and play your guitar. You're not any good at either one. Can you haul us to the home place?" Truva rode in the cab with Razz. Black sat on the tail gate. They turned around in the middle of the road, and Razz delivered them to the Black home place, two thousand acres of paradise.

A tall wooden windmill towered above the house and out-buildings, its round iron holding-tank brimming with fresh water just pumped from the stingy dry earth. Solid as ever stood the large barn, a small shop for blacksmithing and machine work, calf sheds, a chicken house built on stilts and the necessary outhouse. Weathered board fences surrounded the clustered compound and corral, with barbed wire farther out.

The sturdy wood house, basically square with a peaked roof, had an inviting porch that faced the morning sun. A dozen apricot trees grew in the back, mail-ordered from Stark Brothers Nursery in St. Louis and babied. Aunt Jo's apricot pies and jams were a specialty in the area. Her kitchen wall sported blue ribbons to prove it. She also nurtured apple and cherry trees as well as gooseberry bushes. The orchard and her large vegetable garden were completely enclosed with a high fence to keep out the mule deer. She couldn't do much about crows except keep her gun handy. Abe Lincoln rose bushes, also from Stark's, lined the front steps, meeting the morning with glorious red blooms brought about by the judicious use of horse manure.

Inside were five large rooms plus a smaller room fitted with thunder mugs for use during blizzards and sand storms. A strand of stairs led to an open floored attic that could handle a few souls needing a place to bed down. A pioneer in the region, Keith's grandfather, Albert Bellman Black, known as A. B., Albert, or Bert, had built all this with the help of his sons and third wife, Josephine Dwyer, who Keith called Aunt Jo.[6]

An old man stepped out of the shed as Black and Truva approached. He was wearing boots, a collarless shirt, and khaki trousers held up with broad suspenders. A bent straw hat shaded his sun-worn face and gray handlebar moustache. His solemn expression never changed.

"Blackie, how ya been?"

"I'm right as rain, A. B. You?"

"Gettin by, gettin by. Who's your pal?"

"This is Truva McSpadden from Lubbock. We hitched up here. Truva, this is my grandpop, Albert Black."

"How do you do, sir." Truva extended his hand, which A. B. ignored, turning instead to his grandson.

"How's Corwin, Blackie? Good health?"

"Yeah, he's in fine health. He likes working at the Compress." Black hesitated, not knowing whether to add information on his mother's health. He hadn't been asked, and his mother was always a touchy subject. Leave well enough alone. "We've got a nice house, in-door plumbing. Two bedrooms, Joyce has one. I've got my own digs, a little building out back of the main house."

"Any land?"

"No, just the house on a lot." Black kicked a small rock in the loose dirt. He didn't want to talk about land and horses, or rather the lack of them.

"What's you boys' business here? How long you staying?"

"Just a day or two at the home place, A. B. Thought we might get on with one of the branding crews or buck a little hay. Earn some money. I want to go to the Purvines Ranch and look up Ginger. Maybe go on down to Taos for a few days, show Truva the Pueblo. Just mess-ing around."

"Purvines sold Ginger already. Got big bucks from some outfit coming through looking for horses for those western picture shows. He put her through her paces with all those tricks you taught her, and they bought her on the spot. She's long gone."

Black looked as if someone knocked the wind out of him. "But he promised."

"Well, you know about promises when money comes along," A. B. said.

"Money, it's always about money." Black picked up the rock he had been kicking and threw it against the barn. *Thud.*

"Yep, seems to be. You better get on in the house and let Jo fetch you some food before that anger eats you up."

Black and Truva took the porch steps two at a time. Aunt Jo was only slightly warmer than A. B. She instructed them to throw their gear in the attic loft, then sent them to steal eggs from the hens. She cooked bacon, then fried the fresh eggs in the grease and served them with left-over biscuits and apricot jam. They wolfed the food down without too many questions from Aunt Jo. She asked about his mother and sister Joyce but was content with "fine health" answers.

After breakfast, they scurried back outside, shouting thanks over their shoulders. Though Black couldn't bring himself to offer help with the dishes, he pumped the water for Aunt Jo before he left the kitchen. At home his mother would insist he do all the cleanup.

"I don't think they cotton to me too much," Truva said. "I don't feel welcome. Kinda like I feel at your house in Lubbock."

"It's just their way. Some folks hold back, don't show you their hand."

Razz had rescued his brother Lynn from a broken-down tractor and brought him back to the ranch. The family called Lynn 'Wop,' but the people around Des Moines called him Red because of his hair. Yep, Red Black. Tall, big-boned and fleshy with a ready smile, Red must have descended from the Dwyers instead of the wiry Blacks. He bear-hugged his nephew, happy to be in his company again. And when Black introduced Truva, Red bear-hugged him too, just for sport.

"This is the other half of Mutt and Jeff, my two old bachelor uncles." Black said.

"Who you calling old?" Razz weighed in. "You're only five years younger than me and ten years younger than Red. But you're the one who's gonna be a bachelor. We got plenty of women after us, at least I do."

"So it's okay if I call you Mutt but not okay if I call you old, huh?"

"Call me anything, just call me for dinner," Razz snickered.

"That's a girl's line, but you wouldn't know anything about girls, would you?" Black teased though beginning to feel a bit uncomfortable because he didn't know much about girls himself and this little pissing match could get embarrassing.

"You might be surprised what I know about women, Keith Black. They love me." Razz smiled. "I could teach you a thing or two sometime."

"Knock it off, Razz," Red intervened. "Let's saddle up some

horses and show this greenhorn what a real ranch looks like. Can you ride, Truva?"

"Sure. I rode a lot when I was a kid but not much lately. Don't get many chances in town," Truva said. "I'd love to get on a horse again."

Several horses were in the corral. Black made sure Truva got Sadie, a gentle dapple grey he knew and trusted. For himself, he roped a six-year-old spunky sorrel, aptly called Socks, and climbed aboard. Red and Razz had their own favorites.

And they were off, Riders of the Purple Sage, faster than necessary and feeling free. For some people, things are just right with the world from the back of a horse. They climbed Dunchee Hill behind the ranch house, rode past Carr Mountain, Briggs Canyon and Mitchel Springs, then on toward the benches of Emery Peak. Near the top they whoaed up, so Black could point out the features of the postcard landscape. Besides the obvious majestic landmarks of Capulin Volcano, Sierra Grande, and Rabbit Ears, he also pontificated on his favorite smaller spots in the mesmerizing moonscape, then pointed out the home place's wooden windmill and the small cemetery nearby, where folks he knew were planted in the soil he loved.

A full year had passed since Black last stood here. A lot of change had come into his life, most of it good. But this feeling, this one right here, standing on this mountain, this feeling like God was singling him out, showing him His secrets, wanting him to understand something special, this feeling hadn't changed a bit. It still brought tears to his eyes, no matter how many yahoos were standing around. He turned quick to keep them from seeing.

GIT ALONG LITTLE DOGIES
(WHOOPEE TI YI YO)

 Cowboy Ballad. Music and lyrics first published in 1910 in John Lomax's *Cowboy Songs and Other Frontier Ballads.*

The next day Razz toured Black and Truva around the high plains in his old ranch pickup. They picked up Black's cousin, Filthy McNasty, in Des Moines. Filthy's real name was Afton Thornton. His nickname fit because he was just the opposite, spit-polished and scrubbed behind the ears. He and Black rode in the truck bed, staying close to the cab to keep their hats from blowing off. The back window had broken out of the truck long ago, so the four could converse quite easily with Filthy and Black bending in.

The day was still and sunny with buttermilk clouds floating inside a blue dome. Hot.

The fearless four visited neighbors Milo Seaton at his gas station and A. W. "Daddy" Farr, an old civil war vet transplanted from Kansas who was particularly fond of Black. Filthy suggested the Purvines Ranch but Black vetoed the idea, his ire still intact regarding Ginger. Instead they drove through the tiny town of Folsom and then down the Dry Cimarron Valley past Toll Gate Canyon to the legendary Cross-L (Crosselle) Ranch.

The Crosselle, one of the first mega-ranches in the area, was established by the Hall brothers in 1871. They drove 2,600 head of Texas cattle, mostly long-horns, to the beautiful remote canyon valleys of the Dry Cimarron. Over the next ten years they bred those long horns right out of the herd, developing short-horned white-faced cattle on the exceptionally nutritious native grasses. The large ranch house with overhanging verandas looked as if it had been plucked from the Australian outback. The Halls' extensive rangelands were bought out by English and Scottish investors who merged the Crosselle with other holdings to become the Prairie Land and Cattle Company, owning land from the Canadian River in the Panhandle to the Arkansas River in Colorado with over 100,000 head of cattle and thousands of saddle horses. Eventually, due to the financial depression of the late 1800s, the colossal holdings were dispersed, and the Crosselle fell back into private ownership in 1903.

Black, Razz, and Filthy had come to manhood hearing the stories of the Crosselle. Black's father, Corwin, had earned his spurs as a young cowhand on the ranch. Now, as they entered the gates, those cowboy images played in their heads and stirred their imaginations. Reverent quiet descended as the boys surveyed their mecca. The corral boss honored this palpable ethos and allowed the cowboy-dreamers an hour of horseback riding through the cattle herd. Branded on each cow was a prominent long L, crossed at the top.

Afterwards, driving back near Travessier Canyon, Razz announced they would be stopping to cool off at Folsom Falls on the Dry Cimarron.

"Wait a minute," Truva said. "We're going to a waterfall on a *dry* river?"

"Nothing gets by you, does it?" Black teased his friend. "Cimarron *Seco*. It's called the Dry Cimarron because it disappears below ground in some places, then pops up again later in the streambed. Drovers on the Goodnight-Loving Trail could herd cows right over dry ground, bed them down, then water them where the river came up again. Part of the Santa Fe Trail went through here, too, the Cimarron Cut-Off. Swell, huh?"

Three miles north of Folsom in a small arroyo, Folsom Falls drops the Dry Cimarron River about ten feet, just after Pinabete Creek joins the flow. Water pools in a wide rocky hollow, then tumbles amid large boulders and grassland, runs through northeastern New Mexico and kisses Kansas where it blends into the Arkansas River and flows on across Oklahoma and Arkansas, merges into the great rush of the mighty Mississippi and finally into the Gulf of Mexico to mix with the oceans. In this remote isolated place, water falls from the heavens and finds its way into the larger world though its path is long and winding, sometimes turbulent, and its flow is, unexpectedly, east from this western land.

The boy-men took off their boots and shirts and carefully waded into the cool water in their jeans, keeping an eye out for snakes. They cavorted in the shallows because no one could swim except Truva. Not much need or opportunity to swim in dry country. They stuck their heads under the gentle flow of the falls and caught water in their mouths. Razz initiated splash wars and dunked an unwary Black who retaliated by dunking Filthy. Truva backstroked into the deep spots and easily escaped the dunkings.

At the truck, Razz slipped off his jeans, dried with his shirt and slid under the steering wheel in his underwear. Again, he chauffeured the three caballeros as they stood in the back and beat on the cab, wet jeans blowing in the wind.

As they neared the tiny town of Folsom, Keith thought of something important. "Hey, Truva," he said, "did you study the Folsom Man in school?"

"Yep, but don't remember much."

"Well, it's a really big deal. Happened right here." Black hastened on. He wasn't sure if he was trying to convince Truva or just reminding himself that this was the keenest place on the planet. "About ten years ago, west of Folsom, up towards Johnson Mesa in Wild Horse Arroyo, I know the exact spot, been there several times. Anyway, some scientists found a special chiseled arrowhead in the bones of a buffalo. They named it the Folsom Point."

"Wait a minute, you got that wrong," Razz corrected, yelling from the cab. "An old colored cowboy named George McJunkin found that bison bone pit. Credit where credit's due. That was about twenty years ago. It took them scientists fifteen-twenty years to catch up with ole George. Heck, they're probably still arguing about it."

"Cowboys came in colored?" Truva asked.

"Yep. 'Course they did. Old timers called them Buffalo cowboys, after the Buffalo Soldiers in the Civil War," Filthy joined the story-telling. "George McJunkin's famous around these parts. Best cowhand there ever was. He was the foreman over a lot of whites. Everybody loved him. He had been a slave down in Texas, came here after the Civil War freed him. He taught the young yahoos how to cowboy, and they taught him how to read and write. Smart dude. He wore a big, broad-brimmed hat and carried a telescope with him to scope out strays. Always digging up an old fossil he found or some rock. Collected them in boxes and kept them at his house on the Crowfoot ranch. He really knew this country."

"Yeah. I heard he used that telescope to study the stars, too." Black knew the magic of the stars on the dark plains at night.

"Okay, one more thing about ole George," Razz yelled, "he found all those bones because they had been unearthed by the great flood that destroyed Folsom. I think it was aught-eight."

"Yep, that's right, 1908." Filthy said.

"Big rains in the mountains west of here on Johnson Mesa sent a flash flood boiling down the Dry Cimarron. Someone called the telephone operator, Sally Rooke, in Folsom and told her it was coming, would hit about midnight. She started phoning everyone she could and saved a bunch of people but drowned herself because she wouldn't leave her post. Her little operator shack floated away and smashed up. They didn't find her body 'til the next spring. Lots of others drowned, too. The whole town whooshed down the Cimarron. Never was the same after that." Razz made a wide sweep with his right hand, then he turned and pointed his finger at Black. "And that flood washed out Wild Horse Arroyo and left all those bones exposed for ole George to find."

"He knew that what he found was different, that the bones were larger than buffalo nowadays," Black said. "He kept at the scientists at the Denver Museum until they finally figured out that those spearhead points actually stuck in the ancient bones proved that Indians had been in America ten thousand years longer than anybody thought. The Folsom Man. That put Folsom on the map."

"You sure about that, Blackie?" Truva asked. "I don't think I could find Folsom even with a map. And I'm purty sure nobody's looking for it. This is a ghost town."

"I'll make you a ghost, Truva McSpadden, if you don't lay off bad-mouthing my stomping grounds," Black kidded. "Hey, whoa! I know that horse."

Razz stood on the brakes, stopped in the road at the side of Doherty Mercantile. Dust roiled. Beside the white frame building Carlos Cornay, a young lad about ten years old, was dismounting his horse, a sorrel gelding named Keno.

"Amigo!" Black yelled as he put one hand on the side and hurtled over the truck bed onto the ground.

The young cowboy tipped his hat back and squinted, then grinned. "Black!"

The two friends strode eagerly toward each other, hands extended.

"Keno looks good" Black said. He patted the horse's rump. "You're taking good care of him."

"He eats his fill. He's been an easy rider since you broke him for me." Carlos stroked Keno's long neck.

"He looks fast. You don't race him much, do you?" Black teased his friend.

"Only against my brothers." Carlos smiled.

Black glanced back toward the old Dodge. Filthy sat slumped on the edge of the bed. In his black cowboy hat, he looked like a roosting buzzard covered in dust. "Hey, come say hi to the guys."

Black presented his friend, "Truva, this young Frenchman is Carlos Cornay, one of my best compadres."

They exchanged nods, then Carlos stepped to the cab and noticed the bare leg resting on the brake. "Hello, Razz."

"Carlos." Razz subdued a cat-eating-glue grin.

"We stopped at the Falls to cool off," Black explained Razz's missing pants. "You should have been with us."

"Nope. You know I'm not a water man." Carlos pulled back from the truck. "Hey, Black, you still singing?"

"Yep. Lead singing at church. And the guy that owns the drugstore where I work even lets me sing while I'm jerking sodas. It's a lot of fun."

"He sings on the radio, too," Truva interrupted. "Folks in Lubbock love to hear him sing."

"On the radio? A real star, huh? I knew it, had to be. Folks here love to hear him sing too. That voice of his, that's a gift straight from God." Carlos turned to Black. "If you're going to be singing while you're here. I want to come."

"I don't think there's much chance of that. I didn't bring my guitar." Black climbed over the tailgate into the bed of the truck. "*Adios, amigo.* Good to see you again."

"*Vaya con Dios*, my friend."

"*Hasta la vista!*" Razz yelled as he gunned the engine.

On the way back to Des Moines, he stopped in the road again near a cinder plant that was slowly eating little twin lava-rock mountains by grinding, sorting, packaging, and shipping the volcanic materials to less scenic places. As he pulled on his jeans, Razz pointed out the railroad tracks that curved around the diggings, winding to the summit.

"It's over a mile high at the top of the grade, higher than Denver. A long hard pull for the trains," Razz said. "They go really, really slow when they're loaded. Slow enough to be robbed." He pointed at the curved tracks. "Right there is where Black Jack Ketchum committed his last train robbery before he was finally caught. Got shot in the arm. He jumped off the train and just laid there in the dark. Next train in the morning, they caught him. His arm had to be amputated. Then they amputated his head. Ha!" Razz laughed at his own joke. "They hung him in Clayton, sold tickets. Everybody went to see the hanging. Still a big deal around these parts. His head popped right off his body."

"What? That's not true, is it Blackie?" Truva asked.

"Yep, sure is. I saw the picture. His head's laying there right beside his body. The hangman put too much weight on the rope and Black Jack's head snapped clean off when the trap was sprung. Women and little kids were there, watching the whole thing."[7]

The cowboys drove back through Des Moines and continued east to Wiley Hittson's place. Wiley kept fine horses and Black wanted to look them over. At the corral, they happened across a young hotshot summer hand named Max Evans up from Glorieta Mesa south of Santa Fe. Razz had tangled with him before. Max and Razz were like two spokes on the same wheel that just couldn't quite roll along together. Their banter seemed harmless enough until Razz threw his hat on the ground. Black recognized the sign, grabbed Razz and pulled him away before he could throw a punch.

"What's that about?" he asked Razz after Evans had walked away. "He's just a kid."

"Don't like his looks, that's all."

"Guess he didn't like yours, either," Filthy said.

"He just likes to fight." Razz picked up his hat, banged it on his leg to dust it and plopped it back on his head. "Get in the truck. We best get home. Have to wake up early for our Cimarron trip."

"Cimarron? What are you talking about? I can't go to Cimarron tomorrow," Filthy said.

"I'm taking Black and Truva that far. They're gonna hitch the rest of the way to Taos. First we're gonna have us some fun. Pretty women in Cimarron, huh, boys? Pretty Indian women. *Muy bonita chicas.* Those women in Cimarron, they like to pick ripe fruit. I heard they were mighty fond of *cherries!*" There was that mischievous one-sided grin again.

Black suddenly turned red from head to toe. It wasn't sunburn. "What do you mean, Razz? You didn't say anything about women. You just said you would drive us part-way."

"And I will. But no harm in a little *lay*-over, huh? You boys could *get up* for something like that, couldn't you?" He was laughing out loud, holding nothing back.

"Sure, count me in." Truva smiled so wide his tongue almost fell out.

"I'm not so sure about this," Black said.

"You'll be real sure tomorrow. Now get in the truck or I'm leaving you here to deal with Max Evans." Razz skittered down the dirt road pushing the old Dodge all he dared. The truck responded by farting dust clouds back at Max.[8]

THE OLD RUGGED CROSS

Hymn. Written by George Bennard, a traveling singing evangelist. Begun in Albion, Michigan in 1912, first performed in 1913 during a revival at the Friends Church in Sturgeon Bay, Wisconsin, by Bennard and his fellow evangelist Ernest Mieras. Final version first performed by a quartet in 1913 at the First Methodist Episcopal Church in Pokagon, Michigan.

Back at the home place, Aunt Jo had wrung the necks of some chickens, plucked and fried them up for dinner, then served them alongside fresh biscuits and gravy. Her prize-winning apricot pies nailed the finale. "Now when I get the kitchen cleaned up, Blackie, I want to hear you sing. Norman left his guitar in the attic when he went off to Louisiana. You'll have to tune it up."

"Can do," Black said. "You mean Razz and Red haven't been entertaining you?"

"Couldn't get my kids interested in music," Aunt Jo said. "Norman played around with the guitar before he left, but it didn't amount to much. Wait, I think I hear a wagon." She walked to the window, pulled the curtains back and peered out. "Oh, the Larkins are almost here. They wanted to hear you sing. Said they'd sorely missed you at church. There's quite a bit of dust on the road. More coming. Razz, run up to the attic and get the guitar. Ya'll go sit on the porch with them and I'll bring some pie out."

"Your musical talent comes from your ma, you know." A. B. finally had something to say. "Does she still have that old Gibson she taught you on?"

"Yeah. She doesn't play it much anymore though." Black wanted to tell his grandfather about the new Gibson in the store window, the one he was saving for, but he was afraid A. B. might think him a frivolous dreamer.

"She sure had a beautiful voice. Such a shame."

"A. B., enough about that now." Aunt Jo broke in. "Go on to the porch. I'll be right out."

Black knew people had admired his mother's voice, that she used to entertain, singing at school and community events. He also knew she had stopped singing after his birth, except for hymns. Coming to her defense he turned to his grandfather. "She sings in church, even starts it off if I'm not there. Brother Thompson stands up front and pretends to lead, but he can't get the right key going. He waits for her to set the pitch."

"Ain't the same," A. B. said. He stood up and stretched his stiff joints, then picked up his chair and carried it to join the folks who had been gathering on the porch and in the yard—the people Jo had phoned and the ones they had called in turn: the shoppers who told others at the Mercantile and the filling station, the cowboys who passed the word around the stockyard and the feed store and the bars, the diners who talked about it at the cafe, the ones the mail carrier had told.

And yes, Carlos Cornay had heard in Folsom and brought his harmonica, planning to join in. He waited among the crowd murmuring about the exceptional rich timbre of Black's voice, the way it resonated with the land and its inhabitants, the way it brought home into their souls. They had come to experience that again, to touch a piece of raw spirituality simmering, growing, molding into something extraordinary.

Born with perfect pitch, Black had led singing for the congregation from the time he was nine. The Church of Christ does not allow musical instruments in its services, so all singing is *a capella*. The Good Book says in Ephesians 5:19: *Singing and making melody with your heart.* That's proof enough for the Church of Christers that God doesn't want any instruments in His worship service, just voices. Because women are not permitted to be in any position above men of whatever age (1st Timothy 2:12: *Suffer not a woman to teach, nor to usurp authority over the man*), a man must lead the song service whether he can make melody or not. In the Des Moines, New Mexico, Church of Christ in 1930, the man who could set the pitch had been nine years old.

Black sat at the top of the tall porch steps. Norman's guitar was badly out of tune, but friends and neighbors waited patiently, talking quietly amongst themselves with comfort and ease while Black adjusted the strings. Chairs were brought out from the kitchen, blankets spread on the grass. Young cowpokes perched on nearby fence rails.

Black's rich vibrating tenor streamed into the night. He started with hymns out of respect for his church elders saving cowboy songs for later. *On a hill, far away.* He sang the verse alone, then asked everyone to join him and sang it again. By the time the group got to *a world of lost sinners was slain,* many eyes couldn't hold back the emotion. *Cherish the cross, the old rugged cross.* Brother England's deep bass supported the sopranos and altos, as all sang their parts. Black's tears fell as natural as rain. He kept right on singing. *And exchange it some day for a crown.*

Summer evening on the high plains cast its spell. Still dry air clinging to the day's heat, gentle mauve of the setting sun, mellow lamplight, then thousands of sparkling stars in the abyss around them. The land, the heavens, the singer, the listeners: One.

Young Carlos whapped some cowhands from the T. O. Ranch who were making fun of Black's tears. "Have some respect. That's between him and his God. When you can sing like that, make all these people feel something, then you can throw stones."

Black continued, one hymn after another, taking requests. He knew the music and all the stanzas by heart though he wasn't particularly fond of "Bringing in the Sheaves" which one of the Baptists requested. Eventually, he cradled his guitar and transitioned from hymns to ballads, beginning with "Red River Valley" from Gene Autry's movie. *From this valley, they say you are going. We will miss your bright eyes and sweet smile.*

People trickled away as the evening wore on, quietly gathering their things and bidding the young singer and his family adieu. When young folks and those whose hearts were forever young remained, Black picked up the pace with more Gene Autry and Jimmy Rodgers ballads, then threw in "Indian Love Call" singing both Nelson Eddy's and Jeannette MacDonald's parts. Music came like magic to Black. He could pick out most tunes the first time he heard them. Lyrics branded themselves into his mind. *His hat was throw'd back and his spurs were a'jinglin.* Even the most jaded cowpokes couldn't resist the sing-along on that chorus: *Whoopee Ti Yi Yo, Get along, Little Dogies.*

The next morning when they woke and lay talking on the floor of the attic, Black had bad news for Truva, "Pal, we're not going to Cimarron with Razz."

"Are you kidding me?" Truva leaned up on his elbow. "Why not? When are we ever gonna get another chance like this?"

"Well, I don't know, but this isn't right. Wrong time. Wrong place. Wrong people. For me, it's not happening like this. That's not what we've talked about."

"Not what who's talked about? Me and you?" Truva asked.

"No, me and God. We kind of got a deal, you know. I keep up my end. He keeps up His."

"Well, he don't talk to me, Blackie. I don't have a deal. This is as good a time as any to get this over with. I'm seventeen years old. Lots of guys our age have been doing it for years."

"Look, Truva, you can do what you want to do. I won't try to stop you," Black said. "It's mostly Indian women in those places in Cimarron. My Aunt Maybel Thornton, the one who saved my life when I was a baby, is an Indian. It's not right for me."

"Not right for you, eh? Good enough for me, but not for you? What makes you so special, Mr. Goody Two Shoes?" Truva leaped up, his head barely missing the rafters. His hand closed into a fist. "You got a direct line to God, huh?"

Black jumped up too. The rafters weren't a problem. "Get out of my face, Truva. I'm not judging you or anybody else. Not my job. Do what you want to do. I won't think any less of you for it. But I'm not gonna do it. Simple as that. Now get out of my face before I knock you down."

Black might be called short, but inch-for-inch, no one could match the strength of his powerful muscles. It wasn't a fight Truva could win.

They stared at each other with narrowed eyes and set jaws. Finally, Truva unclenched his fist, grabbed his shirt and shoes, and sprinted down the stairs. "I'm gonna talk to Razz," he yelled back over his shoulder.

HOORAY FOR HOLLYWOOD

Theme song for the Academy Awards. Music composed by Richard A. Whiting. Featured in 1937 movie *Hollywood Hotel,* sung by Johnnie Davis and Francis Langford, accompanied by Benny Goodman and his orchestra.

Three days later the driver of a 2-Ton produce truck pushed up the rolling door of the box and there among the tomato crates lay Black and Truva.

"Wake up, sleepy-heads. We're in Los Angeles. If you'll help me unload the truck, we'll call it even on the ride."

Black jumped to his feet and hopped off the back onto pavement. He had slept through the stop and go of city traffic. With the door rolled down except for six inches for air, there wasn't much that could be seen if he had been awake.

The sun was coming up, spreading long shadows cast by tall buildings. He was met by a warm humid breeze carrying the smell of strawberries and bananas, apples and oranges, potatoes and onions, plus the sweet perfume of flowers. This feast had been produced by humans and trucked nonstop from garden plots in Texas and the heartland, or fields in Mexico, or orchards in Oregon and Washington to the hub of the California coast. To Terminal Market, one of the nation's largest produce markets, at 7th & Central in downtown Los Angeles. It was Alive! Loud! Horns honking, people shouting, a train's iron wheels squeaking to a halt in the Terminal Building. The movement, murmur, and wet-cracker smell of hundreds of workers signaled a new cultural experience. Chinese, Mexicans, Whites, Blacks.

"We're really here!" Black could barely contain his excitement. "Come on, Truva. Get out of the truck."

Truva jumped down moving slowly and acting surly. He hadn't yet forgiven Black for missing out on Razz's Cimarron adventure.

"Take a good look, boys. You've made it to the big city." The driver treated them like the greenhorns they were. "They got rules here. You have to pay for what you eat, but plenty of these old hands will trade food for work. Now, you boys go get washed up. There's a public bathroom in the Terminal Building over there. I'll keep your bedrolls here until we unload." While a trusting man, he wanted to ensure he didn't have to unload the truck by himself.

"See that Mexican over there with that little oil stove? He'll make you some eggs with peppers and roll 'em in a tortilla. Got a hot sauce he puts on 'em. Makes a good breakfast. Tell him I'll be over to trade in a bit, bring him some tomatoes for whatever you eat. Then get yourselves back here and we'll start taking off the crates."

A few hours and an empty truck later, the driver shook their hands, gave them a small paper sack filled with tomatoes and bid them Godspeed. Black asked when he was going back to Taos.

"Right now," the driver said. "But I'll be back in L. A. with another load in a week or so. Why? You looking for a ride back? I thought you came to make your fortune in Hollywood."

"Yeah, my uncle's helping me with that," Black replied, "but even if I do get a job, I'll have to go back to Texas and get my things and take Truva home."

"Well, I can take you almost to Albuquerque before I have to turn north. You can find me pretty close to this spot in about a week. Or just ask around the market. There'll be trucks headed back to Texas, too."

"Thanks, we'll ask around," Black said. "Sure appreciate what you've done for us. Mighty kind of you."

A payphone call to Aunt Gertie produced the woman herself

after a short wait. She arrived in her black DeSoto sedan and spotted Black, waving wildly, next to a Phillips Grocer's truck. Her dark eyes darted until she spied a no-parking zone. She pulled in, hopped out and ran, heels clicking on pavement, to hug her nephew.

"Keith Black! I can't believe you're in California. We're going to be in big trouble with your mother. Who's your good-looking friend here?" Aunt Gertie sized up Truva.

"This is my traveling buddy from Lubbock, Truva McSpadden. Truva, Gertrude Clum, my aunt, actually my great-aunt. She's my grandpa's baby sister."

"Pleased to meet you, Ma'am," Truva nodded his head. "You're A. B.'s sister? You've already said more than he did the whole time we were in New Mexico."

Gertrude chuckled. "Yeah, he doesn't say much anymore. He turned out different than he started. Losing those wives and babies changed him. He wasn't the only one who lost, though."

"I want to go see this city, all the tall buildings! City Hall! Man, I saw a picture of it in the Lubbock paper." Black said. "I want to climb to the top floor."

"I want to go see the Pacific Ocean," Truva said it real slow, like it was the dreamiest place on earth. "Swim in that salt water! Dive into the waves! And see all those girls in those skimpy bathing suits! And what about that big roller coaster that goes out over the ocean?"

Gertrude laughed with hearty delight. "That's the Cyclone Racer at the Pike in Long Beach. It's the largest and fastest roller coaster anywhere. You'll get to see it all, guys. I promise. I'll drive you around Los Angeles on the way home, then later this afternoon, Norval wants me to bring you by his office in Studio City."

"We really get to see where they make the picture shows?" Truva asked. "Swell!"

"Today? So soon? I won't know what to do," Black said. "Do they have horses there? I need to find a guitar." Black's mind didn't wait for Long Beach. It jumped on a Cyclone Racer of its own.

"Now calm down. Norval will take care of things for you. He'll tell you what you need to know. Today is just to show you around the lot and let you see what movie-making is all about. You'll meet with a guy who'll give you some music to practice before your audition." Gertrude explained.

"Audition? What do you mean?"

"Norval's got something special set up."

At four o'clock that afternoon, the attendant at the front gate of Republic Studios recognized the black DeSoto and waved them through. "Hi Gert," he said. "Where'd you find those cowboys?" Black and Truva wore their hats, boots, and yoked shirts, just like most days.

"New Mexico and Texas," Gert yelled out the open window, "where the *real* cowboys live."

Norval Clum was waiting inside the compound. A distinguished-looking gentleman of average height, he carried himself with assurance and seemed to be someone who would always make the right decision. He greeted the young men with a firm handshake to each then led them and Gertrude inside a large concrete block building and up a flight of stairs to his austere windowless office. Everything had a place and was in it.

The Depression had put a lot of independent movie companies out of business and threatened to ruin others. Several of these failing companies owed a lot of money to Consolidated Film Industries, a film processing lab owned by Herbert J. Yates. Mr. Yates gathered up six of these so-called Poverty Row Studios, threatened them with closure because of the debts they owed him, then combined their talents and expertise into the collaborative Republic Pictures Corporation. This newly-formed studio concentrated on low budget serials, Westerns, and B-movies. Norval Clum had been in the right place at the right time and knew the right people. Herbert Yates was one of his best customers at the furniture store and had needed a good money man.

"Blackie," Norval began after pleasantries and catching up on family, "Herbert J. Yates owns and runs Republic Studios. He's my boss and my friend. He's had a lot of success with these Western B-movies since the talkies came. He's always looking for good cowboy types. I've been telling him about you for a while now."

"I know, and I thank you for it," Black said.

"Why do they call them B-movies?" Truva interrupted.

"The theatres like to have two movies on the weekend, a double-feature. They can pull more people in that way. The big draw, the high-dollar advertised movie with big-name stars like Cary Grant and Olivia de Havilland, those are called the A-movies. They take a long time and a lot of money to film," Norval explained. "These B-movies are low budget, can be filmed in a few weeks, sometimes a few days. They don't have big names, just actors getting paid so much per day or per week. But lately, the Western Bs have become so popular, people are going to see them as much as the As. They made Gene Autry a star."

Norval stood and walked around his desk stopping in front of Black. "And Blackie, don't thank me yet. You must prove yourself. I can't get you something you don't deserve. I can just open this one door for you. Mr. Yates is a tough man. His language can get a little rough. He suffers no fools. He expects his people to work hard and be loyal. But first, you have to win him over."

"How do I do that?"

"Just be yourself. Flash that big grin but not all the time. You're the real deal. Some of these guys they cast have never even sat on a horse."

"But they all ride horses in the movies," Truva interrupted again.

"Well, they have mechanical horses that sort of rock people. They put a moving scene behind them and on the screen, it looks like they are riding, but they're just sitting there being rocked while they word the script."

"What?" Truva asked. "I don't understand."

"I'll show you the machine later," Norval said. "There are some real riders, of course. The crew goes out and films real horses and riders gettin' country. But not all those riders are actors who can read and recite a script. They don't look good enough or sound good enough."

"And that's what my job would be? To ride the horses for them to film?" Black asked.

"Maybe," Norval replied. He walked around the room again, then sat on the front of his desk leaning toward Black. "I'm sure you can easily get a job riding horses or doing stunts like those I saw you do at the home place in New Mexico. These days, with jobs tight and money hard to come by, that's a pretty good deal itself. But I've got higher hopes for you, Blackie." He stared directly into Black's eyes. "You're smart. You're handsome. Maybe a little young and a mite short, but Hollywood knows how to deal with short. Your movie-star good looks will just get you so far. But your voice, that voice of yours, that's what will make the difference. Music doesn't move me much, but when I heard you sing . . ."

Black turned red. He tried to slow his breathing as he studied the linoleum. He couldn't find any words.

"I think you have what it takes, but sometimes that's not enough. Luck plays a big role. Timing. Who knows who in this town. Right now, I know Mr. Yates. He is willing to give you a shot at something more on my say-so. He's looking for the next big singing cowboy, like Gene Autry. He hasn't found the right man yet," Norval continued. He seemed to know where the words were kept. "The studio has put out a casting call for a new Western film. Mr. Yates is hoping to find his new singing cowboy among these aspirants and build him up in this film. Singing auditions are in three days. He's already honed down the list. I got him to add your name and give you a chance."

Gertrude's smile erupted into giggles. The secret was out. Truva's mouth flew open. Black sat frozen, his heart ba-booming in his ears so loudly he was sure he hadn't heard correctly.

"Uh, I, I don't know . . . What do I do?" Black stammered.

"Anything they tell you to," Truva shouted. "Man, oh man. What a deal!"

Norval smiled but his eyes never left Black's face. "This is serious business, son. I'm going to work your tail off the next few days getting you ready for this. I wish we had more time to prepare, but we'll have to make do. We'll be working from sunup to late at night. Gertrude will entertain Truva. You and I are going to be head down and ass up. Now, in a minute I'll take you to meet the music man. He'll give you some sheet music to learn the songs for the audition. You do read music, don't you?"

"Mostly, yeah. I figured it out from the shaped notes in the church hymnal. Sometimes I do better if somebody just sings it for me. Then I can pick it right up."

"Yeah," Truva interrupted, "he can hear a song once on the radio and pick and sing it all the way through in just a few minutes. Plays by ear."

"Okay, I know a guy who can help with that, too. But don't let the music man know you can't read the sheet."

Black nodded his head. "I didn't bring my guitar, Uncle Norval. Do you or Aunt Gertie have one I can use?"

"Already taken care of. The music man is holding a guitar for you, the best one you've ever played, I imagine, a brand-new Gibson Jumbo Acoustic. It's yours for the next few days, but you can't keep it."

"Sure, okay, sounds swell," Black replied. "I know that guitar. They have one in the window at the Broadway Music Store in Lubbock. I've been saving up to get it."

COOL WATER

 Written by Bob Nolan, 1936. Recorded by Sons of the Pioneers in 1941, for which they won a Grammy Award. Recorded in 1948 by Vaughan Monroe and the Sons of the Pioneers, which became a best-seller. Also recorded by Hank Williams in 1948.

The next day Gertrude took Black for a haircut and bought him a western-style shirt, black with pointed yokes piped in white, and a new pair of 501 Button Fly Levi's. Then she disappeared with Truva in tow.

A studio photographer repaid a favor to Norval by taking pictures of Black in various poses, looking confident in one and dreamy in another. He ran lines from a script with an actor. He yodeled with a voice coach. He polished his boots, his belt, and his buckle. He watched scenes being filmed and others cut and played back. He looked through the lens of a miraculous machine that took quick pictures of people moving and talking. The continuous roll of tiny negatives were then wound onto metal reels. Hours and hours passed, many of them with Black observing, standing stiff in unfamiliar surroundings, an outsider.

Practicing the songs, Black relaxed into the familiar feel of a guitar strapped to him. He studied the sheet music, or at least pretended to, while he picked out the rhythms he could hear in his head, the ones that flowed through his body to tell his fingers to pluck the right string or strum the perfect chord. Sometimes, if others weren't listening too closely, he would add a little riff here and there just to keep it interesting.

The vocals were easy, simple melodies. His favorite was "Dust," written by Johnny Marvin, the man who had given him the sheet music. He also liked "That Pioneer Mother of Mine." He recognized the name of the man who wrote it, Tim Spencer, as one of the Sons of the Pioneers, the cowboy band that had come through Lubbock the previous fall and played their songs over radio station KFYO. Black and Truva and half of Lubbock had bee-lined down to the station to hear them in person and get autographs. The Sons were pretty famous after they performed their "Tumbling Tumbleweeds" song in the Gene Autry movie. Black had shaken hands with them all: Tim Spencer, Hugh and Karl Farr, Bob Nolan, and Leonard Slye.

Now here he was in a sound room learning one of Spencer's songs himself. He wondered if the Sons of the Pioneers would be performing the background music for this new picture show. *Could I be the cowboy singing lead? In a movie!* His head began to spin. He remembered his mother's derision of the movies as sinful, his father's mocking those movie-star cowboys as fake. *Will I be fake if I make a movie? Will I become all those things my parents hate? Will they hate me?*

A quick knock on the door ended his reverie. He opened it. Norval and the photographer stepped in.

"Blackie, I thought you might like to get out of here for a while. Loosen up a bit this afternoon. You've been at it pretty hard." Norval said. "I can't go, but Ronald here will drive you to a ranch in the San Fernando Valley. Toluca Lake, not far. Ace Hudkins keeps a lot of horses out there that we use in the movies. You can do some riding, a few stunts, some roping. Ronald can take pictures of you doing what you do. In case this other deal doesn't pan out, we can still get you a job with the horses. How's that sound?"

"Oh, man! Them's the berries! When do we leave?"

"Right now. Ronald knows a little place on the way that makes thick hamburgers, just like your mother makes. That and some fried potatoes should fill you up. I'm buying." He handed Black a five-dollar bill. "Feed Ronald here, too."

"Hoo, with this much money, I can buy us both steaks!"

"Bring me the change." Norval grinned.

"Thanks, Uncle Norval. I need to get on a horse about now, something solid. Kinda feels like quicksand around here. The horses will fill me up and the food won't hurt none either." Black pulled the guitar strap over his head and carefully placed it in its case. He looked at Ronald. "If you're waiting on me, you're wasting time. Let's go!"

They reached Hudkins Stables about two in the afternoon. Horses and riders were everywhere. Some outfit was filming on an open grassy hillside nearby. As soon as the car stopped, Black headed to the pens which were filled with horses being worked and sorted. Several men were at the corral fence, some sitting on top, some standing with their forearms resting on the wood poles, peering through. They were discussing the headset of a particular horse, the rounded rump of another, a particular switch of a tail, the look in one's eyes. The men looked much like the ones back home standing around a corral, except for newer boots, less dusty clothes, and big shiny buckles. Two wore spurs and ten-gallon Tom Mix hats that hadn't met sweat.

It took Black only seconds to join right in, "That stallion over there will throw you ever chance he gets."

The men turned in unison to look at the newcomer. "What do you know about horses?" one asked.

"Been around them all my life. Name's Black." He extended his hand and shook with each man, as each told him his name.

"What makes you think that gray can't be rode?" asked a curly-haired dude.

"Oh, I didn't say he can't be rode. I said he would try to throw you. That's a proud horse. Solid on all four feet. Shoulders and head held high. Tail high. He's full of himself, an important horse. He's got to like you and respect you to let you ride him," Black answered.

"And you think you can ride him?" Curly wanted to know.

"Sure. Take him a while to warm up to me first, and he'd probably throw me a few times when I wasn't paying attention, but in the end, we'd be great pals."

A Jeep wheeled in and stopped in a cloud of dust. The clean-cut driver unwound himself and confidently strode over to the group assembled at the corrals. Cowboys rearranged themselves as the new man claimed his place to size up the horses. The newcomer was easy to look at, about six-feet tall, sandy-colored hair. His eyes were small and squinty, especially in the full sun, but the squint gave him an earnest appearance.

Black recognized him. "Hey, I know you. You're one of the Sons of the Pioneers, but I don't know which one." He offered his hand.

"I'm Leonard Slye or maybe Dick Weston, depending on who you ask." The man returned Black's handshake, along with a genuine smile. "Sometimes I don't know myself anymore. Have we met?"

"Yes. No. Black's my name. You can't be expected to remember me. I met you at the radio station in Lubbock last year when your band swung through there after ya'll played the Texas Centennial in Dallas. You were the one with the new bride, weren't you?"

"Yeah, that was me. So, you met Arline, too, huh?"

"Sure did. Nice woman, pretty blonde. You're a lucky man. Now, what's this about you having two names?"

"Oh, I got a bit part in a Gene Autry movie last year. The Sons did the music for it and they gave me this little part and someone at the studio decided I needed a better name, so they billed me as Dick Weston. They said Slye wasn't a good name for a cowboy, especially a good cowboy. The studios figure out the names, whatever they think will help sell movies. We've had some fun with it. Just call me Len. My friends call me Len."

"I'd be proud to call you my friend, Len. I love the Sons of the Pioneers' music. I sing a lot of ya'll's songs at the drug store back home. In fact, I'm . . ." He stopped himself. Norval had told him not to tell anyone about the audition or the new songs for the movie.

"Sing at a drug store, eh? So, you're a *real* drug-store cowboy?" Len and the others laughed.

"I guess I am." Black laughed too. "And all this time I thought drug-store cowboys were the fake ones."

"Sounds like you know what you are talking about." Len said. "Did you grow up with horses in Texas?"

"Nope, in New Mexico. My dad was a horse trader. We've had every kind of horse there is, I reckon, at some time or the other."

"What do you think of that palomino over there?" Len asked. He pointed to a sturdy golden chestnut stallion with light mane and tail. "I've been watching that one."

"That's one fine horse. He . . ."

Black was interrupted by the movie outfit returning to the stables. His eyes focused on a strawberry roan one of the stragglers was riding. "No. No. Can't be." He started slowly walking toward the incoming crew trying to get a better look, his eyes glued to the strawberry roan.

As he watched, the roan's head suddenly popped up and shook. The horse snorted twice, then changed its route and cantered toward Black whose steps were quickening toward the roan.

"Ginger!"

Ginger whinnied, nodded her head up and down and scuffed her hooves. Black hugged and gently stroked her neck until she calmed. Then he held her face directly in front of him and pressed his forehead against her nose, eyes closed, as he had done many times before. Ginger made nibbling motions with her mouth but held her head steady for the greeting.

The rider slipped off, handing the reins to Black. In two shakes, he was in the saddle and ready to fly, stopped only by a loud shout.

"Whoa there, cowboy. Hold up." A fleshy-looking man was striding toward them with Ronald trailing slightly behind. "I can see you know Ginger, but you can't just ride off on someone else's horse," the man said.

Black couldn't get words past the lump in his throat.

Ronald arrived and took up the slack. "Smiley, this is the one I told you about, Norval Clum's nephew. How about if we just use this horse. He's already on it."

"She's just come in, been out all day. There are fresher horses," Smiley said.

"Oh, Ginger will be fine. She's been worked a whole lot harder than this. I raised her," Black said. "I sure would like to ride her, with your permission. I taught her a lot of tricks, too. You know about those?"

"No, but she's not my horse. Just belongs to the outfit. I think they got her in New Mexico." He stepped toward Black with his hand out. "They call me Smiley, Smiley Burnette. I help out around here, kind of a go-between for the stables and the movie companies."

"Pleased to meet you, Smiley. I remember your face from some of the Gene Autry Westerns. Just call me Black."

"Well, Black, I guess you can ride Ginger. As soon as Ronald gets his camera ready, you can show us what you got."

Ronald photographed Black and Ginger for almost an hour. It was hard to keep an excited horse and his cowboy still enough for clear shots. Near the end, Black entertained the gathering by guiding Ginger through some tricks. She pretended to fall down, then get up again. She reared up on her hind legs to almost vertical, Black waving with one free hand, legs clamped around her ribs. He rode her backwards and standing on top of the saddle. Holding only the saddle horn, he jumped off her onto the ground, then flipped back into the saddle again.

When Ronald signaled time to go, Black reluctantly turned Ginger toward the horse barn. He ran into Len Slye again near the stable. Len grinned, which made his eyes more squinty.

"Hey, I watched you ride. You're the real deal, aren't you?" Len said. "I won't be calling you a drug-store cowboy again. Heck of a show."

"Sometimes it feels like I was born on a horse," Black said. "I sure hate to leave this one again. Had Ginger since I was a pup. We didn't get much time together with all that palaver going on."

"The hands are saddling up that palomino for me to try, the one we were talking about when you spied that strawberry roan. You didn't get a chance to tell me what you think about him." Len adjusted himself in his saddle and pushed his hat back. "Want to take a ride up into those hills with me? I know a sweet water hole up there. We can continue our talk and it'll give you more time with Ginger."

"That'd be swell. I'll have to ask Smiley, though, and clear it with Ronald. He's ready to go."

"You tell Ronald and I'll tell Smiley. Meet you back here." Len turned toward the office.

"You thinking of buying that palomino?" Black called after him. "What's his name?"

"Golden Cloud. I think I'd change his name if he was mine. I like him a lot. But I don't have the money. Someday, maybe. I'd sure like to find a horse who likes me as much as that one likes you."

After a good run through the amber California hills and a long rest at the water hole, they returned, walking slowly side-by-side, the palomino and the strawberry roan, while their riders talked. Comfortable, unhurried man-talk. About California hills and Texas flatland, New Mexico canyons and Ohio rivers. About horses. About movies. And, inevitably, about music.

"Wish we had a guitar out here," Black said. "I'd ask you to sing 'Tumbling Tumbleweeds' for me. The way the Sons of the Pioneers sing it."

"Who needs a guitar? Why don't we just sing it? You ever just sing without a guitar?"

"Do I ever," Black said. "I lead singing for church, never use an instrument there."

"Let's do it, then."

"You really want me to sing with you?"

"I'm not used to singing by myself, you know. I got the Sons to back me up."

"Okay, then. You start us off."

See them tum–bl–ing down, Len sang.

– pledg–ing their love to the ground. Black joined in. Two voices, fused in perfect harmony, tumbled the lyrics with precise timing, just for the love of music.

As they neared the stables again, Len said, "Bob Nolan wrote that song for the Sons a few years back. He called it "Tumbling Tumble Leaves" at first. We changed the name when we started singing in the Westerns. I like being in pictures, especially when I got that part where they called me Dick Weston. Hope I can get cast in another one sometime."

"Hey, I might get to be in a show. That's why Ronald was taking those pictures. I wouldn't call it fun, though. I like the singing part but remembering those words and spouting them? It don't seem natural. Maybe I just need to work with the horses. I'm more comfortable on the back of a horse." Black hesitated, studying Len, then the words tumbled out, "The audition is tomorrow."

"I haven't heard about any audition tomorrow. For a Western? What studio?"

"Republic Studio," Black answered. "My uncle got me the audition. He works for Herbert Yates. *Under Western Stars* is the name of the show."

"Son of a gun, they're going through with it!" Len sounded surprised.

"What do you mean?"

"I heard a rumor this morning that might happen. I was over in Glendale at the western store getting my hat cleaned, and I ran into a guy who told me the studio was going to teach Gene a lesson, get a new cowboy for that film. But he said the audition would be sometime next week."

"Gene who? What are you talking about?" Black was muddled.

"Well, Republic Studio and Gene Autry are having a fight, a contract dispute over money and some other things like whether Gene has a right to his name and stuff like that," Len explained. "Republic had this movie lined up, called *Washington Cowboy*. Gene was the star. But first day of shooting, he just didn't show up. Said he wasn't going to make the movie until they fixed his contract."

"What happened?" Black asked.

"Yates got mad at Gene. Like I said, there was a rumor that he was going to make the movie with a different name. *Western Stars* was one of the names I heard. But none of my guys knew about the audition, they would have told me. Man, I wish I'd known. I would have thrown my hat in the ring."

"Well, it's not too late. It's tomorrow afternoon. Come on over," Black said. "You sure don't need to practice. They know you from Sons of the Pioneers. I'll bet you already got pictures and stuff all put together."

"Are you for real? We'd be competing against each other, you know. Most guys don't give out this kind of information."

Black's face relaxed into a rascally grin. "May the best man win."

Len laughed. "I don't think I've ever met anybody like you, and I've got some good friends. Tomorrow, huh? I have legal business upstate for the band. I couldn't get back before Republic closes its gates at noon. They're real strict about that. No one gets in without a pass after the gates are closed."

Black shifted in his saddle, then pulled Ginger to a stop. "Any way around the gates?"

Len furrowed his brow in thought, squinting his eyes more

than usual. "There is a side door they keep locked, but it can be pushed open from the inside."

"Tell me exactly where it is and what time you'll be there. I'll let you in."

After a late dinner that evening, Black and Truva stood smack-dab in the middle of the street in front of the modest Clum home on Tamarind Avenue in Hollywood. That vantage point allowed them to see "H-O-L-L-Y-W-O-O-D-L-A-N-D" spelled out in big white letters on Mount Lee in the Santa Monica Mountains north of the house. First HOLLY flashed, then WOOD, then LAND. Some of the bulbs were burned out or missing, but even the missing parts said something about this place.

"I can't believe all this, Blackie. I'm so glad you talked me into coming out here with you. You should have seen those girls at the beach today, like a strong wind would blow off their skimpy swimsuits. I was praying for wind! Oh-la-la, the girls. What lookers! Long legs. Blonds, brunettes, redheads." When Black didn't respond, Truva followed his gaze to the Hollywoodland sign. "Just look at that sign. Ain't that grand? You think we could get up there to take a closer look?"

"I doubt it. Aunt Gertie claims each one of those letters is about five stories tall. Remember a few years ago when that actress climbed up on the H and jumped? Ker-splat. She didn't think she would get some part she wanted and thought that was her only option. A few days after she died, a letter came with her contract."

"Jeez, Black, don't go getting all morbid on me. I thought you had a good day. You found your horse and rode her. Now what are the odds you would find Ginger out here?"

"Pretty good, actually. She was bought for the movies. Hudkins is the biggest supplier of horses to the movies and here I am, training for a Western. Not that big a stretch," Black said. "Hey, that guy I told you about, Leonard Slye, he's a good guy. I think he's got a shot at this."

"What do you mean, *he's* got a shot? This is *your* shot, Blackie. Your chance to make your mark. What do you mean?"

"I know. And I'm going to give it my best, do all I can. Wouldn't be fair to Uncle Norval if I did anything less. But I'm not so sure." Black stuck his hands in his pockets. "This business is like that sign up there, a lot of flashing going on but some of the bulbs don't light up. *Don't tell about this, keep that under your belt, ogle the girls, don't make that guy mad, suck up to Mr. So-and-So.* Maybe I'll get lucky and get a job with the horses."

"Are you crazy? I'd give my left nut to get a chance at something like this. Heck, I can't carry a tune in a bucket. You sing like a damn nightingale and don't want to reach for the brass ring. What's wrong with you?" Truva gave his friend a hard punch on his shoulder.

"Nothing's wrong with me, Truva. I *am* going for the brass ring. Maybe I'll grab it. That's okay. I'm willing to accept the plan. But if I'm on down the list, not the top guy, that's okay, too." Black frowned and rubbed his hair back from his forehead with both hands. "Just saying it's alright to be a sidekick or do stunts with the horses. Same. I'd be just as happy, maybe happier without all those expectations on me."

"Well, I'll be damned!" Truva said.

"Look, I started down this road just to find a job, help my folks out, give us a better life. I figured I could make some money, maybe move home to New Mexico and buy the ranch back. Whatever happens, happens."

"Sure wish you wouldn't talk like that, Blackie. Don't say any of that to Gertie. She thinks you're going to be a bigger star than Jimmie Stewart."

"I don't want to disappoint her or Uncle Norval. They've done a lot for me. That's why I'm going to do my best and let the chips fall where they may. And those chips will scatter everywhere. I don't know how we're gonna keep this trip secret when we get home. Tomorrow could change everything."

Black turned. "Come on, let's get some shut-eye." Then suddenly he chuckled. "Ha! My life is turning into one of those Westerns, like that famous shootout at the O. K. Corral. They should make a movie about that." He put his arm around Truva's shoulder. "My big showdown is tomorrow, pal. Will you be my Doc Holliday?"

"You bet, Wyatt, you bet."

The gunslingers walked arm in arm to the house.

DUST

 Music and lyrics by Johnny Marvin. Sung by Roy Rogers in the film *Under Western Stars*. First song from a B-western to be nominated for an Oscar as Best Music, Original song 1938. Recorded by Roy Rogers for Vocalion in 1938. Also recorded by Gene Autry and Jimmy Wakeley.

Bright morning sunlight pried open Black's eyes, waking him from a fitful night's sleep. White lace curtains in Aunt Gertie's guest room fluttered softly in the open window. Seventy degrees. Another perfect day was dawning in The Golden State where dreams come true, sometimes. Black lay still, watching the moving patterns on the wall, the dance of light and shadow, lace and wind. He thought of the coming day and the ramifications it could bring into his life. *Am I man enough for this?*

"I will do my best," he heard himself say aloud, willing the words to Uncle Norval, to Aunt Gertrude, to Truva and to himself.

"May the best man win," he whispered, sending that mantra to his new friend, Len Slye. "I won't make it easy for you."

Then he closed his eyes to shut out the wavering patterns, to focus on his most important thoughts. After a few minutes, he got up, walked to the window and pulled back the lace curtain. Rich California sun beamed in.

"Thy will be done," he said to the golden sky.

Twenty or so straight chairs were lined up at the end of a cavernous room, about half of them occupied when Black arrived. The space reminded him of a large open barn, but nowhere near as comfortable. Black strode confidently into the group, wearing his new black

BRENDA CLEM BLACK

shirt with V-yokes piped in white. He smelled spit-polish clean and a little nutmeg-y, having used Norval's aftershave, a new brand called Old Spice.

Gertie had helped by providing Brylcreem pomade, which he used to slick back his wavy black hair. "*A little dab'll do you,*" she had teased him.

Black rested the Gibson Jumbo Acoustic in its fancy case on the long wood table where a pretty girl with a blond pageboy was checking names off a list.

"What's your name, cowboy?" she cooed. "Write it on this, pleeease." As she scooted the paper across the table, she leaned forward with her face upturned to give him a better look at the exposure of her low-cut blouse.

Keith LeRoi Black. He wrote in flowing script, then underlined it with a flourished scroll. He grinned wickedly, which the blond thought was for her until he said, "This one's for you, Mother."

"What? Did you just call me Mother? Move along, cowpoke. Others are waiting." The blond straightened her back and pulled her blouse into place.

Black had grinned because he spelled his middle name the way his mother preferred. She had chosen the French spelling LeRoi because her family descended from a Prince of France named Renald Rene LeFors II who had lost the family fortune when he sided with the Brits during the Revolutionary War. With his mother half-crazed after Keith's difficult birth, his father had officially spelled for the birth certificate the only way he knew, the Western way, Leroy, as if pronounced Lee Roy. If Black got anywhere with this madness today, he would insist that, in honor of his mother, Leroy would be spelled LeRoi, the way the family pronounced it.

The hopeful young men sat mostly in silence. Every now and then one of them would uncase a guitar and attempt to tune the strings, strumming a few bars of some song, but there were too many competitive nerves for comradery. After sitting, waiting, walking around and sitting back down again, Black decided he must leave to fulfill his pact with Len. As he picked up his guitar he saw the heavy door open. Three men entered and walked over to the table. Leonard Slye, Smiley Burnette, and a man in a suit.

"Sally, add this guy's name to the audition list," the man addressed the blond.

"Sure, Mr. Siegel." She ramped up the sugar in her voice. "Here, cowboy, put your full name on this piece of paper."

"Which name should I use, Sol? Leonard Slye or Dick Weston?"

"Put them both down. Doesn't matter anyway. If you get this, you'll have a third one. We're working up a name for the lead now." Sol Siegel turned toward the audition room. "Think I'll go sit in, see how it's going."

Len squinted as he scanned the room of cowboy-dressed young hopefuls and grinned when he saw Black waving. They met halfway and exchanged handshakes.

"I was about to go unlock that door when I saw you come in," Black said.

"Yeah, didn't need it after all. When I got here, the extras were coming back from lunch break," Len explained. "It was a big group, so I put my hat on and blended in. I ran into Smiley and we were trying to talk another guard into letting us in this building when Sol Siegel came along and recognized me. He's a producer, knows me from Sons of the Pioneers."

"You going to audition, too, Smiley?" Black asked.

"Nope. I already got the part," Smiley cackled in his trademark squeaky voice. "Playing my same old role as Frog Millhouse, Gene Autry's sidekick. All the parts were cast. They're just trying to find someone for Gene's role now, because of the big fight. Guess I'll be somebody else's sidekick now. This is highly unusual, even for this wacky business. How's it going?"

"A whole lot of nothing so far. Some boys go in, come back out and leave. A few hang around, saying they were told to stay."

Mid-afternoon, Black was called into the small room with a high ceiling and clerestory windows. The blond had given him fifteen minutes' notice, so that he walked into the audition with his guitar tuned, hanging from his body. He wore Truva's Stetson instead of his own sweat-stained headgear. Rays of sunlight through the high windows amplified the swirling currents of smoke, bathing the room in thin milky layers. A handful of men in white shirts and loose ties sat along one side of a conference table spread with packets of pictures and vitae. Heavy metal ashtrays held stubs of cigars and cigarettes. Black was directed to the lone seat facing the group.

The men took turns asking questions while they looked at the papers Norval had produced for him. Black answered sincerely, but solemnly. Then one of the men handed him an open script and asked him to say the marked lines while someone read the other parts. Black's nervousness caused him to stumble with the words.

"Let's hear him sing first," an authoritative voice said, "then run the lines."

Black's hands relaxed as he strummed familiar chords to warm up his guitar. His nervousness dissipated as he immersed himself in the staccato opening lyrics, "*Dust. Dust. Dust.*" He identified with the struggle of drought and dusty days. His soul poured into the music and carried with his voice into the hearts of his judges.

He finished. Silence. Too long for Black. Awkwardness crept back in, but he said nothing.

Finally, quietly, the authoritative voice asked if he could sing another song, perhaps one they knew better.

"How about 'Tumbling Tumbleweeds?'" Black asked. "Everybody knows that one."

"Excellent choice. Proceed."

Black jumped right into the perfect pitch, singing the popular song better than Gene Autry. He held the long notes with precise timing, making his listeners feel the music.

"Well, that's fine! Just fine!" the authoritative voice exclaimed when the song was finished. "That will do, Mr. Black. We are going to dispense with the script reading. Please wait in the audition hall in case we need a call-back."

"Yessir." Black stood.

"One more thing," the voice said. "How old are you?"

"Eighteen years old." Black lied as Uncle Norval had instructed him to do, but the lie stuck in his craw and left a bitter taste.

Leonard Slye was also told to stay, after his audition. Black, Len, and Smiley dragged some chairs together and sang almost all the songs they knew while they waited. They stopped instantly each time the door to the small room spit out one of the cowboys and swallowed up another, then continued where they left off. Black and Len were called back a second time to sing other songs and were again told to stay.

Eventually Smiley took his leave, telling Len, "Call me with the outcome, so I'll know who my new pardner is. Good luck to you both."

Soon only Black and Len remained. Even the blond had gone. Song-less they sat, listening to loud voices coming from the small room. A runner procured Norval Clum who entered and exited ten minutes later with only a quick glance toward Black.

"Isn't this a predicament?" said Len. "I'm sorry, Black. I should have stayed out of it. This was your deal."

"It'll go the way it's supposed to. I believe that. Let's just agree to remain friends no matter how it turns out. Glad our paths crossed. I've enjoyed getting to know you."

"Me too. You're a decent guy." said Len.

The runner summoned Black again.

Black nodded toward Len. "*Once more unto the breach*," he said, then laughed and walked stiffly into the small room.

The man with the authoritative voice dismissed the others and directed the runner to deliver Mr. Slye to his office. Then he led Black to two facing chairs and motioned him to sit.

"Mr. Black, my name is Herbert Yates. I own Republic Studios. I am very impressed with your performance here today." The bald man with intense, beady eyes puffed on a short cigar, then snuffed it out in an oversized pewter ashtray emblazoned with the words: *A Woman is Just a Woman, but a Good Cigar is a Smoke.*

"You have a great future in this business. Your voice is exceptional and were we choosing on voice alone, there would be no doubt as to the outcome. However, there are other factors at play." Mr. Yates talked quickly and precisely, a man with no time to waste. "I regret to inform you that we have selected Mr. Slye for the lead role in *Under Western Stars.*"

Black flushed. A pang of unexpected disappointment accompanied the trickle of relief. "I understand, sir."

"No, you probably don't. But someday you might. You're young. I doubt you are truly eighteen, but I'm not asking. This part needs someone more mature. Mr. Slye has a few years on you and a lot of experience. We are going to shoot this movie fast, in about eight to ten weeks. Everything is set and ready to go. We can't slow down to teach or train. He knows the ropes."

"I understand, sir," Black said again.

"Now I'm going to give you some advice, out of respect for your Uncle Norval. I don't usually talk to the aspirants. I have people for that."

Mr. Yates fiddled with the tiny latch of a fancy wooden box sitting on the table, then lifted a cigar out of the velvet-lined humidor. He bit the plug off one end, spit it out, then struck a match and lit the other end, pulling long and slow. An exotic aroma rolled out with his exhaled breath. He took another and offered it to Black.

"No, thanks. I don't smoke," said Black.

"Well, put it your pocket. You may take up smoking later. Never refuse a good Cuban."

Black put the cigar to his nose and took a whiff, "Well, I do like the way it smells."

"Now here's my advice, son," Mr. Yates continued. "Norval says you want a job working with the horses. There are many possibilities open to you, especially with that voice of yours, but I think you should wait. Take some elocution classes, learn how to get those words out of your mouth easier, gain some maturity and hopefully some height, then come back and go for the leading man role. If you get buried at Hudkin's Stables, you get tagged as backdrop. That's Smiley's problem. He's good enough for leading man, but he's labeled as sidekick and can't step out of it. That crackle voice of his is an act."

"He's been singing with me and Len. Quite a shock to hear him sing so smooth."

"Well, son, that's my advice. Take it or leave it. This is a tough business. Takes a lot of compromise. Eats up good people who aren't ready for it. Talk to your uncle and think it over. If you want a job in the movies, I'll find you one, now or whenever you come back. My door is open to you. That's a big plus out here." Mr. Yates stood and extended his hand. "It's been a pleasure to hear you sing, young man. Norval is waiting for you in his office. Do you know the way?"

"Yessir," Black rose and shook the offered hand. "Thank you, Mr. Yates. I appreciate what you've said. I'll consider it."

"Oh, one more thing. We want to thank you for the name for our new singing cowboy. We had decided on Rogers for the last name, in honor of Will Rogers. The country has a lot of goodwill toward him since he and Wiley Post died in that tragic plane crash in Alaska. But we couldn't agree on the first name." Mr. Yates headed for the door, talking as he walked. "Today, I saw you wrote your middle name LeRoi and thought that would be perfect. But Sol thought it was too French and others were afraid it would be pronounced Lee Roy. We settled on just Roy. Roy Rogers. Has a good ring to it, don't you think? I love alliteration."

Black's trademark grin crept across his face. The irony of his mother being responsible for the name of a movie star deserved a smile.

Mr. Yates departed, his bald head shining under the lights, almost as slick as his suit and himself.

Black stood in the empty room with his thumbs hanging over his pants pockets. A pale glow of light streamed in from the high clerestory windows but not from the sun. The sun had set. He reached into his shirt pocket and pulled out the cigar he had been given, then spotted the humidor still on the table. He flipped open the lid, took out a second cigar and filed it in his pocket with its brother. *One for me, one for Truva.* Then he took a third, slowly turning it over and over in his hand like a baton. He put it to his mouth, wet the end, bit and spit out the plug as he had watched countless others do, then used a match from the box to light the end. A retching cough interrupted the first long pull into his lungs, so he pulled again and again until he could do it without coughing.

"Time to grow up, Blackie," he told himself, watching the smoke spiral up toward the unnatural light.

Early the next morning, Black told Norval goodbye with a firm handshake and promise to return. Gertrude drove the boys to Malibu so Black could stick his foot in the Pacific Ocean. Truva nursed a sunburn from the day before at Venice Beach, so he stayed in the shade. Black rolled up his jeans and walked barefoot across the sand to the water's edge, carrying his cowboy boots. The cold sand squished between his toes and ran out from under him with the waves. A few moments were enough. After all, being a true Westerner, he wasn't much of a water man.

Then she dropped them, their bedrolls, haversack, and Truva's valise near the job boards at Market Square in Los Angeles. She got out of the car to hug them goodbye. "You can always stay with us if you want to take one of those jobs Mr. Yates was talking about. Any time. You are welcome here."

"Maybe later, Aunt Gertie. Really do appreciate all you did for me and Truva. We'll never forget this trip, the trip of a lifetime, even though we can never talk about it," Black replied.

"Call me if you can't catch a ride back. I'll come pick you up. I don't want you sleeping down here."

Finding a ride wasn't hard for two adventurers willing to drive-share through the desert and camp in the back of a dark, enclosed produce truck.

Two days later they landed in east Lubbock near the railroad tracks about four in the morning. The seasoned travelers strolled down Broadway as far as the music store where Black confirmed that his Gibson was still in the window. Their parting was wordless, just mutual grins and a cautionary finger to each lip, indicating silence. Truva walked home. Black headed to his little building out back of the house where his parents and sister lay sleeping.

POMP AND CIRCUMSTANCE

"Land and Hope and Glory" March No. 1 in D. Composed by Sir Edgar Elgar in 1901. First played at graduation ceremonies at Yale University, 1905, where Elgar received an honorary Doctor of Music.

As the school session wound down in January of 1938, Dorris Mc-Spadden received a surprise in the mail. Lubbock High School notified her that she had enough credits to graduate and didn't have to attend the spring session. She wouldn't receive her diploma until May graduation ceremony but could still participate in all the festivities of the senior class. Immediately, she wrote her mother and the girls the good news. A reply soon arrived.

Our Dear Sweet Dorris,

I know that you think we don't care anything for you. Haven't even answered your dear sweet letter telling us all about your graduation and activities, which came last Friday, and oh! how Dorothy and I enjoyed it. And then Monday another sweet letter.

Now the real reason I haven't written, I just didn't have the price of a stamp. I don't intend to make a hard luck story of this but want you to know.

You know that I am thrilled beyond words, don't you Dorris?

I just cried when I was reading the part where you were already out of school. We were so surprised and happy that you were out and made such good grades. Was all just wonderful Dorris and we are so very very proud of you dear.

I just can't begin to tell you how thrilled I am at my first child graduating. I just almost cry every time I think of it.

Just too wonderful about Jess and Vivian giving you the locket and I know it is pretty and know just how proud you are of it. Hurts me so that we can't give you a thing but hope we can soon.

The girls have told everyone at school all about you finishing school and all your honors. They rode to school with Mr. DeLong and Jim Hal this morn. Mr. DeL. said tell her I think she is a very smart girl. His old Mexican died and was buried yesterday. Mr. DeL. said he thought he was about 95, had worked for him about 30 years.

We are getting very anxious to move. I know John and the boys are having a hard time. I want to see them so badly.

Calhouns are fine. We sure like them. The baby is a darling and has taken up with Dot. We have the same front bedroom and our kitchen's in what uster be the living room. They have a good radio in their kitchen, so we can hear it fine and enjoy it very much.

James has taken up with their hens. The old rooster runs him then James runs the rooster.

The graduation picture. I just know that is the best of all and I'm so tickled to know I have that awaiting me at the other end. ha! ha!

Be good and help Vivian lots. Hope all are well. Glad you got to stay so you can go to all your doings. Hope to see you soon.

Lots of love, Mother

Dorris couldn't believe it! Her mother, the No-Tears Queen, crying about her graduation! Since her finishing school days in Birmingham Mama had dreamed that her children would be educated. It thrilled Dorris to fulfill that dream for her. And for herself.

She kept a little record of her activities during graduation week, 1938:

Thursday night — Hollis and I went to the show and saw Jane Withers in Rascals.

Friday night — Truva came over and he and Cecil and I went riding around. Had a good time. I skated some late Friday afternoon.

Saturday — Washed my hair and rolled it up. Hollis and I were going to the Prevue that night but my hair came down, so we had to come home real early.

Sunday morning — Edith came by about 8 and we went up to High School for rehearsal, then back to the Bacculareate Sermon at 3:15 and were we thrilled. After the sermon, I went with Mother to Uncle Coleman's house. Later, Hollis and I went to the show.

Monday morning — I went out to Edith's and we fixed each other's hair. That night, Commencement! Loyd Nunley wanted to bring me home afterwards, but Hollis was there. Hollis and I met up with Truva and his friend Black.

Tuesday — I had my picture made in my cap and gown at Koen's Studio. That night Hollis and I went to the show and saw Mad about Music *with Deanna Durbin.*

Wednesday — When Cecil got off work, we drove home to Christoval, got here about 9:30.

As it turned out, Dorris was the only one of the McSpadden children to earn a high school diploma. Within a year, both Dot and Jean married and dropped out of school. The family moved and farmed a place near Seagraves that year, where Dorothy met Sonny Willingham from another big farming family. They drove to Lubbock in November and married.

After the crops were harvested in Seagraves, Dorris's dwindling family moved to a small frame house on 7th Street in Lubbock. Daddy John had found a nearby place with irrigation to farm. Dorris and Jean shared a bed until Jean married the next spring. Owen and Cecil were there and not, depending on where they could find work.

In December, Dorris celebrated her twenty-first birthday. Helen sent a beautiful birthday card from her home in El Centro, California. There was money inside and the promise of more at Christmas.

Dearest Helen & U.L.,

About an hour ago I received the sweet little card and was I tickled. I wasn't expecting a gift Honey. It's just as you said, too near Santa time. Do you realize that I am now 21 years old? I can't & don't want to. Mother and Jean baked me a real good chocolate cake. Jean gave me a pair of blue wooly gloves and Dot gave me the prettiest little white china vase. I was treated real nice.

Wasn't it grand about the nice Xmas gift Uncle Will Berry sent? We surely have put it to good use. Jean and Mother haven't spent their $5 yet but I have. Dot bought some Christmas gifts and then she bought herself a nice pair of non-run hose and material & pattern for a house coat.

I had a small debt I owed at Hemphill Wells. Then I bought me a pair of Black Fabric gloves (Kayser Brand) they were .69, regular $1.00, a black calf skin bag $1.98, Oh & is it pretty. I bought those at Hemp's then I went to the Sweetbrier Shop and got my hat. It is just precious, black with black vail, and black & white plume on top. It sets cocked over my right eye. It was $2.98 and I got it for $1.00. I'm really proud of my things. I'll get to go to church every Sunday now. I hope to get to work at Ward's some and make some Christmas money. That's the reason I went ahead and got my accessories.

My, but you are surely lucky Helen, getting your job. I certainly envy you. If I don't get to work soon I'm going to leave home. I sure hope I get to work in the Toy Dept. That would be fun.

Helen, I don't know hardly what to tell you about the gifts. Mother needs a pair of gloves but she said she wanted some of those nit underware, snuggies. Daddy needs a shirt or some underware or a tie. Dot & Sonny, I think it would be nice to send a luncheon set, some towels or some kind of linens for the house. She doesn't have any linens yet. Cecil is simply nuts about those pretty wool ties or one of those little narrow leather belts. Owen has gone daffy over long handles. He just has one pair. For Jean and me, if you can spend that much on us, we would like some house shoes, but if you can't we are out of underware and you could send some panties (not like the ones Mother wants, we don't like 'em).

Jean wrote you about me having a date with Taylor Pendly, didn't she? I sure had a good time and I like him a lot. He works in the Furniture Dept. at Ward's. He has the prettiest '38 green Chevrolet. I can go to church with him now that I have my hat. He goes to the Baptists (Mother objects to my going to the Baptists. She says I will marry one because every boyfriend I've had but one was Baptists.) Owen doesn't like him and of course, I don't expect Daddy to, but Dot, Cecil, Jean & Dorris do.

For Christmas. I made some plain fudge and some gumdrops. It sure was lots of fun making the gumdrops. They look like real store-bought ones. Dot made some coconut fudge last night and we put half of that away. I hope we get to have egg-nog.

Love to both of you from all of us, Dorris

BACK IN THE SADDLE AGAIN

 Gene Autry's signature song. Written by Ray Whitley and Gene Autry. Recorded by Gene Autry, released in 1939, Columbia Records.

Black heeded Herbert J. Yates's advice and returned to school. Mark Halsey welcomed him back to the drug store as soda jerk and it didn't take long for the radio station to show up to broadcast Blackie's music on Saturday afternoons. Over the next two years he became a local celebrity.

The secret held. He and Truva reported on adventures in New Mexico and that seemed to satisfy the curious. Norval and Gertie phoned him at Halsey's every now and then. Every few months for a while, Len Slye called to tell him about some opportunity in Hollywood and banter about goings-on. Black stuck to his guns and stayed in Lubbock.

He enrolled in recitation class where his never-shy, engaging manner was put to good use. Although he barely passed English, he won first-place ribbons and trophies in speech competitions. In FFA (Future Farmers of America) he won awards in Beef and Dairy Production and Cattle Judging. For fun, he joined the boxing team and delighted in calling himself a pugilist. He even put together a school-sanctioned "Hillbilly Band" that played at school functions and other venues.

One afternoon, Mark Halsey summoned him to the phone. "Blackie, you get more calls than I do. It's not a girl this time."

"Black, are you there?" The familiar clear voice belonged to Len Slye.

"Yep, I'm here, Len. What's got you wound?"

"I got my horse, Black. I bought Golden Cloud." Len's smile rode the phone lines along with the words.

"Whoa, that is big news! I knew you two were meant to be together. That palomino is one fine horse," Black said. "I'm happy for you."

"Thanks. He's almost mine. I bought him on the installment plan, so I'll have to pay him out. Did I tell you he's half thoroughbred? You didn't see him run full-out at the stables that day. Sometimes I'm just barely hanging on."

"You can handle him. You got good horse sense. And there's something about the trust you two had. He's going to be a great companion. Are you going to change his name?"

"I've been chewing on that. Smiley said the other day that he's mighty fast on the trigger when we take off. I might call him Trigger. What do you think?" Len asked.

"Trigger. Yep, that's a good name. Says a lot." Black replied. "How are you liking your new name, Roy Rogers?"

"It's a name. I like it pretty good. I'll be whoever they tell me to be if they just keep writing the paychecks. Do you go the show much? See any of them?"

"I go to all of yours." Black and Truva hadn't missed a minute of *Under Western Stars* when it showed in Lubbock, then drove Truva's dad's car to Amarillo to see it again.

"How am I doing out there in Texas?"

"Just great. Everybody loves you."

"Could have been you, you know," Len said.

"Not hardly. Hey, I gotta go. Soda orders piling up. Happy for you about your horse. Adios, amigo."

"Till we meet again, friend. Remember, any time you want to come out, I'll help you all I can to get in pictures. Bye for now."

Near the end of Black's senior year, Len called with a bona fide offer. He wanted Black to join the Sons of the Pioneers. Len was no longer a member of the band because of his movie work, but he still worked closely with them on movie sets and sat-in when they were missing a player. The band was about to begin a promotional tour of the southwest and would be performing at the radio station in Lubbock. Len wanted Black to join them and continue the tour, then come back to Hollywood with the group as its newest member.

Black agreed. He would fulfill his promise to his mother to graduate high school, then take this job doing what he loved to do. It paid much better than jerking sodas. His parents wanted him to go to college like his sister Joyce, but his grades weren't that great and he had no desire to go through four more years of waiting for his life to begin.

He kept the offer to himself, didn't even tell Truva, but quietly began positioning himself to leave with the band. He would tell everyone at the last minute, except Mark Halsey who would have to find a replacement to work the soda fountain. He wanted to discuss it with his dad and dared to hope that Corwin might be excited for him. The dad he knew in New Mexico would have been. But in Lubbock, Corwin had shown himself aligned with Black's mother far more often than Black himself.

Black decided to call Uncle Norval and share the news that he would soon return to Hollywood, arriving with the Sons of the Pioneers. He was hoping for a place to stay while he got his feet under him. Uncle Norval and Aunt Gertie were overjoyed. Norval couldn't wait to tell his friend, Herbert Yates.

This article appeared on the front page of the Hollywood Clipper on March 30, 1939, but the paper got Black's age wrong. He truly was eighteen this time, not sixteen:

Black dug the Lord Clinton cigar box from its hidey-hole, withdrew the waded bills and coins and counted. Yep, he had enough. He pushed the little nail shut on the box, put the box under his arm, and walked to the Broadway Music Store. His heart raced as the clerk climbed into the window and picked up the centerpiece guitar from the display. Eyeing the cigar box, the dealer dusted the guitar slowly and carefully before yielding it to his young customer. After a half-hour of tuning, strumming, and negotiating, they settled on $25. Black strutted out of the store, the proud owner of a new Jumbo Gibson Acoustic L-OO. He stored his most prized possession in his locker at Mark Halsey Drug. Even when he wasn't working, he could be found at Halsey's listening to the radio, picking out tunes, practicing.

On the day of the performance, people of Lubbock overflowed the parking lot at the radio station and jammed the nearby streets. The station had put up posters all over town, saying that Blackie would be playing with the Sons of the Pioneers, well-known for their movie work as well as their records. A few select notables were allowed inside to watch and listen up close.

As the band tuned up the door opened, and Black's father was ushered in. Surprised, Black lifted his fingers from the strings to give Corwin a cowboy salute: a loose forefinger touched outward from the forehead. His tall, lanky Dad returned the greeting with a nod and close-mouthed grin.

As prearranged in their practice session the night before, Bob Nolan announced that Blackie would start things off with Gene Autry's theme song, "Back In The Saddle Again." It was an appropriate song for Blackie's debut though he felt a smidgeon disloyal at leading with a song from Roy Roger's rival. But then, if all the Autry songs were cut out, there wouldn't be much left that people recognized. His rich, vibrant voice streamed through the radios of thousands proving he belonged in that saddle.

At the end of the song, the performers could hear the whoops and hollers of all those gathered outside who had listened through special speakers set up for the occasion. Those inside began to clap. Black peered through the crowd and saw his father stand up and applaud, his jaw set and tears trickling down his cheeks. Water rushed to Black's own eyes. *Had there been a better moment in his whole life?*

Afterwards, Black treated Corwin to a banana split at Mark Halsey Drug. Constantly interrupted by congratulations and requests for autographs, there wasn't much chance for conversation. Eventually he led his father to his locker in the back room and closed the door.

"I want to show you my new guitar, Pop. Look." Black unlatched the case and withdrew his treasure. "It's a new kind of Gibson.

A Jumbo Acoustic, they call it."

"That's a beauty. I saw you playing it at the radio station. Thought you borrowed it." Corwin took the guitar but handled it awkwardly.

"Nope, it's mine. I saved up part of my pay the past few years and finally I had enough."

"That's just fine, son. That's really fine. I've glad you got something that you care about. I really hate it that we had to sell Ginger when we left New Mexico back then. I should have found a way. I know a guitar ain't a horse, but it's something." He handed the Gibson back to Black. "Your mother would sure like to see that."

"Dad, I can't tell you what it means to me that you came to hear me sing today."

"Well, I hear you sing every Sunday, Bud," Corwin replied.

"I know, but that's different. Thanks for coming. And I want to tell you something, but you can't tell Mother. Can you do that?" Black asked.

"You know I don't believe in secrets, Bud. I don't keep things from her."

"I know. She'll find out tomorrow anyway. I just don't want her to know tonight. This is going to hurt her. Any way it goes, it's going to hurt her. But I want to tell you. I want you to know. I hope you can be happy for me. Maybe you can soften it for her. I don't want a big scene. If you tell her tonight . . ."

"Just spit it out, son. I can't make you any promises."

Black hesitated, rubbed his hand over his mouth. "I'm leaving tomorrow, Dad. The Sons of the Pioneers have asked me to be in their band. I'm going to finish the tour with them. Amarillo and Fort Worth and I don't where all. They've got room in their cars for me. Then we all go to Hollywood where they've got some contracts to play in the movies. It's good pay."

"You and that Hollywood business. Well, I guess you need to

get it out of your system. How long you going to be gone? Classes start up soon at Texas Tech."

"Forever, Dad. I'm gone for good. Or at least till I save up enough money to buy us a ranch in New Mexico. I'm not going to Tech. I'm not good at that paper stuff." Black stepped closer to his father. "Music is going to be my life. Singing is what I love and I'm good at it."

"You're going to break your mother's heart, Keith. She's had one thing in her mind since you and Joyce came along, that you would both graduate from college. Have a better life than hand-to-mouth all the time. That's what this has been about, selling the ranch and moving down here." Corwin stepped back.

"I know, Dad, but book-learning isn't the only way. I don't mind working hard. I don't need easy. I know you don't follow the picture shows, but the Sons of the Pioneers are famous. They make records and play the radio stations and do background music for the shoot-em-up westerns. I won't be playing in sleazy bars. It's good pay, maybe more than I would make with one of those college degrees. Don't you understand?" Black pleaded with his father.

"I don't want you to ruin your life, son." Corwin put his hand on Black's shoulder.

"You raised me right, Dad. You and Mother trained me up in the way I should go and when I am old, I will not depart from it, like it says in Proverbs 22. I promise."

"You leave tomorrow?"

"I meet them at seven in the morning at the hotel."

"Take care of yourself, Bud. Write your mother and call her every now and then."

"Are you going to tell her tonight?" Black asked.

Corwin walked through the door.

BLEST BE THE TIE THAT BINDS

🎼 Hymn. Written in 1772 by John Fawcett for his congregation at Wains-
gate Baptist Church in Hebden Bridge, West Yorkshire, England, as
an explanation for why he remained their pastor rather than accept a
more prestigious position offered him in London.

Black returned to the soda fountain and pulled the spigot to mix himself a Coca-Cola. The crowd had thinned with the late hour, and the
excitement of the evening's success had waned. Truva sat in a red booth
with two girls and beckoned him over. One of the girls, Susie, belonged
to Truva; the other was Lucille. He realized they had been waiting for
him, Lucille manipulating Truva to worm a double-date. She was ap-
plying bright pink lipstick when he first saw them. Black and Lucille
had dated off and on, but he could take her or leave her. Tonight, he
wanted to take her.

Her auburn hair fell loose and shiny from a pink polka-dot
band held with bobby pins. A tight rosy-pink cotton sweater stretched
over an ample bosom overflowing her bra's constriction. Shoes kicked
off, her body was curled up in the booth with her legs under her. An
elbow rested on the table, her hand slowly twirling the straw in her
soda pop. Her brown cow eyes followed Black's every move. The empty
space next to her waited for him to fill it.

"You're wasting that lipstick on the straw," he said as he sat
down.

Lucille giggled. "It's really pink, isn't it?"

"We're ready to get out of here," Truva said. "How about you?
Had enough grandstanding for one night?"

"You got the car?" Black asked.

"It's Saturday night, ain't it? Thought we might take a little run out to Buffalo Springs. You in?"

"Let me finish my Coke first." Black hoped to get him alone at the end of the night to tell him about leaving. He hated telling Truva almost as much he hated telling his parents.

"Hi, Truva," squeaked a high-pitched voice from a pretty petite girl with clear blue eyes as she and her date stopped by their booth.

Lucille stared at the girl, then laughed. "I know you. You go to our church."

"Yes, I've seen you there too," the new girl squeaked again. "I'm Dorris McSpadden. You spell that with two Rs and two Ds."

Lucille cackled, but Truva cut her off. "This is my cousin from down around San Angelo. You need a ride, Dorris?"

Dorris looked confused. "Well, I'm from here now, Truva, and no, I don't need a ride. I just wanted to say Hi to you and your friend Blackie and tell him we enjoyed his singing. Taylor is going to take me home. You remember Taylor, don't you?"

Truva nodded his head in the general direction of the serious man standing beside her. "You drive careful, Taylor."

"Always do," the man said, taking Dorris by the arm and steering her toward the door.

"Bye," she called back. It sounded like a goose honk.

Lucille cackled again. "What's wrong with her voice? Forget that, what's wrong with her, telling me how to spell her name and all?"

"That's just the way she sounds, born that way," Truva said, "and her pet peeve is people spelling Dorris with just one R."

"There's nothing wrong with her, Lucille. What's wrong with you?" Black shot back, shocking the others to silence with his anger. He noisily slurped the last of his Coca-Cola through the straw, then stood up and said, "Let me get my guitar from the locker and we'll go."

Buffalo Springs was about ten miles away, too far for an ordinary night. But tonight was special, his last night in Lubbock, and the car had enough gas. In the backseat during the drive, Lucille tried to make up for whatever she had said that made him mad. It worked.

At the springs the foursome spread a blanket under the starry sky and pointed out constellations. It was a balmy night following a record high of 109 degrees in Lubbock that day. Lucille offered to take off her pink sweater because of the heat, but no one encouraged her. Black refused to sing though the others continuously requested. "I'm resting up," he said. So, they sang to him, imitating his voice, making everyone hee-haw.

Around midnight, they rolled back into Lubbock. Truva stopped the Buick in the narrow alleyway that ran behind 26th Street. Black's private entrance was near a tall Rose of Sharon hedge he could push through to get home undetected.

"Why did you pull in here? We need to drop the girls off first," Black said.

"Okay, Lucille, you're on," Truva said. "This is your deal. You tell him."

"Well, I thought I might go to your little house with you, like we did before that time. I can be real quiet." Lucille's voice carried a hint of desperation hidden in its sweetness.

"What about your folks? It's midnight," Black asked.

"I'm spending the night with Susie. You can walk me over to her house later. She's gonna let me in her window."

Black hesitated, but it seemed a little girl's "please" was hanging in there somewhere. It was his last night. A little messing around couldn't hurt. "We'll have to be very quiet. None of your loud squeals."

Lucille was out of the car navigating the Rose of Sharon before he could climb out.

Carrying his guitar and a small bag from Halsey's, he stood beside Truva in the waiting car. "I'll give you a call tomorrow early. Something I need to tell you."

"Tell me now."

"I don't think Lucille can wait," Black grinned.

"Well, I'll see you at church. Tell me then."

"Maybe. Good-bye, Truva. You're a swell friend."

"This was her idea, not mine," Truva winked.

"It's okay. I can handle Lucille." Black pushed away from the car. "Till we meet again," he whispered as Truva drove away.

An hour later, Black picked Lucille's purse off the floor and handed it to her. "I'll walk you over to Susie's," he said, directing her to the door. "I've got to get some shut-eye. Have to get up early in the morning."

"Oh, yeah? What do you have to do that's so almighty important?"

"That's for me to know and you to find out," he teased. "Come on, Pinkie." He put his arm around her waist, tugged at her sweater and goosed her ribs. Lucille let out a surprised loud squeal just as he opened the door to leave his little house out back.

"Shhhh," Black cautioned.

Mattress springs squeaked inside the big house. A face appeared on the other side of the window screen in his parents' bedroom.

"Who's there? Keith, is that you?" His mother's voice.

Black put his finger to his mouth, then mustered all the normality he could to speak, "It's me, Ma. Everything's okay. Had to use the bathroom. Just go back to sleep."

They stood frozen. After a long silence, Black turned Lucille toward the Rose of Sharon. They tip-toed across the yard, making as little sound as possible.

Then he heard his father shout, "Loa, come back here! LOA! STOP!"

He turned around just as the back door flew open. A wild banshee emerged, wearing a long white nightgown and brandishing a broom. She cleared the stoop and its steps, running toward him faster than he could have imagined possible. His father trailed behind.

Black pushed Lucille through the shrubs, shouting at her, "Run! Run! Go to Susie's. Don't look back."

She did as he said. She had heard the stories about his mother.

Corwin stumbled on the stoop steps, fell, and lay crumpled on the grass. "Loa! Stop!" he begged.

She plowed into her son full force, swinging the broom, striking him with the handle.

"Mother!" Black crossed his arms in front of his face for protection but didn't fight back.

WHACK! WHACK! WHACK!

"How could you do this to me?" she screamed, as she beat him. "Where is that hussy?" Loa took wild swings, striking the Rose of Sharon before aiming the broom at her son again. "What have you done to me?" The hundred-pound fury struck wildly.

"Keith, stop her. Don't let her do that to you." Corwin yelled from the ground.

Black continued to stand, taking the blows until one connected with his head. He fell to the ground and curled up, covering his head with his hands. She continued to whack him. His body jumped with each blow, receiving the punishment his mother meted out.

Loa threw the broom, then dropped beside him, slapping and pummeling him with her hands. Still he didn't fight back.

Finally, Corwin managed to limp to them on his sprained ankle. He pulled his wife off their son and pinned her arms. Her angry fists kept pummeling the air.

"You've ruined everything! Everything!" she hissed at Black. Her body flailed as Corwin tried to contain her.

"I need help with her, Keith," Corwin said. "My foot's hurt."

Black jumped up from the ground. The two men encircled the most important woman in their lives with their arms and started speaking softly to her.

"Shhhh. It's okay. It's okay. It's okay, Ma."

Gradually she calmed, collapsing into heaving sobs, and when the sobs exhausted her, into soft whimpers. Black picked her up and carried her back into the house. Joyce was standing on the stoop looking horrified. She rushed to help her dad navigate the steps. Black laid his mother on her bed, then stepped back to the doorway. Corwin limped in and adjusted the covers, then kissed her forehead.

"Is Sonny Boy okay?" she asked.

"I'm okay, Ma."

"I'm sorry. God forgive me. I'm so sorry." Loa cried.

"I'm okay, Ma. It's okay."

"Don't leave us," she whined, pulling up on her elbows. "Please don't leave us."

Black walked away.

He walked the rest of the night, crisscrossing Lubbock. Past Mark Halsey Drug, past Broadway Music Store, past KFYO, past Lubbock High School, past Truva's house, past the entrance to Texas Technological College. *Four years for one of those degrees!*

He lingered at the small Livestock Judging Pavilion on the Tech campus, sturdy even in the dark, and on to the large Dairy Barn and Creamery where he had earned his blue ribbons last year in FFA. The Tech Dairy was the driving force behind the huge cream and butter market in the southwest, and when refrigeration came along, the demand for "ice cream makers" catapulted Tech Dairy graduates into high demand. Black had heard that when Tech first opened about fourteen years earlier, they let boys bring up to three cows with them to add to the Tech dairy herd, which served as pay for their education. Didn't matter. He didn't have any cows. He didn't have any horses. He didn't have any anything, except his guitar. *Would they take that?*

Later, oddly enough, he found himself walking past the house on 7th Street where Truva's strange older cousin with the squeaky voice, the one who dated Taylor, lived with her family.

At daybreak, he stood on the corner of Broadway and Avenue K, across from the ten-story Hotel Lubbock. He pulled a fat cigar stub from his shirt pocket and lit it. Slowly pulling the smoke into and out of his lungs, he savored the exotic smell and calm feeling. *A Woman is Just a Woman, but a Good Cigar is a Smoke*, he remembered from the pewter ashtray Mr. Yates had used. *Guess that makes some sort of convoluted Hollywood sense.*

There was still time. He could walk home and get his guitar, the cigar box, an extra shirt.

Instead, he walked into the hotel café and ordered a cup of coffee. When Bob Nolan came down for breakfast, Black told him that his circumstances had changed, and he wouldn't be able to play with the band after all. He thanked Bob for the opportunity, asked him to tell Len Slye about the situation, then shook his couldabeen-boss's hand and took his leave.

Looking flabbergasted, the leader of the Sons of the Pioneers watched last night's star musician walk away.

THE ROCK THAT IS HIGHER THAN I

 Hymn. Written 1861 by Erastus Johnson at YMCA convention at Carlisle, PA, after banking houses fell. Music by William G. Fischer.

Four hours after he had walked away from the Hotel Lubbock, Black stood in front of the congregation of the Pioneer Park Church of Christ at Eighth Street and Avenue T.

"Open your hymnals to page 313, 'The Rock That Is Higher Than I.'"

*O sometimes the shadows are deep, And rough seems the path to the goal,
And sorrows, sometimes how they sweep Like tempests down over the soul!
O then to the Rock let me fly, To the Rock that is higher than I.*

Black looked clean and polished wearing a white shirt, gray trousers and patterned blue tie, his black hair shining in the sunlight that streamed through the windows. His parents, Corwin and Loa, and his sister Joyce sat in the second pew. Lucille sat beside Susie in the back. She tried to catch his eye, but he averted. As he led the singing, Black could hear his mother's beautiful soprano voice clearly above the rest. Pure melody, it soothed his wounds. Her glassed-over eyes concentrated on the music with no hint of last night's distress.

Two mincemeat pies, his favorite, sat cooling on the sideboard in the kitchen at home. A chicken baked in the oven. Loa and Joyce had cooked feverishly before church. Happenings of the previous night were never mentioned.

Another voice in the congregation caught Black's attention, slightly off-key and high-pitched, but robust and full of heart. He hid a small grin of recognition. The sound came from Dorris McSpadden, Truva's odd cousin who was sitting with Coleman and Rilla, Coleman Jr., and Truva. Black had noticed as they entered the pew that she wore red shoes, unusual for church, unusual anywhere. Now he glanced in her direction. A hat with a perky plume of black and white feathers sat cocked over her right eye. Her hands, covered with black gloves, held the hymnal with style and grace. A refined lady singing out of tune. Black liked listening to the strange discord of her high-pitched squeaky voice. It balanced the perfect pitch, the perfect key of his mother's voice.

Fall 1939, Keith Leroy Black, aka Blackie, enrolled as a freshman at Texas Technological College.

GOD BE WITH YOU TILL WE MEET AGAIN

Hymn. Poem written by Congregationalist Jeremiah Rankin, later president of Howard University. Music by Methodist William G. Tomer. First sung in 1880 at First Congregational Church in Washington, D. C.

The McSpaddens had settled in a comfortable house in Lubbock with modern conveniences they had rarely known, the first decent house since the glory days in Clayton before the Depression when Dorris's daddy thought he was making something of himself. Only she and the boys remained after Jean married Howard Noe in March, 1939. Twenty-two years old, Dorris feared she might be an old maid. Daddy John pulled her close and said, "You're my last little woman, Dorris, and I don't care if you stay forever."

Their small house was often full of aunts and uncles and cousins plus Dorothy and Jean and their husbands. The women frothed about, preparing big meals. Dorris landed a job, working in the hosiery department at Montgomery Ward's, or "Monkey Ward" as everyone called it, though it was only part-time. She kept most of the money for herself after Uncle Jesse was paid back. The family was doing better.

The whole country was doing better. After almost a decade of struggle during the Great Depression, life finally seemed a bit easier. Maybe all the bad stuff was behind, although Dorris didn't like what she heard on the radio and read in the newspapers about that big war going on overseas. Russia, Poland, Germany, and Italy sounded familiar from geography classes. But when the radio said Japan had invaded China and started a war in Asia, that seemed far away. She couldn't figure what that meant for Texas, though sometimes she wondered about the "Oriental" people she and Dot had seen in California. Had they really been spies?

Summer came with its Texas dry heat. Daddy John was having a tough time in the fields working the crops with Owen and Cecil. His stomach trouble returned with a vengeance. Mother finally convinced him to go to a doctor. The diagnosis surprised no one: bleeding stomach ulcers. An operation was scheduled at St. Mary's of the Plains, the nuns' hospital.

Dorris and her sisters coddled him, giving him little gifts, rubbing his salt and pepper hair, teasing him about turning gray. Dad had never been in a hospital before. He didn't like the skimpy gowns with open backs and the nuns everywhere in their strange white hats.

He shook the boys' hands, gave hugs and big smiles to his girls and kissed Mama on the lips. He loosely waved as they wheeled him away for surgery. "Bye-bye, little women."

Surgery was complicated. Pneumonia.

Suddenly, Dorris's rock was gone.

John Finis McSpadden's funeral service was attended by a hoard of people. Real people. Farmers. Housewives. Grocers. Businessmen. People who respected the man and how he kept standing through all life had thrown at him. At the end of the procession from the church to the Lubbock City Cemetery trailed a line of wholesale grocery trucks whose vans sported addresses from all over west Texas, along with colorful drawings of vegetables and fruit.

Late evening on the day of the funeral, after guests had left the little house overflowing with brought-in food, Dorris's mother wanted to go back to the cemetery with just the family. They squeezed into the Buick with Owen, Cecil, and Mother up front, all five girls in back. As they neared the plot, Owen stopped the car and peered through the dusk.

"There's somebody at the grave site," he said. "What's that guy doing?"

Dorris peered, straining to see.

"He's fine-raking the grave, making it look better," Cecil said. "I thought about that myself. The grave-diggers leave it pretty rough."

"But who is it?" Jean asked.

Dorris knew who it was. She had noticed him at the funeral service.

"That's Blackie," she said. "Truva's friend."

YELLOW ROSE OF TEXAS

 Folksong from early Colonial Texas. First recorded copy, author unknown, handwritten on plain paper circa 1836, now at University of Texas, Austin. Rewritten and performed by Gene Autry and Jimmy Long, 1933. Performed by Roy Rogers in movie of same name, 1944.

In the spring of 1940 Dorris's cousin, Truva, invited her to a party at his house. She wasn't sure she wanted to go. It would be a Texas Tech crowd. Now that her dad had died and she was on her own, Dorris would never have the money to go to Tech. She wouldn't fit in with these kids. Her job at Monkey Ward was enough, she didn't need a college party.

But Truva had said a friend of his asked him to invite her. *Don't kid yourself, Dorris, you know you're curious who that might be.* She shopped for fabric to make a new dress and found a bolt of polished cotton, the perfect shade of blue to match her eyes. The color reminded her of Texas bluebonnets. The sweetheart bodice had been tricky to sew, but she got it done. Dorris adored the dress but feared the college girls would think it plebian. Some of them would probably show up in trousers.

The night of the party, Dorris felt wrong all over. The curling iron had curled her hair too tight. The Tech girls wore their hair long and loose. And the seams in her nylons were antigoglin. She had been too scared of getting a run to tug them straight. Her new black pumps, the ones with the cute bows above the peep toes, looked too dressy, maybe even tacky. She had hoped they would make her look taller and more grown-up, not so kid-like.

Dorris persevered through her doubts. At Truva's house, she

encountered a tall blond in the doorway. "Hi, I'm Dorris McSpadden with two Rs and two Ds. Do you know where Truva is?"

"He's in the kitchen, but I don't think you can get back there. The living room is jammed. Blackie is about to sing, and everybody's crowding in. You know Blackie?"

"I listen to him on the radio." Dorris didn't mention that she also listened to him lead singing at church sometimes.

"He's going to be in the movies someday. He sings better than Gene Autry," said the tall blond as she dropped to the floor to sit with her friends. "And he's a whole lot better looking."

Young people draped over the furniture, filled the floor, lined the walls. Dorris sidled along a wall and claimed a leaning spot. Truva and Blackie appeared from the kitchen. The Techies erupted in cheers and applause. Blackie sat sideways on the arm of the overstuffed sofa, one knee raised to help cradle his guitar. He looped the wide strap of his Jumbo Gibson Acoustic around his neck, then fiddled with the tuning keys until he got the sound just like he wanted.

"I'll start with 'Tumbling Tumbleweeds.'"

Blackie's rich tenor voice filled the room. The sound was much better than on the radio. His fretwork and strumming made it sound like ten guitars working their magic. Dorris could feel the vibrations of the guitar strings in her bones.

That voice. His voice. Such power it held.

Blackie was beginning to look like a movie star with that wavy black hair combed back, those piercing eyes, and that grin.

Wow! What a grin! Like he knew some kind of secret.

Dorris was mesmerized by the music and by this almost-man she almost knew. Would he really be a movie star someday?

Blackie noticed Dorris and gave her a nod. Then he turned and winked at Truva. She would have preferred the wink.

Blackie sang several more songs, keeping Dorris pinned to the wall with his voice and his eyes. When he finished, the girls rushed him, some of them twirling their long hair in their fingers. Dorris waited for them to clear before she moved toward him.

Before she knew it, he had nicknamed her "Kiddo," learned her favorite song, and had picked up his guitar to sing "The Yellow Rose of Texas."

"One more song. This one's for Kiddo!" he announced.

Dorris stood beside Black. He sat on the arm of the overstuffed sofa and sang straight into her heart: *Her Eyes are Bright as Diamonds, They Sparkle Like the Dew.*

That was the best part, the part that filled her up, when he looked at her like that.

And the Yellow Rose of Texas shall be mine forever more!

Later that night, they held hands as he walked her home.

Keith LeRoi Black and Johnnie Dorris McSpadden.

Black & Kiddo.

PART II

I LOVE YOU TRULY

Parlor song used at weddings. Written by Carrie Jacobs-Bond circa 1900. #1 hit recorded in 1912 by Elsie Baker. First song written by a woman to sell one million copies of sheet music.

Life with its sorrow, life with its tear
Fades into dreams when I feel you are near
For I love you truly, truly dear

Black and Kiddo kept steady company after Truva's party. Cecil, chasing thirty years, started dating a spunky strawberry blond named Marguerite Graham who suited him just fine. Owen didn't date. Man of the house now that Dad was gone, he carried his new responsibility seriously. He ensured Kiddo and their mother were well cared for, quietly putting himself in the background. Owen and Black became buddies, both being hard workers and horse-lovers.

In the summer of 1940, Kiddo's mother rode the train to California to be with Bernice for the birth of the first McSpadden grandchild. She sent a postcard from the Harvey House in Albuquerque.

When Texas Tech finished for the semester, cowboy whispers came on the summer winds calling Black to the high plains. He hitched a ride to his family's home place in New Mexico. His grandpa A. B. had died the previous winter, and Black thought there might be a place for him on the Black Family Ranch, also known by its brand: C Lazy K.

Black needed a place.

He wrote to Kiddo on cowboy stationery pilfered from his uncle, Red Black:

Keith LaRoii Blackie Black
C Lazy K Ranch
Des Moines, New Mexico
June 6, 1940

Dearest Dor,

Once again by golly I'm on the up and up!! The feller I wuz a'gonna ride with yestidy decided to go 'ta Clovis instead 'o Amarillio. Therefore, consequently, although, but nevertheless, I had 'ta hang up a thumb. I started at 11:25 and got to Des Moines about seven. Had to ketch six rides to get here. From Dumas to Des Moines I rode with a doctor from Ohio. He had a wife and small boy. I was the first real cowboy the young lad had ever seen. That guitar shore wuz a lot of company to me while waiting for rides.

The grass, cattle, and crops are fine here. I'm going down the river this afternoon to get on the haying crew (if I can).

The Ranch here has a hundred percent calf crop except for one calf which was lost when 2 weeks old. The spring roundup and branding has not been done either so perhaps I might get some work there.

Everyone is getting along fine here I guess. Russell "Razz" is waiting down at the corral to go over the pastures on the homestead place, so I guess I'd better draw this rambling narrative to a close.

Love,
Bar Room Blackie
Silver Spur Saloon
Out West in the Cactus !!*@!!&#

C Lazy K
Des Moines, NM
June 12, 1940

How's my good friend Owen Mc. now? Tell him I'm pulling for him and if anything shows up I'll let him know pronto. Gee!! I hope he doesn't have to work on that old mixer much longer. Them there things weren't made for humans, especially cowpokes! The W. S. Ranch at Cimmarron is paying $45 a month and board. Also, the C. S. Ranch and Philmont pay the same for riders.

The +L (Crosselle) pays $32.50 for riders and the T.O. pays the same. The price for hay hands varies from $1.50 to $2.50 per day + board. I've never seen this country in better shape, however, we do need rain a little. The spring roundups will start in about a week.

Now, Kiddo, I want you to get these names. "Red" is Lynn, my Dad's half-brother. He is red-headed, about 5'11" tall and weighs about 170 lbs. "Razz" is Russell, another of Dad's half-brothers. He's about my size. They own the ranch where I am now staying.

Most of their cattle are purebreds (Registered). The cows, when just fresh, give too much milk for the calves, so we have to milk them out every morning for about 3 weeks. They surely are fat and the calves are strong, big and healthy.

It sure is nice to be able to climb into that swivel chair on a brisk cool morning and take off after the cattle!! Tell O. I wish he were here. We have been building fence lately. Also, we are building a road into Mitchell Springs Canyon. Just the last few days, in my odd minutes, I have been practicing roping. Gee!! But a fellow can get rusty.

Darling, I'll have to quit now. Be careful and remember I love you. Gosh ain't that mushy!! Anyhow I do. Tell everyone hello for me and kiss all the babies for me too.

Love, Black

Lubbock, Texas
June 17, 1940

Dear Black,

. . . Some day, Black, you will have to spend a day like I did yesterday. I never realized before how terrible it would be. You know Daddy died last Father's Day. It doesn't seem possible that he has been gone a whole year.

Why haven't you written your folks? I saw your mother in town Friday and she seemed so hurt and worried, then yesterday I saw the family at church. Your Dad really seemed anxious about you and wanted to know every thang you were doing. I hope you don't think I've overstepped my place or am trying to have too much say so over you and what you do.

Your cousin [Lavoy Hooker] is a wonderful preacher. The place where the meeting is being held has lots of space for some people to drive in and park their cars. The lighting system is good only I sure hope I don't have to sit near a light again, it is kinda buggy.

All of your Thornton relatives went on a picnic out to McKenzie yesterday. Joyce said there were about 38. They invited me but I didn't go. I was afraid that some of them would think I was trying to get in with the family.

Owen said tell you howdy. He is still sticking to his misery.

Cecil is playing on Hawks ball team (you know the hunchback Hawk). Cecil wears a Pepsi-Cola suit. They played Wolfforth yesterday and won.

. . .and besides that, what did you mean by saying for me to kiss all the babies. What babies, you goof-snoof.

Be good Honey Bee, work hard and write real soon.

I still love you. Dorris

Dearest Dor;

We started into the canyons one afternoon about 2 o'clock. At first going was pretty easy, but after about a mile of rocky, but yet passable roads, we struck the big rocks and timber. We first came in contact with the impassable roads on land belonging to two brothers, Pal and Up Wilson. With strong bars and heavy sledges we moved rocks which were too big to travel over. Soon we came to a narrow wooded canyon. The road ran just along the rim rock which bordered the edge of the woodland. On one side were trees (penones or pingones of the pine family), and on the other was the rimrock which dropped about 30 feet straight down. By driving carefully we made our way about 200 yards. Then what? Porkipines and the drouth had killed many of the trees. The wind in turn, rushing through the narrow canyon had caused the dead trees to fall. In their wake was left nothing but caos and confusion. Rocks, trees of various kinds, brush, vines, and washouts made the way almost impassable.

2.

Then we went to work. For the first time in years I saw tree fall by my own skill and strength with the ax. The entangled mass had to be cut through. Large trees & logs were rolled over the cliff. Others were thrown on the uphill side of the trail to prevent washing out of the road in the future. Some of the larger trees, which four men could not budge by use of chains, cables, + the power of the ranch pickup were cut into in the middle leaving the bottom and top ends as they were, and thus taking out the middle section. You know - like this —

In some cases 2 or three large trees had fallen over one another. in such cases we made a new trail out around them. Only wagons and saddle horses had ever been here before. It had been about 13 years since a wagon had been there. So, you see, in many places we found trees 15 to 20 feet tall which had grown up in the old wagon road.

Passing from this place we came to several deep ravines which ran into a canyon. The old wagon road had been washed out into deep gullies. These places were filled with rocks, and then dirt was thrown on top. Some places we found the road too steep, that is, it ran on the side of a hill. such places had to be cut down like

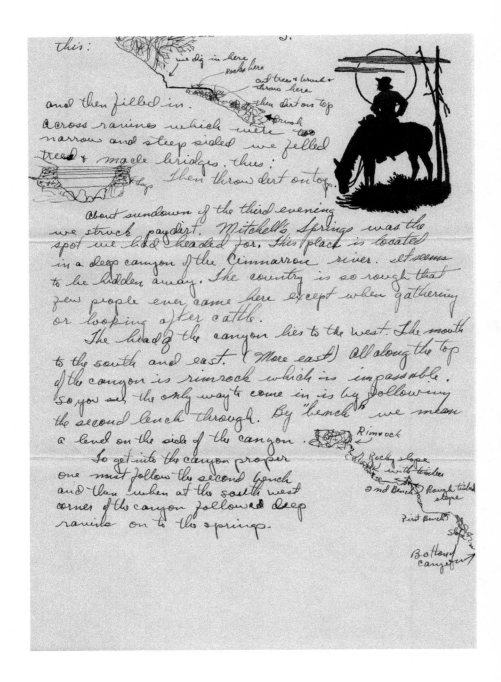

this:

and then filled in.
Across ravines which were too
narrow and steep sided we felled
trees & made bridges, thus:
Then throw dirt on top.

About sundown of the third evening
we struck paydirt. Mitchell's Springs was the
spot we had headed for. This place is located
in a deep canyon of the Cimarron river. It seems
to be hidden away. The country is so rough that
few people ever came here except when gathering
or looking after cattle.

The head of the canyon lies to the west. The mouth
to the south and east. (More east) All along the top
of the canyon is rimrock which is impassable.
So you see the only way to come in is by following
the second bench through. By "bench" we mean
a level on the side of the canyon.

To get into the canyon proper
one must follow the second bench
and then when at the south west
corner of the canyon followed deep
ravine on to the spring.

4.

This place is just paradise complete. Large pine trees that seem to reach the sky & Blue & green cedars spread their scent. The moldering of leaves & pine needles mingled with the scent of the wild flowers and blue grass make a rare perfume. Wind never touches this part of the canyon.

As one stands there under the trees there is deathly silence. Then all of a sudden the wind sings in the pines or above. Then the call of a lonesome coyote, The song of a mocking bird. Then there is music which surpasses all other kinds.

Seven springs run into this valley. Deer come here to drink. We have seen several already. Wild turkeys perch on the branches of the pines. And there play the squirrels in that oak tree. High along the rim rock the bear and mountain lion have their dens. As I stand here and behold nature in its wildest, yet its tamest and most unafraid form it seems that I am dreaming. Everything is so quiet, so peaceful it brings one under a spell.

Well, I guess you have become bored with such "goings ons" so I'll quit for a spell. I haven't received a letter from you yet!! You since last Tuesday had better get on the job. I'll admit, however there is poor mail service between here & Lubbock.

Greet each and every one of the family for me and write to tell me how everything is getting along.

I am to (preach) (?) here next Sunday I wish you could be here.

I Love You —
Black.

Black really loved his New Mexico. Part of that last page bears repeating:

> *This place is just paradise complete. Large pine trees that seem to reach the sky and blue and green cedars spread their scent. The moldering of leaves and pine needles mingled with the scent of wild flowers and blue grass make a rare perfume. Wind never reaches this part of the canyon. As one stands there under the trees there is a deathly silence. Then all of a sudden the wind sings in the pines far above. Then the call of a lonesome coyote, The song of a mockingbird. Then there is music which surpasses all other kinds.*
>
> *Seven springs run into this valley. Deer come here to drink. We have seen several already. Wild turkeys perch on the branches of the pines. And there play the squirrels in that oak tree. High along the rimrock the bear and mountain lion have their dins. As I stand here and behold nature in its wildest, yet its tamest and most unafraid form, it seems that I am dreaming. Everything is so quiet, so peaceful it brings one under a spell.*

Lubbock, Texas
June 22, 1940

Dear Honey Bee,

I really enjoyed the little story you wrote me about your trip into the canyon. When I first started reading it, I didn't know what to think. But it was good (even if I did have to read it twice to get all of the details).

I'm truly sorry that you didn't receive my last letter sooner. I hope I'm never so dilatory again.

It looks like rain again today. I've got to hurry and hang out a small wash and I've also got to iron.

Black, I'm about to convince myself that I'm not a very good manager. I never do get through. Every day is full of work and I always have some left over. I guess I let it worry me too much because I get so tired some time I can hardly make it. Would you have any helpful suggestions to make?

My thoughts and heart will be with you tomorrow especially during church time. I too wish I could be there in person to hear you. I'll know you will do your very best and that your sermon will be a success. Write me the results.

I love you. Dorris

Buffalow Springs Ranch
Felt, Oklahoma
June 27, 1940

    . . . This ranch borders on the lines of Texas and Oklahoma. The bunkhouse where we live was the headquarters of the old XIT Outfit. This surely is a pretty place. There are cottonwood trees a mile? high all around the yard and along the creek. Fishing is good. I'm wrangling horses every morning at four. Sometimes I don't get in in time for breakfast. The vega grows up over waist high all along the canyon here so we are cutting it for hay. I killed a rattlesnake today. It had 7 rattles & a button. If I ever get back to Texas I'll give you the rattles.

    Joe D. Whittenburg, the big boss and third owner of this outfit, came out just after dinner and brought your much wanted letter.

    When I first went to work for this outfit I lived at the Crosselle (+L). Next I went to the Baker outfit & then down here. All of these are owned by the Cimarron Cattle Company.

    Say kid, there is a feller here working who hails from Philadelphia. He is a college graduate. He had never been west before. Clayton is the fartherest west he has ever been. He had a fit the other morning when we saw a couple of coyote!! It almost made him sick when I twisted the rattles off of a rattlesnake. He surely does have some goofy ideas. And can he ask the questions!!

    Hawk (Herman Morrison) and Hawkshaw (Charlie Hendricks) are going to take in the rodeo at Clayton the fourth of July. Hawk took money in Madison Square Garden in steer riding. I think they should do pretty good. There are men working here from almost every walk of life. One can really learn lots of things from a crew like this.

    I am still doing a little singing, you know, as I make the rounds with the rake. I pretend I'm singing to you.

    . . . I'll have to leave you now darlin' so goodbye —
Lots of Love & Kisses from your old man, Black

Lubbock, Texas
July 1, 1940

  . . . Just be careful that some of those snattle rakes don't get you before you do them and "if you ever get back to Texas" be sure and bring me at least one set of rattles. Don't go trying to charm some ole snake by fixing your eye that crazy way – because he might charm you first and then you'd be cock-eyed for good. You know that would be terrible because I don't believe I'd like a husband with a goofy eye.

  Honey, I love you with all my heart and I still miss you terribly. I dream about you too. The other afternoon I took a nap & I dreamed that you sent me a little cub mountain lion in a cage. It was just darling yellow & brown & it would spit & spat at me. Now wasn't that silly.

  Just to show you that I do love you I'm going to close before you get bored stiff. [After nine pages of family and church news]

  Lots of love from Dorris
P.S. Draw me some more little pictures. I enjoy them very much.

Cimarron Cattle Co.
Felt, Oklahoma
July 8, 1940
Dearest Darling Dor,

Did you ever nurse 12 drunk men at one time? That's a job. You see, it all started the night of the third of July when the boys from the Cimarron Cattle Company hit town. [Clayton, NM] Lee, the cook, an old man of about 56 years was first to begin to get woozy. However, be not mistaken, for at the same time Hawkshaw, Hawk, Maynard, Joe Jimenez, Dale Robbins, Bill McKnight, Ern Greys, Roy Barkley, George Hoff, Martain Beasley, and Tracy Sink were also getting a snort or two under their belts.

Soon things started whirling. Men from other outfits, having hit town, had also started tuning up for the next day. Lee was first. The old fellow just went wild. Already the cops had taken several drunks in. I started to the truck with Lee. George, who was little better off than Lee, tried to help me, but soon fell by the way. Lee was shouting and yelling at the top of his voice. The sheriff walked up behind me and said to get him out of town or he would put him in jail.

So, after walking around in the rain caring for the boys for about 2 hours there came the news that Hawkshaw had been in a fight with a Mexican and had been thrown in jail. Also Martain Beasley, the fore-man, in a drunken attempt to get Hawkshaw out had been thrown in also. Martain had the keys to the truck and the law would not let us see him. So, we stayed all night in Clayton. The other lads, some dog drunk and some passed out, just wandered around for the rest of the night.

The sun rose on the fourth. I took the boys 2 & 3 at a time & helped them to sober up. At 8 o'clock we went to the jug to see if we could get Hawkshaw and Martain out. The law turned them out and did not charge them a cent.

At the rodeo Hawkshaw won $12.50 first place in bronc riding and Hawk won $10 first in steer riding.

After the rodeo the boys all went to the dance. I told them that I was going to the show and wouldn't be bothered with them. Ern stayed sober and took them to the truck about 12 o'clock and started home. The show lasted until almost 2, so when I came out, the dance was still going on, but the boys had gone. I just stayed around at cafes drinking coffee.

Sunup came & the crowds started leaving for home, so I hitchhiked back to Felt and a boy I know there brought me to the ranch about noon. Some of those cowpokes were still lit!!

Part of the time I work a team of one high strung, nervous, fast-stepping horse and the other a lazy old meathead. At other times, I work Blue & Bear. Blue is a runaway horse and Bear is mean. He kicks, paws & if you don't watch him, he'll bite at you. I do have fun.

The morning of the second of July I saw a snake fight, a water moxan and a prarre racer. They were twisted & coiled & tangled. Both were trying to squeeze the other to death. At the same time they were slashing one another. Both's heads were just a bloody mass. They would just lay there & twist & bite. It was horrible at times, nevertheless, very interesting. The water moxan won.

A couple of the boys, Mack Margolis (the boy from Philadelphia) and Dale Robbins, wanted me to ride over to starve-out well with them to see about a stud, some mares & some colts. Darling, they were beautiful. The stud is a chestnut sorrel. He certainly is built up nicely. The mares were fat and the colts running and having a big time. It was just at sundown and you can imagine the sight.

Dearest, I've wished a million times you were here. We could do so many things together! You could ride with me in the evening when I don't have to work with the baling crew. You see when I get caught up with the raking, I am sent to see about the cattle. So, I am a "cowboy"? after all!!!!

Mack & I went swimming yesterday. It surely was fine. We have a large clear hole about 120 ft long & 30 ft wide. It is about 18 or 19 feet deep all except for about 5 or 6 feet at one end.

. . . Say, don't let those thinking spells make you blue cause I'll have to run home to comfort you. Come to think about it, I was kinda crazy for

running off from such a sweet little girl to come up here in this cow country where I seldom so much as see a girl. But say, darling, I guess there is no question now as to the girl I want or anything. You know they say the way to find out whether you really want a girl or boy friend for life is just to be away from them for a while. It certainly is working out fine in this case! Gee! I'd marry you tomorrow if I could.

Four or five days ago while driving the team in some swampy country I almost lost a horse. The mowing machine had missed a hole but had cut grass so that it fell over the hole. When I came along to rake, there was no way of telling that a hole was there. I had just swung the team around when woosh!! Jake dropped both hind feet and about half of his body in one of those bottomless bog holes. I started whipping him and also the other horse. By floundering he kept on top and the other horse Browny pulled him out.

The next day the same thing happened to Browny. All of this country seeps with water. The holes vary from 18 feet in depth to almost anything. Lee Thaxton, the cook, said that while he was with the XIT, they tied an anvil onto two 35-foot lariats and never did reach the bottom of one hole.

Often while working I pull over to the edge and watch the schools of fish from a cottonwood tree. There are large cottonwoods overhanging the water and one has only to climb to such a branch to see perch, catfish, bass & some other kind that I don't know the name of. On a nearby hillside I found wild grapes & choke cherries. Oh Boy!! Also, I ran across two graves which Lee told me were the graves of buffalo hunters.

About a ¼ mile from the house is to be found a pile of rocks, which mark the grave of a cowboy. In the early days the punchers were having a sham battle to scare a tenderfoot. A Mexican came up and thought they were in earnest and shot one of the boys as he rode around the corner of the house we live in.

Late this afternoon we branded & vaccinated 32 head of this year's colts. Say they surely are pretty. . . . Sweet dreams to you and goodnight. Love & kisses from your ole man ~ Black

Lubbock, Texas
July 11, 1940

My dear Black, . . . I started the 4th off by nearly urping my head off. Owen, Truva, Doug, Cecil and Dor went to Levelland. The rodeo was simply terrible. It was slow. The performance got mixed up and the performers were all very amateurish. The best time in calf roping was 49 seconds. The only real good thing was the clown. He pulled some pretty good stunts & also some kinda nasty gags. I'll tell you about them when I see you. Black, the cutest thing, this ole clown had an ole paint mule and he would make him lay down on his back and stick all four legs straight up in the air.

. . . Honey Bee, I miss you so much at times that its awful. . . Personally I don't have any desire to go with anyone and please don't think I'm trying to sound conceited or wanting you to know just how many opportunities I've had when I say this. I never go to town, the store or several other places that someone don't ask me for a date. In other words, old Dor still loves ole Black and as far as I'm concerned there won't ever be anybody but old Dor & ole Black, agree. ~ Dorris

P. S. Do you know what one little milk bottle said to the other little milk bottle? Let's go over in the corner and curdle (cuddle). Cute, no?

Cimarron Cattle Co.
Baker Place
Folsom, NM
July 14, 1940

*Darling. . . we have been locked in by a flood on the river since Thurs.
nite. This evening is the first time we have been in touch with the
outside world.*

      *Sweet heart I don't know whether I'll go back to Tech or not. I
got my report which said F,F,D,D,D,D,B,B. Please don't tell <u>anyone</u>
as I'm very much ashamed of it. The folks simply enclosed the report in
a letter but said nothing about it.*

      *. . .The boys here think that we are married & that we are
keeping it a secret from the folks. <u>Believe you me!!</u> As soon as I get
home we <u>are</u> going to be married no matter what the cost (provided
you will). Angel, I miss you much & please don't forget me. I must
leave you now dearest so love and kisses from your hubby (to be).*
~ Black

Lubbock, Texas
July 21, 1940
My dear Black,

 Honey, I'm all confused and worried concerning your present arrangements. . .You know neither your mother or dad said a word about your grades to me either. I haven't told anyone about them. Someone is always asking me if you are going to continue your college work. I always say, well he is supposed to or something about like that. Honey, I'm ashamed of your grades too because I know you can do better.

 I'm terribly worried about what you said about us getting married when you come home. All I can say is, I don't see how two people could get married and make a go of it with one of them going to college and no income and the other one sick a lot and not able to work and help out.

 . . . Honey, that was the first time I'd been out to your little house since you left. Everything was just like you left it. Your mother said she never went out there. It makes her too blue. Ole Feridan [deer head] *is still hanging on the wall and his ears are stiff, at last.*

 Dub and Lozita Flowers come to church a lot now. The baby is so cute. Ole Dub calls me the widder. He sure likes to tease me. One nite he walked up and said, well have you heard from the rancher this week, widder? And do you know ole Lucille was standing near and boy did she look up. If a person could be hurt by angry stares, I'd be dead this minute.

 The meeting ended last nite and I'm kinda glad because Bro. Cogdell preached too long. Honest, Black, it was terrible. He preaches an hour and 15 minutes every time. Everyone was nearly give out after a whole week of that.

 . . . Guess I'd better close and make Owen a chocolate pie for dinner. Helen says if I baby my husband like I do Owen & Cecil that he will be a spoiled, rotten husband.

 Honey bee, I still love you a many and I hope to either see you or hear from you soon.
Lots of love to you from ~ Dorris

Baker Place
August 1, 1940
Dearest Sweetheart,

I love you!!*@*!!@@*&##**!!

Des Moines got preached at again Sunday. That afternoon when I got back, I found my bed rolled, clothes gathered up, my horse saddled, and the rest of the boys primed to leave. We left immediately and gathered 7 carloads of cattle from the Cobert and Scuce Mesas. Then we ran in 300 other heifers besides that and this morning got back to the ranch to cut and weigh them for cattle buyers from Ohio. We cut back 113 of them and sold the rest.

While camped out on top we had two rains. Boy, oh boy, was I glad Pop sent me a tarp.

The shortness of this letter is due to uncontrollable circumstances caused by having to have, after dinner. to take part of the cattle on to the Crosselle (+L) place and on to the stockyards tomorrow at Des Moines.

Last week I drove a truck of night carrying wheat from the combine.

Darling, go out and have a talk with the folks. Ask them what is best for me to do. Explain to them about school, grades too!!! Then write soon.

I have from now until September 1 to register with the army. Also, we have to go to training camp, I think it is eight months. As you know, I'll soon be 20. I have no faults about my body except a weak brain!! Therefore, I would probably be No.1 to be called. If I were in college at that time, I would have to quit and thereby lose the money I had in it. I am doing so poorly in school, it seems that a little layoff might not hurt much. As yet I just can't stand the thoughts of a chemistry lab and a bald-headed professor.

Oh, yes! And if I do go into training camp those eight months, it would be at that time that war would probably be declared. And I'm not going to war!! (I hope.) I guess I could hide out up here in these hills and get by.

After all is said and done I'm a very puzzled little boy. What to do? Gee, I don't know.

Love from ye old man ~ Black

Cimarron Cattle Co.
Kenton, Oklahoma
August 18, 1940
Darling Dor,

    It's mighty pretty here now. We baled hay all day and boy oh boy am I tired.

    . . . Be sure to see the folks soon. I wrote them that I wanted to marry you. Gosh! I don't know what they'll think. But, you see, I explained everything about my love for you. I told them that this summer had proved to me definitely that you were the only girl for me. I won't be surprised at anything that may happen now. Let's look for the best!!!!

    Darling, I'm so nearly asleep. I don't know whether I am dreaming I'm writing, or whether I am really writing. So long for this time. Love, Blackie

No wonder Black and Kiddo seemed unsettled. The whole country was unsettled. Newspapers and the radio reported about the war in Europe every day. When Germany conquered France that summer, it scared a lot of ordinary people. Sure, there was a whole big ocean between France and the United States and then a lot of land before those Nazis could get to Texas, but somehow it seemed possible now. Everyone speculated about the draft and how long the United States could stay out of the fray. Talk shifted from *if* to *when*. Women looked at their men. Husbands, sons, brothers. They prayed, negotiated, made deals with God.

Black returned to Lubbock in early September to figure things out. He came straight to Kiddo before going home to his parents. He picked her up and swung her around, then kissed her on the lips right in front of Owen.

Kiddo's mother returned from California shortly thereafter,

just in time to help Cecil and Marguerite with their wedding a few weeks later. Only two of the seven McSpadden siblings left unwed, Owen and Dorris, and there she simmered in the frying pan.

On September 16th, 1940, President Roosevelt signed what became known as the Selective Service Act. It called for the first peacetime draft in the United States. Everyone knew it was just a matter of time before there was no peace. The general uneasiness, the feeling that something ominous was looming on the horizon, exuded a sense of urgency which made Black and Kiddo believe nothing mattered as much as love. Right here. Right now.

After long talks with Black's folks and Kiddo's mother, brothers, and sisters, they decided to go ahead and get hitched. Black did not return to Texas Tech. Kiddo tried to talk to him about his music, but he would only say, "Maybe. Someday." She worried about how they would live, where the money would come from, but not Black. He assured her that they would be okay, and she believed him.

"Consider the lilies of the field, how they grow; they toil not, neither do they spin," he quoted Matthew 6:28. "He will take care of us. I have no doubt."

On October 6, 1940, Black and Kiddo were married at the Pioneer Park Church of Christ in Lubbock. Black was 19. Kiddo was two months shy of 23. A small spat with Black's mother was settled by compromise: Lavoy Hooker, Loa's sister Ola's son, stood as best man instead of Truva. Kiddo's oldest sister, Helen, who had always been a second mother to the McSpadden squirts, served as her matron of honor.

Kiddo didn't have much time to prepare, but she found a lovely soldier blue dress, the same color as the wedding dress from Mother's trunk. And, of course, a matching blue velvet hat! For something old, she wore her mother's lavalier of pearls.

Black & Kiddo, 1940.

TUMBLING TUMBLEWEEDS

 Written by Bob Nolan, 1934. Made famous in the 1935 Gene Autry movie of the same name. Sung by Sons of the Pioneers.

After the reception at Black's parents' house following the wedding, Black and Kiddo helped with the clean-up, then went to his little house out back for their first night together as man and wife. A couple of weeks later they left on a camping honeymoon with friends, John and Fern Carlisle. Black took some money in a cigar box to help pay for gas. He and John took turns driving with Kiddo and Fern holding down the backseat. Black finally got to show Kiddo his precious New Mexico. She recognized the area around Clayton and told them the story of getting her sisters lost trying to find Rabbit Ears.

Black's folks were gone back to Kansas to finalize A. B.'s affairs there, but the foursome spent a few nights at the home place and rode horses. Kiddo rode astraddle instead of sidesaddle. Mother wouldn't have approved, but she was a married woman and could make her own choices. Black led the riders to his special vantage point on a mountain where they could see forever. He teared up as he pointed out the landmarks but quickly laughed away his tears. Kiddo wished they could have been alone for that. It was obvious this place was sacred to him.

Later, Black took them to an old line shack where they camped for a few days. He called it a batchin' cabin, but Kiddo told him he was a bachelor nevermore. They hiked up and around the rim of Capulin Volcano at 8,100 feet for a God's-eye view of the area then headed toward Taos. They made camp at the spectacular Palisades in Cimarron Canyon on Highway 64, before the climb up to Eagle Nest. The boys caught brown trout which Kiddo and Fern cooked over the campfire for supper. That night they spread the bedrolls right alongside the river. Clear water rippled down the stream, the sound so soothing. Mellow moonlight illuminated the ancient jagged rocks. Above the tall cliffs sparkled thousands of stars in the inky sky. No one could ask for a better honeymoon.

Little house out back, Lubbock. Corwin Black relaxing.

Batchin' cabin, New Mexico. Black standing. Friend John Carlisle seated.

Taos was fascinating. The friends visited the Pueblo and the little plaza downtown where Native Americans were selling homemade jewelry and pottery to tourists. Kiddo wanted a souvenir, but she knew the cigar box was not bottomless. That night, they camped beside Red Willow Creek and were enjoying another trout meal when three of the plaza vendors walked up carrying their wares back to the Pueblo. Their clothing was strange, made from loosely woven coarse fabric. Acting right at home with them, Black offered fish and they stayed to eat. Kiddo was curious but also a bit scared and became uncharacteristically un-chatty.

She heard Black say he was a newlywed, then point at her. The woman in the group dug around in her basket and pulled out a terra-cotta vase with two spouts. She handed it to one of the men who handed it to Black. The man explained that it was a wedding jug, part of their culture's marriage ceremony.

Kiddo's heart jumped. She wanted that jug! Thank goodness,

she wasn't the only one. Trained horse trader Black was already negotiating. Kiddo couldn't tell what he traded besides fish and a beat-up
pan, but he ended up with the precious pottery wedding vase colored
like the land, burnt umber with sienna patterns, the spouts connected
by a rounded braid at the top.

"It is your bond, your joining. Treasure it your whole life," the
man told Black as he handed it over.

Black nodded. "You bet. I will."

The man returned the nod. There was an understanding between them, a shared spirit Kiddo must stand outside of.

Later that night, Black dug clay out of the river bank. Using the
newly acquired pottery as a model, he fashioned a small wedding jug
much like the large one. Kiddo was amazed at what her new husband
could create from nothing. Both jugs would be treasured for years to
come.

Back in Lubbock, Black found what work he could, but nothing
permanent and nothing he liked. Then government jobs cropped up as
the military geared for war. He and Owen heard about white-collar
jobs at Camp Wolters in Mineral Wells over east past Fort Worth.
They drove the Buick.

In December Black wrote:

*No, Darling. I failed. You see, Kiddo, the reason is my age.
For government work of the kind I asked for, men over 21 are eligible.
I was not of that age, consequently that eliminated me. Even though I
was given interviews with heads of companies and foremost of all, the
constructing quartermaster; all was of no avail. Had I been within
six months of the age 21, I could have gone to work last evening at
six. The starting pay for my line of work is $45 week for the first two
weeks and $60 thereafter. Following that time if proper advancement
had been made the next job would have been a supervisor's job paying*

> *$75. Johnson said that a young fellow of my ability and standing could go plenty high with the government.*
>
> *And so, my Dear, with regrets, and at the same time with hopes for the future, I bid you goodbye for this time.*
> *Lovingly yours, Black*

When they returned, Owen told Kiddo that Black had been selected for a job, but when he got to the counter to check in, the man asked for his Social Security Card and he didn't have one. That's when they learned his age. "Go home to your mama, Sonny Boy," the man had said.

Owen said Black became furious and about tore up the place. He badmouthed President Roosevelt and the whole Social Security program, saying he would never sign up and wouldn't accept charity. But Kiddo knew it was the Sonny Boy part that tumped him over. She couldn't imagine what he would be like, that angry, because he was always gentle with her.

Later, on another job hunting trip, he sent a postcard:

> *We have only one more card to play! That is getting the age changed on my classification card. There are three things I would like to do (both Owen and myself)*
> 1. *Go to Arizona to look for the Lost Dutchman gold mine*
> 2. *Go to Arizona or Wyoming to hunt wild horses*
> 3. *Go to Alaska!*
>
> *Ain't that awful?? Love, Black*

Kiddo wanted her mother-in-law to like her, but she never knew what to expect. Loa was sweet at first but could turn on a dime. It didn't help that they shared a kitchen. Kiddo loved to cook, but Loa wanted to fix her son his favorites.

Harder for Kiddo to understand, having come from a family of loving little women, was how hateful Loa could be to her own daughter Joyce. One day some friends stopped by to pick up Joyce for an outing to Buffalo Springs. They had all agreed to wear trousers. Girls were just beginning to wear trousers then, so Kiddo thought it exciting to see her new sister-in-law be so avant-garde. But when she came into the room wearing pants, Loa threw a fit.

"You are not leaving the house like that," she screamed. "People will think you are a queer if you wear men's clothing in public."

Joyce looked stunned. "Mama, they are just pants. All the girls are wearing them now."

"Not my daughter," Loa yelled. "Go back and put on some decent clothes."

"No. I'm grown, Mother. I've graduated college. I can wear what I want."

"Oh, God! Oh, God!" Loa wailed and threw herself into a chair. "What have I done to deserve a daughter like this? You are nothing, nothing! I raised you. I gave you everything and you treat me like this."

Joyce's friends pushed each other and quickly left. Kiddo didn't know what happened after that because she ran for the little house out back and locked the door behind her. She was still sobbing when Black came home a few hours later. She begged him to explain his mother to her.

"I've never seen anyone behave like that, to be mean to someone they loved," she said.

"It's my fault," Black said.

"What? You weren't even there."

"I know, but it's because of me she's like that. I was too big. When I was born, I was too big."

"What?"

"Look, Kiddo, you know how sometimes a cow can have a hard time birthing. Say it's a really big calf. The cow can just go loco from the pain and all. From then on, she gets spooked easy and has a wild look in her eyes and just isn't quite right. You know about that?" he asked.

"Yes, I guess so, but what are you saying?'

"Well, I'm what happened to my mother. She was small and I was a big baby, over ten pounds. She had a terrible time bringing me into this world out there at the ranch house near Des Moines. No doctor. It went on and on. Her insides tore up. After I finally came out, they took her to the hospital in Raton, but the docs couldn't do anything for her. They put her stretcher on the train to the Lubbock hospital. She was there for five months. Several operations. Barely lived."

"Five months?" Kiddo asked. "Were you with her?"

"No. I stayed with Uncle Dee and Aunt Maybel Thornton. Dee is one of Mom's brothers. Aunt Maybel is Choctaw Indian. They had a baby a couple of weeks before I was born, a girl named Hazel. Aunt Maybel had a lot of milk, so she offered to become my wet-nurse, nursed me and Hazel side-by-side. She saved my life. I lived with them for almost a year. Joyce was just two. She stayed with Grandma and Grandpa Thornton. Dad went to Lubbock with Mom." Black had a pained far-away look in his eye. "People said she was never the same after that."

"Black, you can't think that's your fault. It just happened. These things happen sometimes." Kiddo tried to soothe him.

Tears fell down his cheeks. "You should hear how people talk about her, the way she was before, her voice, the music in her soul. All gone. It is my fault. If I hadn't been born . . ."

"You didn't have any say about that. Shh, shh," she kissed his tears.

Black baffled Kiddo. Crying men were new to her. The men in her family weren't criers. Neither were the women. No tears. That was the rule.

"Black, God knows what He is doing." She didn't know what else to say. "He has a plan we don't know about."

"This wasn't His plan," he shot back. "He wouldn't do this to me. Or to her. Not my God." Black started for the door. "I better check on her, make sure she's okay. I'll be back in a bit."

Kiddo sat in the dusk, feeling abandoned and confused.

Not long after that, Black's dad found a used electric cook stove on the cheap. He and Black installed it in the little house out back, and Kiddo could cook meals just for the two of them. Made them seem more married.

Well, that and the little one growing inside.

There was a small hitch when Kiddo was hospitalized during a sick spell with her stomach. The nuns took good care of her, but she and Black were devastated when the doctor told them she had lost the baby. He said her pelvis was tilted and that she was unlikely to become pregnant again. But weeks of despair turned to joy as it became evident that the doctor had been wrong. Their baby was alive and Kiddo's tummy kept growing.

Black hadn't been able to find sustaining work and the future was a big question mark. He hadn't performed at Halsey's or on the radio since he came back from New Mexico.

Kiddo nudged him about his music. She told him some people made a living with their music, playing the guitar and singing. "Maybe you could try that?"

Black grinned. "I'll think about it," he said. He went quiet for a few days, out of the house most of the time, just saying necessary words. Kiddo could tell he was chewing on something and gave him his distance. Eventually, he was ready to talk.

After mincemeat pie one night, he sat Kiddo on the side of the bed. They didn't have a couch and the conversation seemed too important for the kitchen table.

"Kiddo," he began. "I've been trying to come up with a plan, so I can provide for you and the baby. It's hard because there are so many unknowns. Mostly it's this war situation and not knowing if I'm going to be drafted."

"I don't think they will draft you, Black. Not with a wife and a baby to support." She stroked his arm, hoping to soothe his fears.

"If it gets bad enough, who knows who they'll take? They're after Owen hot and heavy and he's your ma's sole support. Besides, maybe it's my duty to go. Protect the country and all. Truva plans to sign up. Douglas says he'll quit Tech and enlist if war is declared. I never thought of myself as a coward. I just don't think I could shoot a human being." He was fidgety for a man who mostly sailed through life showing no worries.

"Oh, Black, you could never be a coward. You're not afraid of anything. You're the bravest, most manly man I know." Kiddo meant every word. He didn't back away from anything.

"I'm afraid of war. I'm afraid of killing somebody. I'm afraid if I was standing there and it was him or me . . . well, I'm afraid of not coming home to you. I'm afraid of not doing right by that baby."

A few tears fell. He pushed them away. "But that's not what I wanted to talk about. I don't have any control over that," he went on. "I want to talk about what you said about making money with my music. There might be a way to do that if I don't get drafted. It could require some sacrifice on your part, and I want you to know what you're getting into."

The setting sun sent long slants of fading light across the bed. Black got up and pulled the cord turning on the light bulb in the center of the room. Kiddo waited, a little breathless.

"I have some connections in the music business. If I call up some people, I might could get hired to be in a band, maybe even a band that plays music for the movies. Have a regular paycheck."

Kiddo's mouth dropped open. "What connections? You've never said anything about this. I didn't think we had any secrets between us."

BRENDA CLEM BLACK

"Not a secret exactly. Just something I didn't tell you. I made a promise to a friend that we would never speak of it. But I'm telling you now," he said.

"Then tell me."

"Well, I have a great uncle out in Hollywood, works for Republic Pictures. And then I know a man out there named Leonard Slye who's in Westerns, a singing cowboy. He's getting pretty well known. Both of them will help me, if I ask."

Black grinned that slow enigmatic grin, the grin that had been holding back a big secret for a long time and must let it out slowly. After suspenseful hesitation he said, "Len's screen name is Roy Rogers."

"Roy Rogers? You know Roy Rogers?" Kiddo asked. They had just seen the picture show *Red River Valley*. The Sons of the Pioneers had been in that movie also. "How can this be, Black? Roy Rogers is famous. You've never been anywhere except Lubbock and New Mexico. I don't think I believe you," she said to the man she knew would never outright lie to her.

Then Black told the story of his big adventure with Truva, swearing her to secrecy. She couldn't even tell her sisters.

"If I go for this," he said, "it will be a big change. It means moving to California. It means I will be gone sometimes, off on some tour to promote our music. You'll be alone, or rather, alone with the baby. I know how you love Texas and how important your family is to you. I don't want to take you away from that."

Kiddo pulled him down beside her. "Black, you are my family. You and the baby. We are our own family now. I will be happy where you are, wherever that is. Besides, Bernice and Everett are still in California and I think Helen and U. L. will be moving back there soon. Good grief, Dot and I keep the postal service humming just between here and Seagraves. We can keep close with letters." She stopped to gather her run-away thoughts. "This is fantastic news. A chance to make something of yourself. Our baby can have a better life. We could maybe get a house of our own someday. My parents never owned a home of their own, you know? Oh, Black!" She jumped up and danced around. "I can't believe this. This is swell news. How soon can we go? Wait, we don't even have a car. How will we get there?"

"Kiddo, Kiddo, calm down." He grabbed her hands and pulled her back down. "There's a lot to think about, to plan. First of all, we have to stay here until the baby comes. Your mother would kill me if I took you off somewhere before it's born. She'll want to help you and you will need her. I know you don't want my mother here all the time."

"Oh no, please, no. No, I wouldn't."

"Here's the plan." Black laid it out. "I went to the dairy at Tech today and talked Professor Stangel into giving me a job. Remember, I won all those ribbons in Dairy Judging? Well, he set up those contests. He remembered me and said he could use me. I figure we can stay here in our little house until the first of the year, no rent to pay, and save up all we can. The baby comes in October, so your ma will have a couple of months to spoil the two of you. Meanwhile, I'll write some letters or phone California and see what I might can work out. Then we take the train out there in January. How's that sound, Kiddo?"

Black wasn't just grinning this time, it was a full-blown, all-out smile. He picked up Kiddo and swung her around, heavy and lop-sided with child as she was.

BLESSED ASSURANCE

 Hymn. Lyrics written by blind hymn-writer Francis J. Crosby. Music by her friend, Phoebe P. Knapp, 1873.

Perfect submission, all is at rest
I in my Savior am happy and blest,
Watching and waiting, looking above,
Filled with His goodness, lost in His love.

This is my Story. This is my Song.

Black and Kiddo fell asleep cuddled like spoons. Finally, they had a plan, a grandiose plan that seemed more like a dream and, like most dreams, ephemeral, hard to get hold of.

In October when Kiddo's labor pains came close together, Black, Corwin, and Loa took her to St. Mary of the Plains Hospital. She struggled through the day and night, through forty hours of hard labor and no baby. Black wasn't allowed to be with her. No men in Labor or Delivery. Kiddo was alone with her pain and her fear.

The waiting room filled with family: his parents and sister Joyce, Joyce's fiancé Bert Milam, Kiddo's mother Ida, her brother Owen, her brother Cecil and wife Marguerite, her sister Helen and U. L., her sister Dot and Sonny, her sister Jean and Howard, her cousins Truva and Douglas and Verlene. Everyone laughed and patted Black on the back calling him Papa and Daddy, telling him his life would change now. Lots of smiles.

Time passed.

The crowd grew with various aunts, uncles, cousins, friends, and church members. Nuns in their wide sailing hats wandered through with reports and coffee.

Time passed.

The doctor came and pulled Black aside, along with his parents and her mother. Problems, he said. The infant had started delivering, but the head was unusually large. Complications. The wife was being kept as free from pain as could be managed. He hoped to have better news soon.

Time passed.

People smiled and told Black not to worry. The doctors know what they are doing. Sometimes it just takes a while longer. You won't even think about this when it's all over and the baby is in your arms. Why, once I had a cousin. . . Things people say when they don't know what to say. Smiles accompanied by crinkled foreheads and sad eyes. They began to hold each other's hands and give gentle hugs. Some nestled together and fell asleep scrunched in uncomfortable chairs.

Time passed.

The doctor returned, pulled Black aside and told him the baby was finally delivered, but there were additional problems. A blue baby. Not enough oxygen. They were doing everything they could. Also, there was difficulty in getting the wife's bleeding stopped. Prepare yourself. The doctor stepped away, then turned back and placed a firm hand on Black's shoulder.

"It's a boy," he said softly.

Silence filled the room as family members read the seriousness of the situation from Black's face. No smiles, no congratulations, just muffled weeping and clinging to each other.

Sister Maureen had been standing beside the doctor in her black habit, white starched pinafore, and hat. She took the young man's arm and stared directly into grief-stricken eyes. "Mr. Black, what can I do for you?" As he stood frozen and didn't answer, she asked, "Would you like to pray with me in the chapel?"

"Yes, I want to pray," he said with a small bit of relief. Yes, that was the thing to do. That was it. "But not with you, Sister. I need to get outside where God is. We got some talking to do. Just me and Him."

Sister Maureen led him outside to a small garden, then left him alone. A few marigolds were still hanging on, clustered at the base of a concrete birdbath. A small statue of Mary and baby Jesus stood inside a wooden alcove. Seeing it pulled tears from his eyes. He sat on the heavy iron bench and took a cigar from those he had earlier crammed in his shirt pockets. Feeling its realness in his mouth was enough, he didn't need to light it.

Wrangling with himself until he got a hold, he stood and walked. He talked, not where anyone could hear, but having a conversation nonetheless. He acknowledged the cottonwood trees and the pale grass, then stepped out from under the tree canopy where he could see the sky. Evening clouds lay in milky gray layers, like a vast turbulent sea above the flatland. He imagined himself on a ship, sailing with white starched sails on that sea.

"You can't do this." He looked at the far horizon, captaining his ship. "You're not that kind of God. I'm a good man. You took my mother from me, but you can't have my wife. Nor my son. It's not fair." Anger came first, then pleading. "Please, please, let them live. Take me instead. My life for theirs.

"We don't talk like we used to, out there on the plains when I was a boy, just you and me, when I was learning all those hymns. I know you remember me and I haven't forgotten you. I'm still singing hymns. I go to church most Sundays." Black dropped to his knees. "Why? Why? What do you want? I have nothing to offer except myself. Take me instead, please, take me."

Clunk! The heavy door pushed open. Owen stepped out. "You okay, Black?"

Black waved him back inside.

Knowing it was unlikely that God would strike him dead on the spot in trade for his family's life, Black's mind struggled for an acceptable offering, a solution, some sort of control. He scrambled to his feet and addressed the gray sea sky.

"I want to make a deal," he said, still sailing along. "I'm not asking for myself, but for the sweetest person I've ever known.

"Let her live. My baby, my son. Let him live. Take my voice instead. My singing. It's all I have. I'll give up this show-business stuff. I'll sing only in church. Maybe I forgot my voice was a gift from you and I've been too puffed up about it. Seems music wasn't your plan for me anyway. You've been telling me that. I'm listening. I'll never speak of show business again. I pledge to you. Never speak of it again. Please. Let them live."

Kiddo lived. As did Richard Corwin Black, their son. After six weeks of loving care from the nuns at St. Mary's, they came home to Black and the little house out back to experience all the joys and woes of new parenthood. The doctor warned the new parents that they should never have another child. Two miracles were more than anyone could expect.

A few days after they came home, on Kiddo's 24th birthday, December 7, 1941, "a date which will live in infamy," Japan attacked the United States, bombing Pearl Harbor in the Hawaiian Islands. The nation was stunned. War was officially declared, the draft amended to include all men ages 18–64 to serve for the duration of the war plus six months. Young people's dreams were abandoned as the United States geared up for an uncertain wartime economy.

The government began construction of a military base near Austin, Texas, named Camp Swift. It provided jobs for many men, old and young alike, waiting to hear from the draft board. After more than a decade of dearth and depression, steady jobs. The McSpadden clan traveled across the state to Austin and landed paying jobs: Uncle Coleman and his son Truva, Uncle Jesse and his son Douglas, Kiddo's brother Owen and his big farm truck.

Owen wrote home:

My job is hauling supplies to the ditching machines on the water and sewer lines. Have nine machines running now, scattered all over. Sure is a jungle out there. No roads much yet and the trails we use are blocked every day with new buildings starting. Ninety miles of pipe lines plus the disposal plant. Am working 10 hours a day. I got in a full week this time, made $115.50 for the 7 days, got 30 hours overtime. I get .70 cents an hour. The truck gets $80 a month, gas and oil furnished.

Money order: take $40 to the bank for the truck payment and the rest is for you, Ma.

They are building a magnesium plant here and are going to build a bombing plant seven miles out of Austin starting sometime soon, so there will be a lot of work here for some time. There is about 9,000 men working there now and will be a lot more soon if they can get them.

Black and Dorris came for visit. Dorris is feeling fine, walked a little yesterday, hasn't been fainty anymore.

Don't worry about me being drafted. It won't be so bad.

Love to all of you, Owen

Owen McSpadden was drafted into the U. S. Army in 1942. He was 33 years old. Trained as an Army Medic at Ft. Knox, Kentucky, he served on the battlefields of France and Germany, attached to an ambulance just behind the line of fire. He gathered dead, dying, and wounded men like kindling. During the bloody Battle of the Bulge, he tended soldiers for three days straight with no sleep. Owen wrote over 300 letters to his mother and six siblings and sent almost all his pay to his family. During training at Ft. Knox, he had fallen in love with a woman he met at a USO dance. She waited for him. But the war changed Owen. When it was over, he came back to Texas and wrote the woman that he had seen too much and had nothing to offer her.

He leased land and farmed all over West Texas, as his father had done, often with his brother Cecil. He shared his home with his mother, his dear motherless mother, and took care of her until her death. He never married but was always included in the family plans of his sisters and brother, an old bachelor eternally revered for his sacrifice for his family and his country.

Truva McSpadden served with the First Marines at Guadalcanal. Kiddo's cousin, Douglas McSpadden enlisted in the Army Air Corps and served in the Pacific. Lynn "Red" Black joined the Navy and spent most of his service with the Seabees in the Philippines. Red missed the official military photographer when he was allowed leave to return to New Mexico for his mother's funeral.

Owen McSpadden, U.S. Army.   Truva McSpadden, U.S. Marine Corps.

Black registered for the draft but puzzled over what to do when the official notification came to report to duty. Kiddo and the baby needed him. Professor Stangel, his boss at the Tech Dairy, offered an alternative. As it turned out, all those newly drafted military men must have milk, cream, and butter. Stangel had been asked to recommend a manager for a dairy at Chickasha, Oklahoma which supplied milk for Fort Sill. The manager would not be a military employee but the job, considered a soldier-support function, would defer military service.

Black and Kiddo left the little house out back. They got a ride to their new home in the cattle truck hauling milk cows to the dairy. Black loaded their few belongings, mostly clothes and baby paraphernalia. Kiddo placed the orange crate they used for the baby's bed on the bench seat between them. Sight unseen, Black, Kiddo, and baby Richard moved to two rooms in one end of the low block building used as a dairy barn on a farm near Chickasha. The use of an old pickup truck, or 'kick-pup' as Kiddo called it, was included in the deal. Kiddo registered for their first War Ration Book at Ninnekah. It listed her as 5'2" tall, 112 lbs., blue eyes, brown hair, 24 years old. She was glad to get the rations. Black's pies needed more sugar.

Kiddo didn't ask what happened to the other plan, the music plan. She knew the Earth had turned over. That Black had gone through some passage. That he had offered his life for hers. That he had given up his music. That was enough. Let the plan unfold by itself. For now, she was thankful her husband didn't have to go to war, thankful to have a growing baby to love, a house without in-laws outside the door, honest work for her man, and solid ground under her feet. And this man, this man she would stand beside for her whole life.

A week or so after arriving in Chickasha, Kiddo received a letter from her friend Edith who described the scene at the Black house when they had left Lubbock. She said Black's mother Loa, who the moment before had been loving and gooey and bidding everyone good luck, fell into a fit on the floor as they drove away. Apparently Loa had screamed, "They're going to kill that baby! I'll never see it again. Neither one of them has the sense God gave a goose. They can't raise a baby!"

Richard thrived. Kiddo had his picture taken when he was six months old by a professional photographer. He lay naked on a pink blanket that his great-grandmother Thornton had knitted. Black sent one of the pictures to Kiddo's mother with this note:

From your grandson Richard

Granna, I hope you like me like this 'cause my Mother, Daddy and all of our friends here think it is just like me. My hair is dark brown, my eyes are dark blue, my eyelashes and brows are Black. I'm kinda fat and have a big chest (which my Pop is very proud of).

I love you. R.C.B.

Black didn't mind the hard work of the dairy. Twice-a-day milking and dairy herd management kept him busy and provided a steady income. He beamed with pride the day he loaded Kiddo and baby Richard into the 'kick-pup' and drove to a store in Chickasha where they bought their first real furniture: a rectangular dining table with six chairs and a matching china hutch. Golden Oak. Heavy. Solid. Proof that he was providing.

A year later, they moved to Hobart, Oklahoma, where Black was transferred to manage a larger dairy, still providing milk for the Fort Sill soldiers and the 700 Japanese-Americans interned there. For entertainment, they watched Grasshoppers and Bird Dogs take off and land at the air field.

Black and baby Richard with milk cows. Dairy, Chickasha, Oklahoma, 1942.

I'M AN OLD COWHAND
(FROM THE RIO GRANDE)

 Written by Johnny Mercer for the film *Rhythm on the Range*. Recorded by Bing Crosby with Jimmy Dorsey and his orchestra, 1936.

In August of 1943, Russell (Razz) called from New Mexico. He had roped some military contracts to grow beef for the soldiers and needed Black's cowboy help to help him fulfill the contracts. Red was fighting in the Philippines and their mother, whom everyone called Aunt Jo, had died earlier that year. There were more acres and cows to tend than Razz and his sister Hermona could wrangle.

Dairy herd or beef cattle, same difference. Black could still serve his country by providing food for its army. A chance to be on the home place, the Black Family Ranch his grandfather pioneered, to be part of the legacy his father had turned his back on when they left for Lubbock. Maybe dreams come true after all.

Seven years. Seven years since he rode Ginger to Emery Peak and said goodbye to the land that lived in his soul. He hadn't expected it would take so long to get back.

Black hired a truck to move their oak table and chairs and other belongings from Hobart, Oklahoma to Des Moines, New Mexico, about 350 miles. Leaving the dairy's kick-pup behind, they rode in the cab alongside the driver. After the move, Kiddo wrote her folks round-robin letters which they could send on to other family members, so that she wouldn't have to write everything seven times.

Dear Mother and Kids,

    I would have written sooner, but <u>I have been sick</u>. One of my urpy spells and a pretty bad one. We sure were worried but I believe I'm gonna be alright now. That was a pretty hard trip up here. We rode all night and had to hold Richard and too we couldn't find anything decent to eat, just plain ole slop.

    I was at my row's end and urped for two days. I took a big dose of Milk of Magnesia so maybe I'll be o.k. now. Goodness, I just gotta. We have been over here all this time and me practically a stranger and have to be waited on. I'm so mad at myself. Russell (Razz) bought all kinds of juices trying to find something I could eat.

    Say, it has just started raining and we are having a regular cloud burst. Black and Russell went over in the canyon after wood. Oh me I'll bet they nearly get drowned. Black and Russell finished sowing the fall wheat yesterday. They will be tickled pink over this rain.

    I really believe I will like it up here. It is cold! We have been sleeping under a big heavy comfort. Our house is o.k. not too pretty but it has nice sized rooms, a small built in cabinet, sink and the water piped in. I'm sure glad of that.

    Mother, did I tell you we sold our fryers? We got .35 cents each for them. That was good, wasn't it?

Razz leased a small house for them on the west side of Dunchee Hill, a few miles from the ranch house on the road to the Purvines Ranch. In Raton, the Colfax County seat, almost an hour away, he bought them a wood cook stove, a blue linoleum rug, and blue paint for the floor around the edges of the rug. Kiddo busied herself with fixing up the house and chasing Richard.

Years later, for a church bulletin, she reflected on that time:

So, there we were. Everything, and I mean everything was strange and foreign to me. I felt as if I had landed in an alien and unknown world.

Black, well, Black was ecstatic with happiness. At last he was finally back in his beloved New Mexico where his heart had never left. I tried but could not enter into his enthusiasm.

I knew no one. We had no car, telephone, radio. Our nearest neighbor was Milo and Flossie Seaton that lived two and a half miles away. Black left early each morning riding his saddle horse over to the Black Family Ranch headquarters and there I was with baby Richard all the long, long day. It was the very first time I had known true, deep, empty loneliness. Having come from a large, loving, close-knit family, there had always been someone with me and there for me.

Then came the evenings. The coyotes would start their usual evening serenade. Oh, mercy me, the chills would run all over me. It was frightening! I would get Richard ready for bed with his Bearie and Banket, then hold him close, rocking and singing as loud as I could. He would grow weary of my screeching for soon he would say, "Maw, I want to go to feep." I would put him to bed and wait for Black, listening every minute for the sound of his horse's hoof-beats.

When he finally got home we would have a wonderful, happy reunion, kinda like he had been gone a week. He was always ravishingly hungry and bone-weary from the ride and the many hours of hard demanding work. But let me add, he loved every minute of each day! We exchanged happenings of our day as he ate then soon jumped in bed.

It didn't take long for Kiddo to realize that her urpy spells might be something more than bad food or a nervous stomach. She was in a family way again.

Panic filled Black's heart. She was his life. He couldn't lose her. They made an appointment with Dr. Elliott in Raton. Trained in obstetrics, he assured them that advancements had been made. That he could perform an operation, a Cesarean, if necessary. That he would monitor Kiddo carefully throughout gestation. Those assurances plus a few talks with the Man Upstairs calmed them. Another child to include in their lives, what a gift!

Des Moines, New Mexico, to Lubbock, Texas:
Dearest Mother and Kids,

Have I written you guys about my hens? We bought 24 Austro-Whites from a lady. White with black specks and splashes around on them. About half of them are molting and yet I get 11 or 12 eggs a day. Sunday when we went into church I took 4 dozen and sold them. They brought .55 cents per doz. I was so tickled.

Say Mother, if you have time I wish you would sit down and write me just exactly like you use to make light bread! The bread we get here is awful it molds so badly.

Richard keeps me in a constant trot. He just takes off across the pastures or out to the barn. He brings in the eggs, one in each hand, yelling thank you to the hens. We found a dandy little wagon here all smashed up and Black fixed it for him.

Black and Raz went to the timber and killed a deer. Boy it sure is good eating. We put it out and let it freeze three nights straight before we started eating on it. It is so tender.

Black has gone into the tanning business. Deer season is just over here. He is going to tan two for one man and get $3.00 each. He has ten in all to fix. Black is going to make Doogan (his nickname for Richard) a pair of buckskin chaps for Christmas to go with his rocky horse that we plan to get him for his Santa Clause. We are going to fix him a whole cowboy outfit.

I wish you all could come for Christmas. We will have fresh beef then and get another deer or wild turkey and it would do me so much good to see Cecil fill up on all the meat he wants.

I'm beginning to show quiet a bit now and am going to have to get some dresses made. I've made one dress and a slip on the "Mamma style."

Dr. Elliott told me to get a maternity girdle now. Sure hope I can find a good one.

You know I may be wrong, but I believe that it's going to be another boy. It's high up and in the same place as Richard was and oh boy is it active already. If it's a boy part of its name is going to be Owen.

Wish you all could see how much this change of work and climate has helped ole Black. He is already gaining weight and Mother what do you know he just gets up every morning when I do without having to be called. He goes out and chops up a lot of wood before breakfast. Do you need a wet rag on your forehead after reading that? Ha-ha!

Well, we just got back from a flying trip to Raton in a big snow storm.. The dentist all but killed me this time. I nearly fainted once. Sure hard to take such treatment but if you gotta, you gotta. I'm sure nervous now. After all he did to me we had to drive home in a blowing snow. Lots of love to all of you, Black Kids

One day that winter, Black was herding cattle alone near Carr Mountain. Razz had ridden the train to the stockyards in Kansas City, taking the latest carloads of cows to market. A fast-moving blizzard swooped down from Colorado. Black spurred his horse and headed for home, but within minutes became enveloped in such dense snow that he couldn't see landmarks, a complete white-out. He searched blindly for a fence line to follow or a windmill to read direction, but he could see absolutely nothing, barely the horse on which he sat. A pure white world. In sub-zero weather he wandered, trying to find his way. Out of options, with icy snow sticking to his face, he dropped the reins and buried his head in his horse's mane to conserve body heat.

"Take us home, Bay," he said to the horse. "I can't find the way."

Black and Bay arrived home just before nightfall when Bay bumped into the closed barn door, waking his rider. Black forced his stiff, almost-frozen hands to unsaddle, feed, and bed her down before stumbling through the drifts into his own warm house where anxious Kiddo waited with dry clothes, a blazing piñon fire, and loving arms.

Another vicious blizzard hit in late March of 1944 and lasted for days. Head-high drifts made it difficult to clear a path to the barn to feed the animals. Everyone hunkered down inside by a cozy fire.

Then Kiddo's water broke two weeks early. Roads were covered in snow and ice. Even if Razz's pickup would start, it couldn't track over the drifts.

"Black, I'm scared." Kiddo's blue eyes puddled with tears. She stood in the doorway of the kitchen with her legs apart, staring at the water on the floor.

Black rushed to her. "Don't be scared, Kiddo. I've got you. We're gonna figure this out." Wild what-ifs raced through his mind as they stood embracing each other.

He pulled away. "We're going to need a lot of quilts. Do you feel good enough to gather up every quilt we own?"

"Black, I can't have this baby here. We'll both die. I need Dr. Elliott."

"I know, Honey Bee. I'm gonna get you to the hospital, one way or another. Right now, I'm going to the home place and get the tractor and Razz. We need him to stay with Richard and he can help me hook up the hay barge. We'll lay you in the hay and cover you up real good. I'll pull you into Des Moines and we'll see what the roads are like there, find somebody to drive us on to Raton."

"But that will take a long time, Black. You'll freeze out there. Don't leave me alone. What if . . .?"

"No!" He pressed his finger to her lips. "No more what-ifs. Like your mama always says, we're just gonna take things as they come." He rubbed her huge tummy and leaned down to kiss it. "Russell Owen, you calm down. We need you to stay put as long as you possibly can."

He put his arm around her shoulder and led her to the bedroom. "Just lay on the bed till I get back. If you feel like it, between pains, get yourself dressed in the warmest clothes you have. And gather up all the quilts and blankets." Quickly, he pulled on three pairs of socks, several shirts, then two pairs of jeans and tied his leather chaps over them. He grabbed his heavy buckskin jacket, gloves, and his fur cap with earflaps. No weather for a cowboy hat.

Kiddo sat on the side of the bed and watched him dress. As he started for the door, she bleated, "Blaaack . . ."

He quickly pulled her up to him, embracing in a tight hug. He gave her an intense kiss. "I'll be as fast as I can." Then, reading the fear in her eyes, he added, "I will come back, Dorris with two Rs. I will come back."

He opened the front door and kicked away the accumulated snow, then disappeared into the blowing blizzard. Following the rope line to the barn and after that, the fence line, Black made his way to the home place in leaping heaves through the drifts.

After rousing Razz, he fired up the sturdy F20 Farmall and they started down three miles of snowy, frozen dirt roads. Arriving home, they located the hay barge in the frigid barnyard, cleared the hitch and secured the tongue to the drawbar of the tractor. Then they shoveled snow from the bed of the barge and stacked bales of hay from the barn onto it, forming a small nest lined with saddle blankets and gunny sacks.

Black hurried back inside to Kiddo. He hoped the tractor noise had given her comfort.

"I'm okay!" Kiddo yelled as soon as the door opened. Wearing ten layers of clothing she stood, a very fat statue in the middle of the room with quilts piled beside her.

"I knew you would be, Tuffy." A momentary grin glued them together.

Razz took the mattress from the bed and laid it in the hay. Black carried round, wrapped Kiddo through the snow to the nest and laid her gently inside, then covered her with quilts and threw a tarp on top. After a few last-minute instructions to Razz concerning two-year-old Richard, Black climbed on the F20 and pulled Kiddo's hay barge four miles through blinding snow into town. Des Moines was buttoned down for the blizzard. There was no traffic on the snow-covered main highway. Black stopped at the first house near the railroad tracks and used their phone to call Dr. Elliott in Raton.

A second call to the Union County Road Department informed him that the county snowplow was working near the small blip town of Capulin. Black pulled his praying wife another five miles through the blinding snowstorm, his navigation guided by feel and his connection to the land. He located the snowplow. After he explained the situation to the driver, they transferred a fearful but toasty mother-in-labor and a fearless, half-frozen expectant father to the big truck pushing the plow. Then another thirty miles of icy highway.

By the time Kiddo reached Dr. Elliott at The Miners' Hospital in Raton, her labor was too far along for a Cesarean. Again, she struggled for many hours.

Alone in the stark waiting room, Black ignored the stiff wooden chairs. He stuck a half-smoked stogie in his mouth, then walked across the oak floor, leaned against the windowsill, and stared into the blizzard still raging outside. His expressionless face belied the fear simmering in his soul. No tears, no pleading, no negotiations this time. Not even a prayer. Just a conversation, a friendly reminder that he whispered to the white nothingness on the other side of the glass, "Here we are again. I've kept up my end. I'm trusting you to keep up yours."

For two-and-a-half years, Black had refused all requests for his music except to lead the a capella singing at the Church of Christ. Countless friends, including Carlos Cornay and Filthy McNasty, had asked him to entertain at other gatherings, but he held steadfastly to his promise. His tenuous phone connection with Len Slye had been lost when they moved from Lubbock, though he figured he could always find Roy Rogers if he really needed him.

But he never would.

He had closed that door. Part of the bargain. It was worth it. Now the Big Fella had to keep up his end again.

Looking exhausted, Dr. Elliott finally appeared. "Congratulations," he said, shaking Black's hand. "It's a boy!"

"I know." Black grinned. "That's Russell Owen Black, named after his uncles, two of the best men in the country."

The doctor said the baby was healthy, with a little round head and all his fingers and toes. Six pounds, six ounces. As for his wife, she was torn up inside and would need to stay in the hospital for several weeks but would slowly recover. Then Dr. Elliott used his fatherly voice to explain that she would not come through this again and could not, ever, become with child again. An operation would be performed after she had some time to heal, just to be sure. Not asking for permission, stating a fact.

"Your family is complete," he said.

Complete. Complete. Black remembered telling Kiddo that he wanted a whole football team first, then they could start on the girls.

But right now, in this moment, two healthy boys sounded perfect.

Black realized that he was now responsible for four people. The money Razz could pay him would not be enough for his family to have the things they needed. Time to figure out something else, some way to make extra money. He decided to start building his own dairy herd and set about collecting cows. Kiddo's mother came to help with the baby and Richard stayed with his Black grandparents, Corwin and Loa, while Kiddo remained in Miners' Hospital at Raton, forty miles away.

In May of 1944, Black wrote to her:

Dear Mother,

How are you feeling? Maybel said that they told her that you were doing OK. Sure hope you are. Do they let you eat anything yet? We had an "up-siderds" pineapple cake for supper tonight and I liked to have made myself sick on it.

We brought the cows home today. All three of them, so now we have four cows. Now you will have to learn to milk!!! Raz said that if we wanted the other cow that he would pay us another month's wages, so we could get a separator, some cans etc. Bought $10 worth of feed in town today.

Oh yes!! Our barley is coming up!! We came by today when we were bringing the cows home and started to walk out into the field to see how wet it was and sure enough! It was coming up. We have about 22 acres of barley and 17.5 acres of wheat in. Have to get some more wheat seed.

Doogan is having the time of his life ordering grandpop and granpom around. They feed him candy and stuff all the time. The folks really get tickled at him the way he acts and talks. He still calls himself "Mr. Black."

Little feller sure is growing. Your ma is rasseling with him now trying to wake him up to finish his bottle. Guess I better quit and get some shut eye.

Much love,
Black, Doogan, & Bubba

Russell Owen Black, dubbed Bubba, landed softly in this young family full of love, a joyous baby grinning even in his sleep. Richard took serious responsibility for his brother, once reporting to Ma that the goat had jumped in Razz's old wicker carriage where baby Bubba lay sunning. Horrified, Kiddo came running but found Bubba enjoying this new experience, laughing and flailing his tiny hands. Sam, the hairy white goat, had treaded carefully around the baby, then lay down beside him in the narrow carriage. Thus began Bubba's lifelong kinship with animals wild and tame.

Black holding baby Russell on Horned Hereford bull.
C Lazy K, Black Family Ranch, Des Moines, New Mexico, 1944.

The boys grew up calling their father Black as often as Pop. Besides Ma and Mom, they also called their mother Kiddo or Greasy (for her cooking skills) or whatever endearment suited her in the moment.

Cowgirl Kiddo holding baby "R." Family fisticuffs over which "R."

HOME ON THE RANGE

 Anthem of the American West. Lyrics from a poem titled "My Western Home" by Brewster M. Higley, first published in 1873. Music written by his friend, Daniel E. Kelley. Adopted as the official song of the State of Kansas in 1947.

In New Mexico, rumors were rampant about what the military was up to in the state. Huge unnatural clouds and eerie colors filled the southwestern skies now and then. Phone lines buzzed. Neighbors speculated that the government had decided the few people in the sparsely populated state were expendable. Atom bombs being tested by scientists in Los Alamos, New Mexico, were eventually dropped on cities in Japan, ending World War II. Peace was declared late in 1945. The soldiers were coming home.

Truva came to visit as soon as he got back, surprised to find that Black and Kiddo had two children and a life mapped out. His dreams had been on hold while he fought for the right to have dreams.

Red Black returned to New Mexico and the Black Family Ranch, the home place that his brother Razz (five years younger) and his nephew Black (ten years younger) had held together while he was away. Red had seen the world and was ready to run it. He and Razz immediately locked horns about how to manage the ranch. Red declared himself in charge, entitled by being the eldest, and bullied taciturn Razz with his much larger physique and world-wise language. With America's army standing down, the military contracts for beef were phased out, ending the reliable stream of cattle profits. These harbingers drove Razz from the ranch and into the arms of the first of three wives.

When Razz walked out the door, any agreements about Black's participation in the ranching enterprise or inheritance of the land went with him. Red would honor no promises, though he loved his nephew and really loved Kiddo's cooking. Everyone remained cordial. Black still helped Red with the ranching, as did Razz when hands were needed. No pay was expected, just family helping family. Black hoped that things might change over time, when he had paid his dues and proved himself to Red as he had to Razz.

Sharpshooters, the three hunted together and shared the spoils, keeping them in plenty of venison. The hunt often included Corwin, Black's dad. He and Loa had moved from Lubbock to nearby Raton, where Corwin took a job with an appliance company. Black understood that his father was getting older, but the injustice of the best horseman in the country becoming a Maytag repairman was unsettling.

The huntsmen: (L to R) Red, Russell, Corwin, Black, Richard.
The trophy: Tickie Boy.
The gun: Winchester .30-30.

Always striving for a better life, Black looked for land to start his own cattle operation. Good land, like the home place, had been grabbed up long ago by large ranchers and tied up in huge parcels. No way could he afford that kind of land. He would have to start small. Eventually he found a half section north of Folsom near Tollgate Canyon. The land went up the backside of Emery Peak almost to the top with three benches partially cleared where cattle could graze. Piñon trees and white cedar covered most of the mountain, a big plus. As Black cut trees to clear patches for cattle grazing, he could sell the wood as fence posts, poles, or firewood. The parcel didn't include river land. In fact, he had to ford the Dry Cimarron to reach it. There was no bridge. Heck, there was no road.

That didn't stop Black's dream. He envisioned their home nestled in a small canyon where, in wet weather, a small stream tumbled. Never mind that it was rarely wet weather in New Mexico.

Using his last earnings from the government beef contracts, Black made a down payment on the bare land, financing the rest with Federal Land Bank. An easement allowed him to build a road and low water bridge across the Cimarron near the old ghost town of Madison, now just the foundations of a grist mill, wagon wheels, and a few old windowpanes. He cut cedar posts with the only tool he had for the job, a hand axe. Working tirelessly, he sold enough posts to buy them an old pickup, the first vehicle they owned. Then he taught Kiddo to drive.

His friend Carlos Cornay spied the young family at Fred Honey's gas station in Folsom one day. They had stopped for Grapettes.

"Hey, Black," he shouted as he crossed the empty street. "You make your wife chauffer you around? You're getting lazy, my friend. Where's your horse?"

"Where's yours?" Black sparred.

"Getting lazy like you, grazing in the pasture." Carlos stepped back. "I see you bought a truck."

"Yep. I've been cutting fence posts with an axe. Sold enough to buy us this pickup. Next I'm gonna get us a house."

"That's a lot of fence posts, friend, especially by hand."

"Sure is. But the work ain't hard, the boss ain't mean, just ain't no place for a jelly bean."

Carlos laughed. "You're feeling no pain today. Hey, I got a buzz saw with an engine I can loan you. Makes the work go faster on that cedar."

"Yeah, but the buzz saw runs better with two" Black said.

"Well, the hombre that owns the saw might help with that. He might could use a truck himself. When do we start?"

In time, working with Carlos, Black earned enough to arrange for an old house to be moved from Des Moines to a small bench on the side of the draw. He hauled red rocks from the booster station on the Cimarron to make a foundation, then patched up where he could. A rectangle with two large rooms, it wasn't a fine house, but solid and theirs. Black hired a well drilled, then cut poles and built a tower over the well to support the Aermotor windmill and its gears which drove the sucker rod that pulled the water from the depths. He built an out-house. In the kitchen he installed a Warm Morning wood stove for Kiddo's cooking. In the other room where this little family of four would sleep, a pot-bellied stove would keep them warm.

Moving day in 1946 was thrilling, even if the house was not. Black and Kiddo, Richard and Russell moved to a spot of their own in the majestic New Mexico landscape. It had been ten years since his forced removal to Lubbock. Black had made his dream come true, though it was a slightly different version and a bit ragged around the edges.

Over the next few years, he continued to better their place. He added a kitchen and a bedroom and built a wind charger that produced electricity to burn the light bulbs hanging from wires he strung in the center of each room. He built a house for Kiddo's chickens, then a small barn for the cows, and after that a larger barn. Three years later he designed and built a gravity-flow water system, bringing water into the house and finally an indoor bathroom, but no electricity until 1952.

When Kiddo found a picture in *Good Housekeeping* magazine featuring a turning Lazy-Susan for the kitchen corner, he incorporated the design into the cabinets he was building. Then he built a larger one in the corner of the boys' room to use as a closet, near the bunk beds he made of cedar.

He dug a cellar for food storage into the hillside. In the kitchen, to make firewood handy for Kiddo, he fashioned a wood chute with the door about two feet off the floor. But there was a major problem with the wood chute. A "Germit" took up residence there. Russell Owen would pull the firewood out, climb inside, close the door and yell for his mother to find him. When she would fling open the door and say, "I found you, Bubba," he would answer, "No, you didn't. I not Bubba. I a Germit."

Black didn't build all of this alone. Kiddo was by his side, doing what she had strength to do, which was considerable. They trusted and believed in each other, that each would do what needed to be done. Red and Razz and Corwin helped when they were available. Carlos assisted, as did others among their new Folsom friends and neighbors. Supplies, tools, labor, and expertise were bartered. Black was an excellent scavenger. He often stopped his own projects to help others. For several days, he helped fight a prairie fire near Des Moines that burned over 30,000 acres.

When the red brick, two-story Folsom school burned, Black and his fellow school board member, Frank McNaghten, arranged for classes to meet in the old boarded-up saloon, then set to work building a new school. Kiddo and Frank's wife, Alma, orchestrated pie suppers and other fundraisers.

Black's work ethic and skills became known. He began to get job offers from the community building a fence or a barn, adding on a room, building cabinets, cutting timber. There seemed to be nothing he couldn't or wouldn't do.

For a few years, they had enough. Sporadic cream checks from their fledgling dairy (hand-milking twice a day, separating the cream and scrubbing the DeLaval separator, hauling cream cans to the rail depot at Folsom to ship to the creamery in Trinidad, Colorado). Cash from odd jobs. Barter. Chicken, eggs, and egg money from Kiddo's chickens. Beef, their share from Red, at slaughter-time. Plenty of venison and turkey from Black's hunts. Ham and bacon from Oinkie and Poinkie and their offspring. Rabbit from Mumpsy's litters in the boys' rabbit hutches. Fresh and canned vegetables and fruits from Kiddo's large garden, produced and preserved through her own unending work ethic. Furniture, clothing, and toys made by loving parents.

One Christmas, Black cut cedar, stripped the poles, and made the boys a table and two chairs, just their size. A string of small wagons and wheelbarrows followed, getting larger each year, for the kids to haul their plunder. Another Christmas, Black and his friend Frank McNaghten built a small tractor for the boys. They painted it red with official Farmall paint and adorned it with Farmall decals that the dealer in Clayton special ordered from International Harvester, then welded a hitch on the back to pull the boys' wagons. Black skinned and tanned the hides of calves that died, which Kiddo made into vests and chaps and rugs for their play. She sewed their pajamas, their shirts, their wagon blankets, and clothes for their never-ending parade of animals, live and stuffed.

Kiddo made that Warm Morning hum and quickly earned her reputation as best cook in the county. Her high-pitched, giggly tee-hee-hees made their home friendly and welcoming, perhaps too much so. People dropped in unannounced for a visit and a meal. With no phone, there was no method for advance notice. Relatives showed up from Texas or California or Colorado to stay a few days, friends and neighbors happened by, church friends came visiting. Plus, Corwin, Loa, Red, and sometimes Razz and current wife, followed them home from church every Sunday, ate a big meal and stayed the day.

GHOST RIDERS IN THE SKY

♪ Written and recorded by Stan Jones, a forest ranger, 1948. Published by Edwin H. Morris & Co., Inc., 1948. Recorded in 1949 by Burl Ives for Columbia Records, Vaughn Monroe for RCA Victor Records, Bing Crosby for Decca Records, Peggy Lee for Capitol Records and Spike Jones (altered lyrics) for RCA Victor Records.

Those were halcyon days in the wilderness. Black and Kiddo were building their own world with their own hands. Raising joyous little boys. It was a lot of hard work, getting up at four to milk before the rest of the day started and milking again at night, often after dark. But, gee whiz, they were young and strong, full of themselves. They had a basketful of friends and neighbors to count on. Everyone helped each other, striving to make life better for all.

Kiddo never felt alone at Folsom, not even when the boys got old enough to ride away on the school bus each day. There was so much to do, plus people dropping in all the time, and reasons to drive to Folsom or Des Moines or Clayton or Raton a few times a week. The closest neighbors, Colonel Frank and Persis Bannon, lived only a few miles away. Older than Black and Kiddo but such dear friends. Persis taught Kiddo about gardening and canning and, well, life.

Nearer her own age, Kiddo's best friend was Alma Newkirk McNaghten. She and her husband Frank and their son George lived on Newkirk land in Oak Canyon. Kiddo and Alma were homeroom mothers at school, always making cupcakes. They went to PTA meetings and Home Demonstration Club meetings together, gave each other Toni permanents and took their sons on picnics to Johnson Mesa or Folsom Falls or wherever one of the husbands was working that day.

Once, helping out when both families tore down an old barn to get the lumber, Kiddo and Alma backed off in a panic and drove their boys home. Too many rattlesnakes kept crawling out of that old barn.

Kiddo started writing things on the calendar, just to keep up with the goings-on:

1948 May 17 – Took Bantam hen off nest with five chicks. Set out pepper, cabbage and cauliflower plants.

July 29 – Black worked for Bannons. I canned 8 pts peas, 3 quarts beans, 2 pts spinach, 5 pts beet pickles. Killed a fryer. Red and Raz came down. We went on a picnic.

Aug 4 – I canned 12 pts of peas, 14 qts green beans. Made my first chiffon cake. Killed fryer. Did a hand wash.

Nov 14 – Went to SS and church. All the gang came down for dinner. The men hunted in the afternoon.

Nov 19 – Black worked at the River crossing. Started on Bridge. The kids and I helped in the afternoon. Red, Raz and Mr. Yarger came down to hunt. Stayed for supper.

Men came every fall to hunt. Not local people. Businessmen and bankers from places like Amarillo and Dallas. Texas oil and gas men, the locals called them. Oil on their hair and gas in their stomachs. They paid to hunt on Black and Kiddo's land. Black liked taking others along while he laid in a supply of venison, showing those big shots the ropes. He talked about building a cabin for them to sleep, but Kiddo put a stop to it. *For cat's sake*, it was enough that she had to cook dinner and supper for whoever showed up. She didn't want to add breakfast and cleaning duties to her roster. The hunters savored her cooking and some of them left extra money for the food, like a tip, which she kept for herself. After every hunting season, Kiddo bought a new hat or a special outfit that she didn't have to sew. Or maybe some shoes. Red, if she could find them.

1950 Nov 15 – Black worked for Doc Morrow. I baked pies, made apple and cranberry sauce, jelly. Wrapped meat, took to freezer in Des Moines. 5 guys from Albuquerque came to hunt.

1950 Nov 22 – Washed windows and curtains, cleaned house, made rolls, pumpkin pies, etc. Mother, Owen, and Jean family got here at 3 a.m. Cecil family at 6. Big Thanksgiving Day.

1951 Nov 21, 22, 23 – We worked like Eager Beavers all morning. Red brought beds & bedding down after lunch. Went to Folsom to school program. Cecil, Marguerite and girls came at 10 pm, the Wards and the Willies at 2 am, and Mother, Owen, and Jean's bunch of girls at 10 am. Big Thanksgiving Dinner. Took pictures with flash bulbs. Had a big time visiting, kids riding Jenny and the tractor. On Friday, Dot put a Toni in mother's hair. Then the whole gang left for Texas!

1951 Dec 24, 25 – Got up early to get things ready to go. Black got up sick. Milked. Dick Murray came over to see about chores. Went to Pueblo [Colorado] to Joyce and Bert's with Red. Got there about 5, ate supper, kid's program and then the tree. Had great fun. Went for ride to see the Christmas lights.

When their families came to visit, it was a continuous party, especially for the kids. Richard and Russell were the only boys. Kiddo's sister Jean and her brother Cecil liked *Little Women* so much, they made their own passels. Six girls for Jean (Bobbie Jean, Ida Lynn, Ann, Leesa, Pam, Beth) and five for Cecil (Amy Helen, Cecilia, Marikay, Barbara, Debra). Cecil quit when his sixth was finally a boy. The child was named John Owen Graham McSpadden. Helen adopted a daughter (Dana) and Bernice birthed both a boy (John) and girl (Marilyn), but they lived in California and later Idaho, so couldn't visit often.

Dorothy didn't have children though she was a powerful mother figure to Jean's two oldest, Bobbie Jean and Ida Lynn. She helped raise them when Jean divorced and later, when Ida Lynn contracted polio. Out of seventeen grandchildren for John Finis McSpadden and Ida Esta Berry, there were thirteen girls and four boys, two named John.

When Jean left her abusive husband, she brought her two girls to spend the summer with Black and Kiddo on the ranch. Her daughter, eight-year-old Bobbie, seemed depressed and confused. One morning Kiddo cut a beautiful rose and placed it beside the young girl's plate at breakfast. When she saw it, Bobbie's face lit up brighter than the New Mexico sun.

Amy Helen, Bobbie Jean, and Cecilia were closest in age to Richard and Russell, so they helped the boys corral the younger feminine cortege. The small Farmall tractor Black had built pulled a wagon full of little women. The kids rode Jenny the mule and Dolly the horse and petted the goats, dogs, cats, and Bambi the deer. But mostly they played Cowboys and Indians on Indian Rock.

Four young cowboy cousins: (L to R) Richard Black, Marilyn Foster, Russell Black, John Foster.

One fall Black was cutting cedar on the mountain. A limb hit his eye, which later swelled and became painful. The doctor in Trinidad said that his eye would heal, but that he should use safety glasses for protection. He didn't have safety glasses, so he used a pair of mirrored sunglasses that Frank McNaghten gave him. Russell called him Hollywood when he wore them, which made Black grin that secret grin of his.

On the mountain again a few months later, he was cutting cedar poles with his double-bit poleaxe. The boys played outside on Indian Rock. Kiddo walked out to check on them and heard a noise in the woods. Black stumbled down the track into the open, his hand covering his left eye. Blood streamed through his fingers and down his chin onto his clothes. He looked like a monster and breathed in moaning heaves.

"Black, what happened? Are you okay?"

He gasped for air and couldn't answer. Kiddo pulled his hand away. A shard of mirrored glass protruded from his eye. The sunglasses had shattered from a flying chip of wood.

"Oh my God, what do we do? Should I pull it out?"

Black shook his head slowly but didn't speak. The pain, evident by his grimaced expression, had addled his thinking. He struggled to stay conscious.

Terrified, it dawned on Kiddo that she was in charge. "Don't panic, Dorris!" She said out loud, then yelled to the boys. "Richard, bring two wet washrags and a towel and move those cherries off the stove. Russell, get my purse and Black's wallet from the bedroom. I'll get him in the truck. Go fast." The keys were always in the truck.

She drove like a maniac to Miners' Hospital in Raton, over forty miles, with two little boys too scared to talk and their silent father, frozen and limp at the same time. The doctors cleaned and bandaged Black's head but did not remove the shard. They gave him pain medication, then referred him to an eye specialist in Walsenburg, Colorado. Kiddo filled the gas tank and headed north through Raton Pass, another sixty miles of wild driving.

When they arrived, Black's limp body was carried to a gurney and wheeled away. Kiddo yearned for her man to take charge of all this craziness. Her legs started to buckle. It took almost all she had to keep from breaking down in front of her boys. She set her jaw and heard her mother's voice inside her head: No tears. Be a strong woman.

Kiddo grabbed Richard and Russell tightly in a hug.

"Is Black okay?" Russell asked.

"You bet he is," she answered with all the perkiness she could muster. "Your daddy is the strongest man I know."

Black was okay.

But he lost the vision in his left eye.

Black wore a patch over his eye for a while. If someone expressed sympathy, he grinned and said, "No need to be sorry. My right eye can still see. Besides, I always wanted to be a pirate."

He always looked good to Kiddo, with or without his patch. How did she get such a handsome man, so distinguished? Every Sunday Black stood up front, leading the singing with his magical voice and sometimes giving the talk if the preacher got misplaced, just talking to the people, real-like, not bouncing up and down on the balls of his feet, hell and brim-stoning like some preachers do. Kiddo was proud of him and their two sons, scrubbed clean, starched and ironed, standing there singing with hymnals in their hands. She made sure the boys had little books or toys to occupy them through the long sermon, especially Russell who was a fidgety little thing. Richard was a perfect little man taking his cue from his Pop, never doing anything wrong. His singing was like Black's, too, rich and on key. Poor little Russell's voice was like his mama's, but he hit the right notes occasionally.

And Kiddo? Well, Kiddo looked good too. Stylish. Might as well be honest. She studied pictures in magazines of how women looked in other places, in cities, and wore nylons and heels with her dresses. She tried to coordinate jewelry, purse, and gloves with each outfit. And always a hat! A real lady wears a hat when she dresses up.

Sometimes, as she put on her finery, Kiddo looked in the mirror and saw her young mother, back east in Birmingham, when she wore those lovely dresses from her trunk.

Kiddo spent a lot of Saturdays washing, starching, and ironing, getting ready for Sunday church, so the family could hold their heads high. Sunday mornings they rushed around getting the milking and other chores done and getting gussied up. Then Black put the pedal to the metal and off they flew to the Des Moines Church of Christ. The boys called their old truck a Fodge because Black had put it together out of both Ford and Dodge parts.

One Sunday morning, hurrying to church, they piled into the Fodge and took off. Black driving, Kiddo next to him, then Russell balancing on the front of the seat and Richard by the window, like they always rode. Kiddo made them roll up the windows, so her hair wouldn't mess up, but Black got hot and opened his door a bit to get some air. The door hinged on the backside and well, the wind caught it and blew it clean off. It landed in the bar ditch on the other side of the road.

The Fodge kept rolling.

"Pop, aren't you going to stop for the door?" Richard asked.

"It'll be there when we come back." Black grinned. And it was.

Sometimes after church in the summer, as the Fodge bounced over the rubboard caliche road, Black would stare into a cloudless sky and declare, "It's about to rain!" Then he ran the truck in the shallow bar ditch, clipping the heads off tall sunflowers growing there. To the boys' delight, Ping, Ping, Ping! could be heard on the Fodge's roof. Flower heads flew over the top of the cab and landed in the bed, raining sunflower seeds as they traveled.

Black & Kiddo, Russell (L), Richard (R).
Folsom, New Mexico, 1946.

What Kiddo didn't like about church was Loa. Black's parents made the hour drive each Sunday from Raton to the church in Des Moines, then came to Black and Kiddo's for the day. Does any young woman want to spend one whole day a week, every week, with her mother-in-law? Especially when those days are filled with criticism for the clothes she wears, the food she cooks, the way she keeps house, the way she raises her children? Kiddo could do nothing right.

"It's a nice dress, but the pattern's too flashy and it's too short for a decent woman."

"Why don't you fix the roast the way I told you?"

"Your new curtains are the wrong color for the house."

Kiddo took most of it, as her mother taught her—being nice, not fighting, but going her own way. For Black's sake, because of Loa's condition, so she wouldn't have a fit. But when Loa told her that her hat looked silly or that it was her responsibility to keep her man satisfied so he wouldn't turn out to be a rounder, Kiddo ran to Black for support.

There wasn't any. He wouldn't confront his mother either.

"Just ignore her," was the only advice or comfort he gave. "She doesn't mean it."

Then at a Sunday dinner when the Milams had come down from Pueblo (Black's sister Joyce, her husband Bert, and their children Loyd and Judy) Loa picked on Joyce instead. Kiddo was relieved until some slight mention of her family prompted Loa to say that her mother was going to hell because she wasn't a member of the Church of Christ. Kiddo's perfect motherless mother, who was a Methodist.

Last straw.

"I know my dear little mother will be in heaven when I get there. I can't say the same for you with the venom you spew, criticizing everybody and everything. Going to church every Sunday doesn't give you a free pass through the Pearly Gates." Kiddo ran from the table in tears to escape the coming fit. She hoped Black would fight for her.

He didn't. Why would he never take her side?

Loa smiled at everyone, finished dinner, and asked to be taken home. No more Sunday dinners for a while. Later, through Corwin and Black, she asked for an apology.

Kiddo steadfastly refused. "I will go with you to the Church of Christ till the cows come home," she told Black. "But no one, no one, can tell me my precious mother will not go to heaven!"

Eventually Black's parents came back to Sunday dinners. Nothing more was said. Loa had no more fits after that, none Kiddo saw anyway. She wondered if old age had mellowed her mother-in-law, or if her taking a stance made the difference. Regardless, though the fits stopped, the criticism didn't. Even Black grew weary of pretending not to notice.

August 30, 1951, a day etched in memory. The Black family stood on their mountain and watched a big truck far away down the Dry Cimarron Valley. The truck would pull forward for some distance, stop a while, and pull forward, then stop again, repeating this strange action over and over. Finally, they solved the mystery. The Rural Electrification Project was dropping power poles that would eventually bring the area into the 20th century with electricity. Indoor water that didn't have to be pumped, a flushing toilet, a refrigerator instead of ice box, an automatic washer and dryer, a toaster, plug-in iron and lamps. Light, real light, to read and sew. No more coal oil lamps to clean.

Russell perched on Indian Rock and watched them drop the poles day after day. It took another seven months before the first spark of electricity came into the Black home and another month after that, April 1952, before running water and Kiddo's first automatic washer got hooked up. She did seven loads that day.

By that time, Black and Kiddo were making plans to leave.

WHITHER THOU GOEST

Music and lyrics by Guy Singer, published in 1954. Words based on Ruth 1: 16-17. Recorded by Les Paul and Mary Ford for Capitol Records, 1954. Later recorded by Perry Como, Bing Crosby and Mahalia Jackson, among others. Also known as the Song of Ruth. Popular wedding song in mid-century America.

Federal Land Bank held the mortgage on the land. Farmers Home Administration (FHA) had loaned money to upgrade their house and buy chicks. The Water Facilities Board extended a loan to drill a new well and pipe water indoors. Black and Kiddo had charge accounts at several merchants, such as Tovy Smith's Grocery and George Larkin's Feed in Des Moines, Parley Roach's Raton Distributors, and others. All that hard work and couldn't get ahead. Always robbing Peter to pay Paul.

1951, June 26 – Black worked at Dohertys 10 hours. We weighed 47 chickens and put in a pen to kill. Black & I dressed 30 chickens after supper til 1:30 am.

June 27 – Took 54 chickens on foot & 30 dressed to Raton. Had a blowout, bought used tire.

July 6 – Took 35 chickens to sell in Raton. Came home and dressed 24 more.

July 7 – We dressed 25 in the morning. After dinner we took the chickens to Des Moines and put in the deep freezes.

July 9 – Loaded chickens for Raton. Had a blowout. Took washing and got it done.

The chicken business wasn't any easier than dairying.

By 1952 Black's odd jobs had dried up along with the weather. Drought lingered from year to year: dried-up grass, cows giving less milk, lower cream checks. Scientists declared that, in New Mexico, the drought of the early 1950s was far worse than the Dust Bowl drought of the 1930s. Neighbors started to talk about finding greener pastures, but no one knew where those pastures were.

1952, July 4 – The whole gang met here. We all went up on the mesa for our 4th of July picnic, 20 of us. We sure had a grand time! Everyone came home with us. We visited, ate, and SANG, then milked cows.

Red gave them the old dust-covered piano from the home place. Black could pick out any song on it, but he used only the black keys. He said the white ones muddled things up. His Jumbo Gibson was too large for the boys, so Loa donated her smaller guitar for them to learn on. Richard was a natural, working through the strings and teaching himself. Russell was too impatient and didn't have the ear, but his rhythm was flawless. He beat on anything he could find, keeping time with Black and Richard's strumming and singing, so they bought him drumsticks.

With hard circumstances, Kiddo tried to talk to Black about his music again. Was Roy Rogers still his friend? Could he be asked for assistance in finding a job? Something a little easier? Black refused to talk about it and asked Kiddo never to speak of it again. He seemed angry that she asked, like when his Uncle Norval and Aunt Gertie Clum had come to visit a few years earlier. He had barely spoken to either of them.

This time he went silent for days, taking extra time to bring the cows off the benches in the evening. Kiddo knew he was sitting up there on top of the ridge, looking at Capulin and Sierra Grande in the setting sun. Thinking. Figuring. Hoping the spirit of the land would reconcile his dreams with reality. She gave him his space and waited.

With Black on the Folsom school board, people often showed up at the door looking for a teaching job. In the summer of 1952, Everett and Mary Ann Dame came calling. About the same ages as Black and Kiddo, they had a son named Woody who seamlessly fell in with the Black brothers. On behalf of the school, Black hired them to teach.

Mary Ann had grown up in Lincoln, a small town on the western outskirts of the Ozark Mountains in northwest Arkansas. Her father grew tomatoes and was well known to everyone there as Tomato Brown. Mary Ann talked about how different Arkansas was: green from frequent rain, huge trees, orchards, wildflowers, cardinals and eastern bluebirds, on and on. Not at all like the sere high plains desert in drought. Neighbors, Colonel Bannon and Persis, drove to Arkansas to see for themselves. They reported that it was a beautiful place with friendly people, good farmland, and frequent rain where a go-getter could make something of himself.

1952, Aug 21 – It really rained today. The river got on a big rise. R.E.A. went out, as usual! No lights!

Aug 22 – Rained again. Pump acted up. R.E.A. went off again. The River got in a bigger rise. Biggest one yet.

Aug 23 – Our River crossing is out! There were just two rises too much for it. Bannons fixed their phone line. We can at least phone now.

The ground was so hard-packed, it couldn't absorb the rain. It seemed everything was going wrong. Something had to give.

Black fixed a camper thingie on the bed of the pickup. Kiddo packed and arranged for the Bannons to do chores, then they took off for Arkansas to see for themselves. It was the family's first real trip. The boys were excited. So was Kiddo!

1952, Sept 10 – Got up at 4:30. Stopped in Clayton, got new battery for the pickup. Got to Amarillo about 11 Texas time. Spent the night near Clinton.

Sept 11 – Really had a grand time today. Got to Browns in Lincoln, Ark. about 4. Was sure tired.

Sept 12 – Had a good time today seeing the country around Lincoln.

Sept 13 – Left Browns. Went to Fayetteville. Bought the boys some shoes. Went on to Rogers. Got a cabin at the Apple Blossom Courts. Went to the show.

Sept 14 – Went to Sunday School and Church this morning in Rogers.

Sept 15 – Stopped in Fayetteville. Black went to see F.H.A. man. Back to Browns, helped pick tomatoes. We went looking at some more places. It was real dusty. My tooth started hurting.

Sept 16 – Picked tomatoes again. Mrs. Brown and I washed. Black took me to Prairie Grove to dentist. I really felt bum.

Sept 19 – Ate breakfast in Dalhart, Texas. On to Clayton. Got to Bannons about 10:30 a.m., came on home.

Now what? Arkansas was beautiful, but Kiddo knew how Black felt about New Mexico, its spirit flowing through his veins. How peace settled within him when he walked the large stone circles on the first bench where teepees used to sit. How he studied the petroglyphs on Indian Rock, the antlered deer, the stick men with bows and arrows.

She loved Texas, too, but she didn't have a choice. She expected to live where her husband lived, to be where he wanted to be.

Black finished up the milking one evening while Kiddo drove the boys to spend the night with their friend Woody Dame. Near the house on her return, she heard a loud commotion in the barn: cans clanging, cow bawling, Black's angry voice. She ran to investigate. Milk buckets and cream cans flew as he kicked them again and again. He yelled and cursed at Jezebel, one of their Jersey cows, who frantically zig-zagged to get out of his way. He swatted at her with a lead rope. She slid on a manure pile and down she went. Black rushed in and violently lashed the poor thing with the rope.

"Black! Stop it! What are you doing?" Kiddo ran to him. "Stop! Stop!"

He turned with his arm still in the air. She could see his rage. For a moment, she thought he might hit her with the rope.

"She kicked over the milk can!" He screamed through hard breaths. "We're just scraping by and she ruined what little we have. Gall dang, cantankerous hussy!"

"Black, put that rope down. Don't treat her that way. She's just a dumb cow." Kiddo put her hands on her hips to show him she meant business.

Jezebel scrambled up and took the opportunity to escape. Black dropped the rope and stomped out of the barn.

Kiddo straightened up the buckets and cans, getting them ready to wash, giving him time to cool off. When she left the barn, Black was sitting on the tailgate of the pickup. She walked over and sat beside him. Neither spoke. The gentlest of breezes whispered the cool dry air of evening. Sundown on the high plains sent its last rays of peach and gold streaking across the sky.

"Nothing works," Black broke the silence. "I try and I try and I can't make anything work. I'm thirty-one years old and don't have much to show. I thought I was gonna be somebody. I thought I was special. I have failed you."

Tears came easily to him, but not this time.

"Black, don't talk like that. You haven't failed. There's no contest here. We're just trying to live, make a home for our boys."

"That's what I want to talk about. I've been doing a lot of soul-searching."

"I saw that happening."

"Now I know how my father felt all those years ago, when he sold the ranch and moved us to Lubbock, how it must have torn him. Here I am, facing the same dilemma." He pushed off the tailgate and stood to face her. "How would you feel about selling out and moving to Arkansas?"

"I don't know." Kiddo stared at the pink-bottomed clouds over Johnson Mesa, holding her breath. "How do you feel about it?"

"I think we need to do this for the boys," Black said, "to give them a chance at a better life. Richard will be eleven next month. He's been milking for over a year. Russell feeds those calves on the nipple bucket every morning and night, some of them bigger than he is." He scuffed his boots at the rocks. "This rocky dry mountain land won't ever be any more than it is right now. I've pulled all I can out of it. But if we can get a good place where there's enough rain, I think I can make a go of it. Have something for them to hold onto, to have a future. That university there in Fayetteville . . ."

Now the tears brimmed his eyes and rolled down his cheeks.

Kiddo took his hand. "But what about you, Black?" she asked. "This is where your heart is. Your dream. All you've worked for all these years. You've built us a beautiful home here."

"I can give this up," he said, pushing the tears off his face with his fists. "I can live in Arkansas. For the boys. For you. You deserve better, too, Kiddo. You deserve a crown for putting up with my mother and all those others who think food just magically appears here. For putting up with me. For living this way. Dang it! It's the 1950s. Time for us to stop living like pioneers!"

"Yes, but people make fun of Arkansas, how backward it is. Barefoot hillbillies and all. Will it be any better?"

"It sure looked good to me," he said. "They call it the Land of Opportunity, you know."

"Well, like it says in Ruth, *whither thou goest*, Black. My place is with you, wherever you are." She was used to him making the decisions. She didn't like the responsibility of it. "Whatever you decide."

"No, Kiddo." He pulled her face up and touched her cheek with the back of his hand. "My Dorris with two Rs. You have to say, too. Tell me what you want to do!"

Oh, she could feel herself breaking Mama's No-Tears Rule. How could she help it with a man like this?

"I want to go to Arkansas," She mumbled between sobs. "Those boys of ours can be anything they want to be. We just gotta get them to the right jumping-off spot. I don't know how to do that, but I don't think it's here."

Black pulled Kiddo close to him and unleashed the flood gates. Through crying heaves, she ranted on. "I'm so sick of the criticism, so much family pulling us this way and that, giving advice. They treat us like we're still kids. I don't think Red's ever gonna let you be part of the home place. You could really do something with good land like that. But he pushed you out and Razz is barely holding on. And my family, oh how I love them, but there's so many. I get so tired doing for them and they still think I'm kooky. Then there's your mother! Don't get me started. Sometimes I just go in the closet and cry when you and the boys aren't around." *Oh, fiddle-de-dee!* Kiddo's pent-up flood of tears was worse than when the Concho got out at Ben Ficklin years earlier.

Later, as they walked toward the house, Black said, "You know, I always thought, if we ever left New Mexico, our next stop might be California, since our families have moved farther west for over two hundred years. Hope we're not backtracking. Kiddo, do you suppose they have cowboys in Arkansas?"

"They will when you get there!"

Black set to work, trying to sell the place. With the improvements, it was worth more than they owed, but finding someone who wanted that droughty backcountry wasn't easy. A man came from Dallas and another from Amarillo to consider buying it for hunting purposes. No offers.

The Colonel and Persis made their decision to move and put their place up for sale also.

In the Arkansas Ozarks, Tomato Brown bought a farm in the Dutch Mills area, southwest of Lincoln near Salem Springs, hoping to convince his daughter and husband to move back and farm but the Dames weren't interested. He offered to lease this farm to the Blacks until they found something, but they couldn't go until they sold their place.

1953, Feb 15 – So much snow and so cold. We decided not to have school.

Feb 18 – Black went to work. The boys worked on their skis and skied in the afternoon.

Feb 19 – Snowing this morning. The wind started blowing real hard about 9:30. Black and the boys came home at noon. We really had a blizzard!

Snowed in, they hunkered down and made the best of it. A few days later, here came Corwin and Red on the tractor, bringing food and supplies. The house was empty when they arrived. Black and Kiddo were on the mountain with the boys, sledding and skiing. When Corwin and Red figured it out and found them, both were angry as hornets.

"You're acting like children," Red yelled. "We thought you might be starving. We came through freezing weather to bring food to you."

"When are you two going to grow up?" Corwin asked.

Black's last straw.

"Right now," Black answered. "You can just go on home. We're fine here. We have plenty of food, always do. You've eaten a lot of it. The house is warm and toasty. Plenty of firewood, cut and stacked. The wood chute is full. We can take care of ourselves. Go home."

They stomped off, climbed on the tractor, and rode twelve miles in the cold back to Des Moines. Kiddo couldn't have been prouder of Black, but it made them more anxious than ever to get away. Black figured harder, scribbling numbers on the backs of envelopes. In the end, he worked a deal with Otis Bray from the Hayden area that involved taking over some loans, some cash, and several Holstein heifers for their future dairy.

1953, March 22 – Russell's 9th birthday. Corwin & Loa, Joyce & Bert and Loyd and Judy came down. We had a big time visiting.

March 23 – Went to Frank & Alma's. Black and Frank worked on our pickup. The boys and George played. Alma & I put a permanent in my hair. The Dames and Shorts came for our get-together. Had a big time.

March 24 – Went to Clayton, finished up our trade with Otis. Boys got haircuts. Paid some debts. Russell spent night with Woody.

March 25 – Went to Raton. Tended to a lot of business. Got back to Folsom about 2:30. No truck. Black & Everett went to get us a truck.

March 26 – We got up early. Milked. The trucks came at 5 a.m. Frank came at 5:30. Alma & George, The Dames, Bannons, Red and Corwin all came. We got everything loaded and left "home" at 10 a.m. We are moving to Arkansas!!!

Off the mountain, down the lane, across the Dry Cimarron where the bridge had washed out, the Black family followed the bob truck loaded with their belongings and the semi tractor-trailer loaded with 23 cows, Dolly the horse, Sam the goat, and several crates of chickens. Black pulled the pickup onto the caliche road and turned southwest for the first leg of the journey that would resettle these Westerners farther east.

Black stopped, one foot on the clutch, the other on the brake. He dropped his head for a moment, then slowly turned and looked back. Kiddo and the boys turned to look also. The house wasn't visible, tucked into the side of the little canyon as it was, among the cedars. Only a piece of the windmill and tip of the barn could be made out, if you squinted, but Indian Rock still towered above the piñons. The mountain looked the same as it had for 30,000 years. Ten years Black and Kiddo had lived in New Mexico. Except for the slice of road, you couldn't tell they had been there.

A small, anguished sigh escaped from deep within Black. Silent tears betrayed four stalwart faces. Black, Kiddo next to him, Russell perched on the front of the seat, and Richard by the window, the way they always rode.

They didn't wallow long. Black wiped his eyes, put a stogie in his mouth, then let out the clutch and said, "Here we go!"

PART III

ARKANSAS TRAVELER

Traditional folk tune appearing before 1840. Early barn dance. Credit given for arrangement, but not composition, to Colonel Sandy Faulkner and Mose Case. Sheet music first published in 1847, arranged by William Cumming. Various lyrics. Recorded by Len Spencer on cylinder and disc in 1902 for Edison Records, most popular song of 1902. Official state song of Arkansas from 1949–1963.

The Black convoy drove all day and all night arriving in Lincoln, Arkansas, about seven the next morning. As always, cows before humans. Tomato Brown led the entourage to the farm near Salem Springs, where they unloaded and milked the cows. Exhausted, but full of excitement and anticipation, the family got its first look at their new Land of Opportunity.[9] Green pastures lay mostly flat amid small hills, decent land though rocky and overgrown with brush. The tired house was little more than a shack. Four squeegee rooms with a tiny front porch. Old wallpaper swooping down from the ceiling. Outhouse. Hand-dug well. Disheartening.

For four nights the Blacks slept and ate with the Browns while they made the house livable. They enrolled the boys in Lincoln school. The first week, Richard's class went on a trip to Siloam Springs and Russell's class had a picnic. Black fixed the radio and built a cozy fire in the stone fireplace.

No time to mope. There was a life to build. Again.

Kiddo scrubbed and scrubbed, hung curtains, and displayed her knick-knacks. Black enclosed part of the porch and built bunk beds for the boys to have their own bedroom. The barn was barely standing, so he bargained the use of a barn for milking from his neighbors, the

Villines, an inconvenient mile down the road.

Within a few weeks, Black and Kiddo had located the sale barn at Fayetteville, the milk association offices (P.M.A.), Farmers Home Administration, the Soil Conservation offices, and the University of Arkansas Agriculture Extension Services. They made friends at church, at school, in the stores, and introduced themselves to all their neighbors and invited them to dinner.

Their closest neighbor was Lafayette Little, known as Fate. Fate Little was a young man, overgrown like the brush in the fields between their farms. A hard-working farmer, he lived with his mother. Black borrowed his mules to plow their garden and in return drilled his field with oats. Soon Fate was helping with chores and joining them for meals the instant he was asked. After savoring Kiddo's cooking, Fate repaid the gracious gesture by bringing her a treat. He plopped two small stiff animals on her kitchen table. "I brought you some nice dressed possums, Miz Black. Just caught 'em last night. They'll be real fresh."

"Well, thank you very much, Fate." Kiddo said through her pasted smile. "We'll enjoy those. That's very kind of you."

As soon as Fate took his exit, Black, who had been standing in the doorway, turned to Kiddo and said, "Possum for supper, Miz Black?"

"Get those fool things out of my kitchen. I can't stand to look at them," she replied.

Black disposed of the critters, but the "Possum for supper, Miz Black?" stuck around for decades.

Within a month their New Mexico friends, Colonel Frank and Persis Bannon, moved to a farm near Lincoln. Later, the Bannons' daughter Delphia and her husband Dick Murray moved to a farm at Cincinnati, Arkansas, just a few miles from the Oklahoma border. Both families remained lifelong friends.[10] Other New Mexicans they knew also moved to Arkansas to escape the drought, including Otis

Horton who became a professor at the University of Arkansas.

Conditions weren't the greatest and the work was physically hard, but the family was happy making its own way without interference or criticism. They immersed themselves in their new community.

1953. April 11 – We went to Earlene & Alvie Spears after supper to watch TV. Our first time to see TV.

April 24 – Black built fence. Field Day at school today. Russell won Blue Ribbon in Penmanship! Shipped 4 full cans of milk this morning. First time!

April 28 – Our new tractor was delivered! The boys were really happy over 'their' new tractor. John Deere 40, a Poppin Johnny.

May 8 – Richard & I set out strawberries and planted garden. Black plowed corn field. Went to school house for Band Round-Up. Russell played in rhythm band. Was all real good.

May 17 – Sunday School and Church. Home with Fritz and Grace Khale for dinner. Sure had a nice time. Went to Baccalaureate. Black helped sing.

May 18 – Black and I picked some "Poke" (our first offense). Took it to town and sold it.

Black focused on being a farmer instead of a rancher. With spring coming fast, he plowed and tilled a large garden plot for Kiddo less than two weeks after they arrived. Then he started on the fields so that the cows would have a nice menu next winter. Tomato Brown had advised in his deep scraggly voice, "Lespedeza, Bud, Lespedeza," in much the same way "Plastics" would be bandied about a few years later. Black plowed and sowed lespedeza, Sudan, millet, hegari, corn, barley, oats and sorghum. He hired a bulldozer to dig a trench silo. When it hit rocks that wouldn't budge, he finished the job himself with dynamite. He attended farm meetings and reread his text book from his freshman year at Texas Tech, *Morrison's Feeds and Feeding*. He scouted out University of Arkansas pamphlets and subscribed to farm magazines, teaching himself all he could.

1953. May 25 – Still working on silo. Rich and Bubba each grew up a notch today. They drove tractor and plowed corn ground.

May 29 – Black & the boys plowed. Mr. Brown and some more guys came out to "witch a well." Fate and Mrs. Little came over to visit. Really hot today. I sure felt bum.

July 1 – Bannons came to visit, stayed for dinner. I finished the boys shirts. Made 4 shirts in two days. Black finally got milk cooler to going. Well drillers got down to 100 feet and water!

Richard had a tough time that first year. Besides coming down with measles and getting the flu, he broke his arm at school. *They had to re-set his arm. It sure hurt our Little Man!* But the worst was the wasp attack. An innocent trip to the outhouse turned into terror as wasps dive-bombed the unsuspecting youngster, stinging his head. He was mighty sick for a few days.

Fall came, time for the Washington County Fair in Fayette-ville. Black built a ramada enclosed with saplings to use as a practice show ring. He taught the boys to groom, position, and lead a cow for conformation and showmanship contests. Russell was too young this first year, but with Black's guidance, Richard (almost twelve) entered the Dairy contests. They chose Lady, a solid attractive Guernsey that had made the trip from New Mexico with them. The boys groomed her and put her through the stances for weeks.

1953. Sept 21 – Sure had a big day, lots of fun. Got Lady all settled in her 'stall' at the fair at Fayetteville. The Halls said they would milk her, so we came home.

Sept 23 – We all went to the fair again. Really had a full day getting Lady ready to show tomorrow. Watched Beef Judging today. Black and boys got new Levis.

Sept 24 – Black & I got up at 4 and milked. We left for fair at 7. Richard showed Lady. GOT 1ST PLACE IN SENIOR CLASS and SENIOR CHAMPION! Hurrah for Rich and Lady!

Sept 25 – Got up at 4:30. Got to fair early. Lady was really glad to see us. Groomed Lady and Richard showed her at 11. Oh boy, what an hour we spent. RICHARD AND LADY WON FIRST – WON A HEIFER CALF! A great day!

After the fair Black was convinced that Guernsey was the breed for his boys. He sought out every Guernsey herd in western Arkansas and eastern Oklahoma, seeking cows with the best features. Richard and Russell were right by his side on most of these quests, as was Kiddo. Every week there was a sojourn to a Guernsey farm. Money was tight, but Black became as adept at cow trading as his father had been at trading horses on the high plains. He could usually figure some trade, some way, to work better genetics into the herd.

1953. Dec 7 – Happy 36th Birthday, Dorris! I went to town after lunch. I got birthday cards and letter from Mother telling of Jean's baby, my new niece named Pamela DORRIS – spelled with two Rs!!!

1954. March 27 – WELL, WE ARE ARKANSASERS NOW! Arrived here one year ago.

April 10 – Artificial inseminator came. Killed ole Cock-A-Locky. Black beheaded him and I had the pleasant (oh, yeah) task of dressing the old buggar.

April 28 – Black plowed potatoes. Then we hoed peas and onions. Then we planted cantalopes, watermelons, sweet corn, black-eyed peas, and pumpkins. We really enjoyed the gardening. I went barefooted all morning (Shhh, don't tell anybody but it sure was lots of fun!!!)

May 25 – Black hauled rock. He sure is getting fed up with this rock business. Wish he would just let those silly ole rocks alone. No one would do that much for us if we owned a place and someone else lived on it!

June 30 – Black rushed to town early to get millet, sudan, & milo maze seed. Persis, boys & I picked wild plums. Cooks came over. Cookie & I put rhinestones on my hat.

August 25 – Went off on a little look-see trip (chasing butterflies ha-ha).

Trading expeditions weren't just for cows. The Blacks were also looking for a place. Their place. Occasionally they found one that spoke to their hearts, but somehow, try as they would, it slipped from their grasp.

Black once made a deal for a beautiful piece of land just west of Prairie Grove on Muddy Fork. He approached the Farmers and Merchants Bank in Prairie Grove about financing and was told to come back in three days. Before the three days were up, the landowner drove to Salem Springs to tell Black that the deal was off. He had just sold the land to a board member of the bank who showed up out of nowhere. Nowhere. Yep.

Staying connected to her Texas kin was important to Kiddo. She wrote many letters and instructed her boys to write also. Russell, age 10, wrote the folks in Lubbock:

Dear Granna and Uncle Owen,

I'm very busy these days getting my heifers ready for the fair. My Guernsey heifer is registered. Her name is Queen Ann.

Remember Richard won $100 to buy his heifer. The man he

bought his heifer from, Mr. Owen Thurman, let me have my heifer for a $100 and gave me a whole year to pay for her. I hope to win first money.

Wish you could come to see us in fair time and see us when we show our heifers.

Uncle Owen, I hope your and Uncle Cecil's crops are still doing good.

Say, we have a pet goat. He really is a pest. If you need him to weed your cotton, write and tell us and we'll send him right down.

Hi to Uncle Cecil, Aunt Marguerite, and the girls.

Love, Russell Owen

(L to R) Queen Ann, Russell, Richard, Maiden.

The dairy business in northwest Arkansas was just getting organized. There was no way to know where the milk would be processed once it left the farm. All the farmer could do was wake up before dawn, milk his cows, pour the milk into cans for the milk hauler truck to pick up daily, and wait for a check to come through the mail. Sometimes the wait was long, two weeks or more, and sometimes it didn't come at all, like the time Black found milk running down the ditch. The hauler had poured it out to lighten his load, so he could climb the big hill out of Salem Hollow. The check might come from Coleman, Meadowlark, Pet, or Monette Creamery, wherever the milk was sold on any particular day. Meanwhile, the farmer must feed his cows and thus run up a huge bill at the Farmers Co-Op. Often when the check finally came, the farmer had to choose between paying the cattle feed bill or feeding his family.

1954. July 26 – No milk check. No calf feed. We had planned to go to Fayetteville, but NO money, no go. We made a freezer of chocolate ice cream.

July 27 – Got ready to go to Fay. Met Bro. Cook to get mail, but NO milk check yet! Nurtz! Dumb ole milk company! Came back home. Field man and inspector came. We got flung off Grade A. Kinda hurts in more ways than one.

July 28 – The milk hauler brought our belated milk check today, so we went to Fayetteville. Went to the University farms. Visited stud barn. The boys enjoyed it all so much.

July 29 – Fate came over and told us about Gerald Hamilton having polio.

August 4 – Well Tut Tut, hot again. Boys finished planting maze after milking. We went out and looked over the dear fields, some millet and sudan coming up. We could use some rain, if you please.

August 23 – Put the cows over in our new pasture we leased from Fishel. The cows were so happy to find some good grazing. President Ike made a speech tonight on the radio. Poor guy sure has sorry delivery.

August 27 – Oh, Fuzzy Lee, but it's hot today. This ole dumb, dry, hot country. Shore getting boresome. Will it never rain? Sometimes I wish we were in Alaska! We were trying to relax and do just as we pleased but of course the "inevitable" [Fate Little] *had to come over and spoil our plans. The dear Ugh said temp was up to 108 today.*

Arkansas heat could be humid and oppressive, especially in the still of night with no breeze. In desperation, they dragged mattresses into the yard and slept under the stars. In winter, cold penetrated the uninsulated house. With only the fireplace for heat, Black came up with a wild idea to get them through the frigid nights. He positioned a large empty oil can in the back of the fireplace to act as backlog. It worked. The oil can radiated warmth into the room throughout the night.

The mistake was telling his neighbor Gerald Hamilton. Gerald altered the plan a bit. He threw an old tire in his fireplace, figuring it would do the same, get hot and keep the room warm. It worked all right. Boy, did it work! The Hamiltons opened all their windows in freezing weather and still kept warm. Paint liquefied and ran down the walls.

"We're going to have the best Guernsey herd in the state," Black announced one evening at the Family Council around the heavy oak dining table bought in Chickasha long ago. "That means we need a modern milk barn with this new automatic milking equipment and coolers, the whole works. A parlor-type pit barn, so we don't have to squat to attach the milkers. A bona fide dairy that we can keep in grade-A status. No more cans of sour milk returned to us. Full production. Full milk checks. Enough to live on. We're gonna build us a modern barn. How hard can it be?"

Kiddo had baked chocolate chip cookies that she served with milk. "What's it gonna look like?" she asked. "I don't like those low-slung, concrete block affairs. It should be a pretty barn."

"Let's figure it out," Black said. He passed around paper and each drew a different barn. They poked fun at Kiddo for wanting a pretty barn, but that's what they eventually built, on land they didn't own. A beautiful white barn with gabled roof and cobblestone trim on the sides under the windows, a barn constructed from salvaged lumber, bartered materials and durniks (Black's euphemism for the ubiquitous stones) picked up from the fields.

1955. Feb 26 — The boys milked. Black and I started putting up sheetrock on ceiling of milk room. It were a job! Boys helped Black when they finished milking. I painted barn doors on inside after supper. Ran out of paint. Rawleigh man came. We listened to the radio. All so tired tonight.

Feb 27 — After church, we buzzed around and got lots of things done. Fixed some gates. Cleaned barn and got everything assembled to milk over here tonight. Really kept us all jumping but we dood it! Got started at 5:30. Cocoa first cow milked in new barn, Josie 2nd, Jeannie was last cow milked. We were all so relieved when Pauline acted okay. Finally got through with all chores at 9:15. Ate some supper and hit the hay, a real tired bunch of milkers.

As fair time neared in 1955, Richard, age 14, wrote to the family in Lubbock:

. . . We have about 30—35 acres of grain sorghum of our own and half of our neighbor's crop, which is about ready to cut for ensilage if we don't wait and bind it. Looks like we might get quite a little winter feed, sure hope we do.

Russell and I wonder if you could send us that cot you asked about bringing Christmas. We could use it for the fair because last year we took a bedroll and it got gravel all in it and that wasn't so good. Ha! Ha! We are sending money to help pay for getting it back here. We think we can get our neighbor's cot, so that would be two.

We are going to take 11 head of cattle to the fair this time. Russell and I may take some of our crops, too.

We have bought 2 cows, 1 registered and 1 grade. Russ and I borrowed the money from the bank and pay back as the cow produces. Russell and I have a pretty good little bunch started, which is around a dozen head, all the way from baby calves to mature cows. We've had a little bad luck, such as my registered heifer getting bred to our neighbor's scrub bull!!

We wrote to the Guernsey Cattle Club and got an official herd name, which is "Dutch Garden." How's that for fancy?

We are starting a new community 4-H Club at Dutch Mills and I was elected President at our first meeting last night. There were about 15 kids there. I sure do hope we get a good club going.

Tell everybody Howdy for all of us.
Lots of love, <u>President</u> Richard (Ha! Ha!)

Within a couple of years, Black and Kiddo and the boys had greatly increased their milk production through better genetics and nutrition. Black became highly regarded as one of the county's foremost dairymen. Men showed up at their out-of-the-way farm near Salem Springs seeking his council. He freely gave his knowledge, taking others on a tour of his modern dairy, showing them what to look for in a good milk cow, scribbling a quick barn design on the back of an envelope. If he wasn't available, Kiddo or Richard or even young Russell filled in, taking pride in what they had built.

Kiddo's light also began to shine. Her spunk was quickly recognized and rewarded. Installed as Lincoln PTA President in 1955, just two years after moving to Arkansas, she wore a hat with her new dress for the ceremony and loved the corsage her guys gave her for the occasion. She became a role model for young girls at her school and church, and a patient teacher of homemaking skills to the girls in the 4-H Club at Dutch Mills, which she and Black organized and led.

While Black taught farming skills and leadership activities to the boys, Kiddo taught the girls to can, cook, sew, and how to dress like a lady. Without a daughter of her own, she developed a small hoard of little women to nurture.

In 1955 the Blacks were selected Arkansas Farm Bureau's Farm Family of the Year for Washington County. A banquet was held in their honor. Kiddo wore red shoes.

Even their steadfast faith and support of the Church of Christ brought notice to the family, as each moved into leadership positions. Black often substituted for a missing preacher, giving a talk instead of a sermon. He served as a deacon and attended church business meetings, lending his two-cents of pragmatism to the precarious politics of religion. Both Black and Kiddo taught Bible classes in Sunday School. They dropped something into the collection plate, even when money was at its tightest. But the family's most significant contribution to the church was music. The unique rich timbre of Black's voice led many to a Come-to-Jesus moment.

Richard, his voice carrying its own richness, first led a hymn at a Sunday afternoon singing at the Lincoln Church of Christ with 228 in attendance. He was 13. Not long after, he began to entertain at school and community functions. Later, he performed with a quartet that included Russell on drums.

Unfortunately, the recognition they garnered in their new state didn't translate into monetary success. Cash remained elusive. Hat in hand, Black borrowed a few dollars from Owen "Buster" Thurman, a fellow Guernsey breeder, for the family to take cattle to their first State Fair in Little Rock. The following year Richard, age 15, attended alone, traveling with Carl Rose, the County Agent. So, Black and Kiddo and Russell weren't with him in Dinky Durnik when Richard won 1st place in the Arkansas Dairy Judging Contest!

A week later, Richard's 4-H records won 1st in the State and qualified him for a trip to Chicago. It was the beginning of a long line of wins for both Richard and Russell and annual treks by both boys to Chicago for the National 4-H Congress. When Russell made his first trip out of state, his excitement was evident in the letter he wrote home, addressing it to his cat and dog:

Harrison Hotel
Chicago, Illinois
October, 1958
Dear Soks and Judo,

Boy, you ought to see the big city! It is dirty but kind of pretty. All the buildings are dark and smutty. You ought to see the farms on the way up here on each side of the road. There are big red or white barns with tall silos. They are all real neat. I have never seen so much corn ready to pick at one time. Each farm has at least two huge corn cribs.

We went by the surge farm where they have the glass front parlor-type barn with large model cows in the stalls with milkers going to each cow. Then we stopped at the Northern Illinois Breeding Co-Op where they have a lot of Holstein bulls, real near kin to some of the Arkansas bulls. They have some McDonald bulls and a real good Burton Lane bull. Then we went back to a BIG Holstein farm, Clanyard #2, that has the highest producing herd in the country. Then we judged a class of two-year-old cows. We headed for Chicago and passed by Rosewood Farms where we will stop coming back. Boy, you ought to see the barns and silos!

Today we registered for the conference and I almost didn't get to enter, because I am 14 instead of 15, but they went ahead and let me enter.

Today I watched part of the junior shows and man, is it rough. There were 21 head of Holstein heifers in our class. The Grand Champion Guernsey Cow was a three year old owned by a girl in Indiana.

Tomorrow we get to go through the barns. Each animal up here is estimated at $1500 each. Well, it's 12:00 o'clock and I'm pretty sleepy so bye for now. Hope everything there is okay.
Love, Russell

Somehow the money was found for these trips, for whatever the boys needed to uplift themselves. Even when things were bad, when the milk check wasn't enough, when the butane was out and Kiddo had to cook in the fireplace, when the water froze and they couldn't scrub the milkstone off the cans to pass inspection, when the truck needed gas to go after cattle feed which would be put on a charge ticket, even then, the Black family heard the music.

1954. March 16 – The boys had a good time today playing on the guitars. Richard taught Russell a lot. The sawmill guys brought another load of lumber. Some real pretty walnut and ash.

June 15 – The boys and I went shopping. I got new white shoes, hat and purse. Goody, goody, goody. I really am proud of my new things.

1955. April 2 – Happy Birthday old Father Bear. (Black always said he was durn near a fool, since his birthday was the day after April Fool's Day.) The boys and I had a big time giving Black his birthday spankings. I made Black a mincemeat pie and baked his birthday cake. It was the "Tackiest" cake I've ever fixed anyone for their birthday. I hated it so much.

July 17 – After church Black went to the Legion hut to sing for Mr. Beaty's 100th birthday bash.

August 25 – Milked in record time. Went with Luginbuels down to Evansville to Kiwanis meeting. Black did good with his singing.

December 6 – Just as we started to eat, here came Grace and Fritz Khale, Cundiff, and Jadie & Inez Allen for a surprise birthday party for me and was it ever a surprise! Grace brought a fruit cake, Inez a devil's food cake. We had a big time. Black played his guitar. Black, Fritz and Rich all sang.

1956. March 25 – Got through milking about 7:30 p.m. Then we went out to Bushes. Maxine had supper ready. We had a nice visit. Black,

Bill, Maxine, and Richard all played some music. Really had a good time.

March 26/27 – Black found out he needed to inoculate the alfalfa seed. So that put a stop to the alfalfa sowing. He went to town after goop to fix seed. Richard sang at school today for freshman assembly. Did real good. The wind is really blowing now. Makes it bad for Kadiddle Hopper's alfalfa sowing.

July 8 – Church. Changed our duds. Went on picnic other side of Westville on Barron Fork. Oh, boy, we got to go swimming. First real swim we have had since we have been in Ark. Had a real good picnic dinner then another swim. Everyone had so much fun!

December 8 – When the guys went to milk and do the chores, I made mince and cherry pies and Russ helped me fry doughnuts. After they came in we all ate too much. Richard played the guitar.

I WALK THE LINE

 Written and recorded by Johnny Cash. April, 1956. Sun Records, Memphis, TN. His first number one Billboard hit.

Christmas Day, 1956. Black's family had come for the holidays: his parents, Corwin and Loa from New Mexico and his sister Joyce, her husband Bert Milam and their young teenagers Loyd and Judy from Colorado. Cots and bedding had been borrowed from friends. Kiddo prepared a fat turkey and set a fine table with tablecloth, candles, and a centerpiece made from pine cones and greenery she gathered in Salem Holler. With her now legendary pies and cakes pulling off a grand finale, everyone left the table stuffed to the gills.

1956. December 25 – Merry Christmas to each and all! Got the Turk on at 8. He cooked real nice. At Russell's request, we froze a freezer of ice cream. It was a real treat for Christmas! Took some flash bulb pictures of table, turkey, etc. After dinner and dishes, all of us but Loa went over west and got some small trees for the folks to take home with them. Finished ice cream and then it was milking time. Again!

After the evening milking, Black invited their neighbors, the Paul Connors and Bob Fields families, for a music session. Bob played a mean fiddle and Paul could really handle his rhythm guitar. Black picked up the Jumbo Gibson that lived beside his favorite chair. Richard brought Loa's old guitar from his bedroom. Russell uncased his school band drum. Cousin Loyd, becoming a fine musician himself, had brought his own guitar. Cousin Judy's lovely soprano reminded the family of Loa's voice. The crowded little house filled with the sound of family and friends *pickin' and a singin' and a grinnin'*.

Christmas hymns came first. "Joy To The World," "Hark The Herald Angels Sing," "Silent Night," "Away In A Manager." Songs everyone knew well and could sing along. Loa and Judy took center stage on the high notes of "O Holy Night."

"Rudolph the Red-Nosed Reindeer" was repeated several times in a little contest to see who sounded the most like the popular Gene Autry recording. Next Black led with well-known old western songs, starting with "Git Along Little Dogies." Of course, he did a solo "Yellow Rose of Texas," which required that Kiddo come stand beside him while he sang. The best part was when they looked at each other the way they did. It brought light to every heart in the room.

Then the four teenagers clamored for some of the more popular country and western songs, the ones being played on the radio. The musicians picked out "Mexican Joe" which had been recorded by Jim Reeves, then tried "Take These Chains From My Heart," recorded by Hank Williams, Sr. and his Drifting Cowboys. That led to a couple more Hank Williams' sing-along songs. "Hey, Good Lookin'" and "Jambalaya." Rock and roll came next, songs by a wiggler named Elvis Presley. They tried three of his recent releases: "Blue Suede Shoes," "Don't Be Cruel," and Russell's favorite, "Hound Dog."

With complaints that the new songs were too hard, the strummers fell back to Tennessee Ernie Ford's "Ballad of Davy Crockett" and "Sixteen Tons," then Richard soloed with Marty Robbins' "White Sport Coat." As the evening wore down, Black tried a song he'd heard only a few times by a newcomer from Arkansas with a unique deep voice, Johnny Cash.

"Kiddo, come over here and stand beside me again," Black said.

"Why?" Kiddo asked.

"Because you're Mine," Black sang in a bass voice, his face wearing a rascally grin. He strummed the opening chords of Johnny Cash's "I Walk the Line."

When he finished, the neighbors declared it a fine evening and took their leave. The family shuffled around, ready to call it a night also. All except Loa, who hadn't moved from her spot by her son's chair.

"Keith," she said.

"Yeah?"

"I think you missed a good one. If you can play it, I might, well, I might . . ." Loa twisted a blue flowered handkerchief in her hands. "I might would like to sing it with you."

Stunned, Black sat back down and propped his Gibson in position. "Sure, Ma. What do you want to sing?" He studied her face.

"It's just a pretty little ditty. Patti Page, I think. Called 'Mockin' Bird Hill."

The house fell silent. This family's matriarch only sang hymns.

Black's eyes brimmed with tears. "Never played it, Ma, but together we can figure it out. Richard, hand your grandmother her guitar."

Mother and son worked through the keys and chords, hitting wrong notes, changing them to the right ones, conversing in a language deeper than words, until the discord vanished and harmony was reached. Together they peacefully sang their song: *Tra-la-la, tweedlee-dee-dee.*

Under a clear black Arkansas sky, well cared for cows lay in the fields on this warm Christmas night, their shapes lit by a million bright stars in the Milky Way. An idyllic barn with cobblestone trim and gabled roof stood nearby. On the rocky Ozarks hill farm a small house squatted, surrounded by pastures cleared of brush from Little's Ridge to the top of Salem Holler. Big Boss, the boar hog, lay against the door on the front porch, asleep.

Inside the house, people made music.

QUE SERA, SERA
WHATEVER WILL BE, WILL BE

Composed by Jay Livingston. Lyrics by Ray Evans. Recorded by Doris Day for Columbia Records. Introduced in the Alfred Hitchcock film *The Man Who Knew Too Much*. Academy Award for Best Original Song, 1956. The words "Que Sera, Sera" appear on a brass plaque in the Church of St. Nicholas, Thames Ditton, Surrey, 1559.

1957. April 7 – Well, I guess a person never knows just what a new day will bring. This one started out very ordinary. About 9:30 we got a phone call from a Mr. Gordon Phillips. We went to church, came home, had a quick lunch, then Mr. Phillips came. Looks like we have a big deal on. Dick and Delphia Murray came after King, so we had a big time planning and talking. We didn't have too good a night. Too excited to sleep.

April 8 – Oh dear! Winter, winter, winter. Almost freezing rain and the coldest wind. What a day to go look over a place, but This is The Day! Boys didn't go to school so they could go with us. We went by Bannons' store and told them the deal, then we went on to the farm. Mr. Phillips came out and we talked and figured, looked at house, etc. Then Mr. Phillips and us went to Fayetteville. Luck was with us. Fred Nettles [Farmers Home Administration] *was in, so the deal was discussed and agreed upon right there. Afterwards we went to Heflin's and ate dinner and talked some things over. Went back out to "PHILDALE," talked over some more things, then we came on back to Lincoln, stopped and told Bannons.*

Nestled in the heart of the Prairie Grove Valley, Phildale was a four-hundred-acre dream farm spread just outside the eastern city limits of

Prairie Grove. Bordered by U.S. Highway 62 on the west and Arkansas Highway 170 on the north, the cleared bottomland, sliced by the Illinois River, was rich enough to grow anything. A storybook white barn stood as a landmark: two stories, eighty by fifty feet with Dutch Gambrel roof, 18" thick concrete walls, floored loft and open staircase. It had been built by Mr. W. E. N. Phillips, a wealthy patron who had recently donated land and a new gymnasium to the Prairie Grove School. Besides the Big Barn, Phildale included a dairy barn, granary, machine shed, and other outbuildings plus two houses. The plum was Mr. Phillips' home, called the Big House, a modern rock ranch house with large windows, hardwood floors, TWO tiled baths and an enormous kitchen with all the latest appliances. The other house, the House on the Hill, was a two-story white clapboard Victorian.

Mr. Phillips had passed away leaving the farm to his two grown sons, Gordon and Jonathan. Their lives elsewhere, the sons had hired poor managers and now sought better leadership for the farm. With visibility and high regard throughout the farming community plus a strong recommendation from Carl Rose, Washington County Extension Agent, the Black family was a natural choice.

For Black, Kiddo, Richard, and Russell, the move was a game-changer. In Arkansas four years, they hadn't been able to obtain a place of their own. They had cleared brush, picked up rocks, run fences, fertilized pastures and built a barn for someone else's farm. In the previous few weeks before the offer, their well pump had gone out, the hot water heater stopped heating, the tractor died, the pickup wouldn't start, and Kiddo's sewing machine quit sewing, prompting Kiddo to write in her journal: *Wonder how much more of this kind of stuff we can take and still be in business?*

Phildale seemed God-sent. Fronting the major highway, it was only ten miles from Fayetteville and the University of Arkansas. A complicated deal that would merge the two dairy herds and lead to the Blacks' gradual purchase of the land was worked out. The only disappointment was that they couldn't live in the Big House. It was rented to Barry Parks, part owner of the Prairie Grove Telephone Company, and his new bride Betty. Ten days after the deal was made, Black and Kiddo were sanding floors and painting cabinets in the Victorian House on the Hill, preparing to move.

Farming started immediately. That first spring was hectic, back and forth between the two places at Salem Springs and Prairie Grove, fifteen miles apart, bringing in the hay and silage crops, wrangling equipment and three Black men. As part of the deal, Black hired help for the twice-a-day milking. With over a hundred cows, there was no other way to get it done.

They soon learned that farming the luscious river bottom brought its own set of problems. Heavy tractors sank in soggy soil after spring rains, plus the volatile Illinois River headwaters could turn into a raging torrent in the matter of a few hours after heavy downpours—overflowing its banks, ripping out fences, leveling riverside crops, and flooding Highway 62 at the bridge. Accustomed to stumbling blocks, the family made adjustments for whatever Mother Nature threw at them.

Every fall, the family made the fairs: Washington County Fair in Fayetteville, Fort Smith District Livestock Exposition, Arkansas State Fair in Little Rock, all within three weeks.

1957. Sept 9 – Black brought cows in from back on Lucille Morton's and he had a time getting them home. Russ was elected Class President today. Congratulations, ole kid! Boys made show blankets for the little heifers tonight. We had a family talk-talk.

Sept 16 – This is the day we moved in at the fair. Took 17 head. Got the same stall again, goody for that. Jack Hall brought 12 head this year, business picking up in Guernsey division. I went over to little store and bought lunch stuff. Jack ate with us. Flies terrible! Got everything fixed pretty good. Little heifers sure dirty. Black and I came home about five.

Tired, oh so tired. Boys stayed with the cows.

Sept 19 – Show day at the Fair! So much crowded into one day. Otis Horton was judge. Boys had stiffest competition ever and they really had to work for everything they got. Didn't get their Guernsey trophy back, but they did splendid in the fitting and showmanship contests, with Richard placing 1st and winning the Trophy (for keeps) and Russell placed 2nd. We were sure proud of our little men!

Sept 28 – Nice sunshine. I washed boys clothes real early this morning so they would be sure and get dry. Fixed black-eyed peas, roasting ears, Swiss steak and baked apples for dinner. Black and the boys clipped and bathed King and worked on his horn. He sure looked pretty. Mac took hogs to sale ring in the Dodge. I ironed and ironed and ironed in afternoon.

Sept 29 – Real nippy this morning. I got up at 4, got Black and the boys up at 4:30. This is the big day. Off to Little Rock and the State Fair. Jack Arney didn't get here till nearly 11. We loaded his pickup with plunder, went on down and loaded the two little heifers. Little Blondie was kinda sick, all swollen up around the eyes, gave us a scare, but Black decided it might be a reaction to the penicillin shot, so they loaded her. Spot Wilson didn't get here till nearly 12, had to reshape the cattle. Boys and cows got off at 12:30. Black went over to get cows off the highway, then to mow millet in the afternoon but he bogged down, couldn't mow, then decided to plow other field, well, that ground too dry to plow. I went to garden and picked veg. I never will get all these vegetables taken care of.

Russell, age 13, and Richard, barely 16, were off on their own to the Arkansas State Fair and Livestock Exposition in Little Rock, along with several head of cattle to manage. Black and Kiddo stayed home to work the farm. No money to pay for help and no money to pay for a motel room for a week while the show was going on. The boys slept in the barn stalls alongside the cattle.

Their Guernsey bull, King, took top honors, Arkansas State Champion, as did two of their heifers. The huge purple ribbons were centered with a plastic button showing a picture of the perfect Guernsey and in large gold letters, the word "CHAMPION." Besides the top-level purple ribbons, the boys earned dozens of blues (1st place), reds (2nd), whites (3rd) and lower level colors. The cattle were judged in various categories, and the boys were judged in showmanship and for how well they themselves could judge.

The Blacks claimed the Arkansas Razorbacks as theirs from the first year they landed in the state. When Razorback football was aired, the day was planned around game time. Church and Razorback games were pretty much the only reasons to stop work. Kiddo fixed treats, Black made a fire, and the whole family glued to radio station KGRH out of Fayetteville and heard Willie Ingalls, and later Bob Cheyne or Rip Lindsey, do the play-by-play.

"Gee fuzz, you should hear three Black men yell and scream at a little box," Kiddo wrote her Texas kin. When the Hogs played Texas Tech, she rooted for the Red Raiders just to add some excitement.

At night, they tuned the radio to music over KRMG out of Tulsa or WLS in Chicago when the skies were clear.

The family lucked into its first television in 1957. No more running off to neighbors to watch TV. Black was given an old RCA that had quit working. He took it to a repair shop, then bought an antenna. The day he brought it home, he climbed the big oak next to the house and attached the antennae to the tree, leaving two strings of baling wire hanging down. Cords clipped to the back of the TV ran under the windowsill to the antenna. Excited, Kiddo made popcorn balls and the family got comfortable to watch TV in their own house. A snowy picture finally came in along with whooshing sounds. The reception was sorry, no matter which direction the antennae was turned.

"A little more toward the south," Black would direct. "Now, back to the east. Just a little more, a little more. Now back. WHOA!

Stop right there!" The boys argued about whose turn it was to go out-side and yank the baling wire, tuning in the best signal. "I did it last time!" Hopefully, at some point, they could tune in KFSA out of Fort Smith or KTUL from Tulsa and get decent images. Most kids watched the Cowboys and Indians serials on Saturday mornings, but not Rich-ard and Russell. Farm work and social activities kept them busy even on weekends.

The boys rarely watched the "Roy Rogers Show" and didn't re-alize how famous Roy Rogers and Dale Evans were. But from rodeos and other publicity, they learned the names of Roy's palomino horse Trigger and Dale's horse Buttermilk, their dog Bullet, and the 1946 Jeep called Nellybelle.

One Saturday morning when the guys were out of the house, Kiddo watched the show. She studied Roy's face and tried to imagine Black in that role. How different their lives would be if Black had become Roy Rogers that day long ago, instead of Leonard Slye. Then she imagined herself as Dale Evans, his wife. *Ha! Me on TV! For cat's sake, that would never have happened, not with my high squeaky voice.* She never mentioned Roy Rogers to Richard or Russell. *It isn't my place to tell them. That's Black's deal, if and when.*

After people got their own televisions, they didn't visit so much. No more dropping in without notice, coming home with you after church, or going to someone's house to just talk and get the news. A bit of community was lost.

When Barry and Betty Parks moved from the Big House, Black talked to the Phillips about buying it but couldn't get an answer. Life went on.

1957. Nov 1 – While the guys were milking, a silly ole cow swatted Black in his good eye with her ole tale and it was full of cockleburrs.

1957. Nov 26 – Went visiting around to find things to use for Thanksgiving centerpiece. Stopped at magnolia tree house and lady gave me some clusters. Stopped at a rock house. Met Shirley Sharp's grandmother. Got red berries and real holly branches. Later saw a beautiful Siamese kitty. Stopped and visited with it. And its lady.

1957. Dec 27 – Got up early and really bizzled about. Got everything ready for the baby chicks. Weldon (Farmers Co-Op) brought them about 10 am. Oh, but they are so pretty. And the way that guy dumped them out just like they were so much garbage! We got 4,080. Lots of babies!

1958. Aug 25 – Russ worked with show cattle. Rich started mowing in old corn field, supposed to be lespedeza, but mostly weeds and bind vines. Russell received a letter from Cecil saying they had shipped his bulldog. Was he surprised! Didn't know he was getting one.

Kiddo's brother Cecil knew that Russell loved bulldogs, so he put one on the bus in Lubbock, Texas and sent it to Russell. The trip took almost a week. The family went to the bus station in Fayetteville every day and finally the bulldog puppy arrived. Kind people had fed and watered her along her journey. She was thin, but happy, and quickly become part of the family. Russ named her Judo. Snubby nose, white wriggly skin, and spots on her tummy which could be seen when she squirmed on her back. They all loved her, but she was definitely Russell's dog, the first in a long line of bulldogs he kept throughout life.

The only problem with Judo involved Mr. Clark, the milk inspector. He came once a month to inspect the dairy barn and cows. Farmers were expected to feed him and house him overnight. One night while he bunked in Russell's room, a horrible loud scream woke the whole family. Black investigated and found Judo had crawled into bed with Mr. Clark, giving him a rude awakening!

Mr. Clark was also the source of a family saying. Kiddo always buttered the toast when she made breakfast for the gang. The first time they shared breakfast with him, she asked, "Mr. Clark, would you like your toast buttered or plain?"

"Butter my own toast!" he gruffly replied with Arkansas independence. They liked his answer and took up the saying whenever someone wanted to do their own thing. It's kin to what Black told the boys when he separated them in one of those brotherly fights, "Bud tend to Bud!"

And by the way, Kiddo bought a kitten from that Siamese cat she stopped to visit. Sing-Fu was the first of many Siamese in the Black household. Kiddo liked their autonomy.

1958. Nov 14 – Tonight Black and I had a nice long visit, one of our deals where we talk over everything from A to Z and back.

1958. Nov 15 – We went to Fayetteville to meet the boys coming back from Little Rock. Everything and I mean every thing was closed up in town for Homecoming game. Razorbacks played Texas Tech. We waited and waited. Boys were late getting back.

1958. Nov 28 – Got the Guernsey Journal in today's mail. Boys picture is in it.

1959. Jan 14 – Boys, posters, atoms, etc. got off to school okay.

1959. Jan 20 – Black went to Russellville for Guernsey Breeders board meeting. Tornado warnings for late evening, first of season. Sure do hate tornado season.

1959. Feb 10 – Gordon Phillips came out and we talk-talked and figured and made our deal. He was really nice and we got along fine. So here's to the future here on this place. May it be a good one. We know it will be a busy future that will take lots of planning and good management, but with work, determination and the blessings and guidance of our heavenly Father – WE WILL MAKE IT!

With teaching and support from both parents, Richard and Russell Black showed cattle at the various fairs for nine years. They amassed over six hundred ribbons plus numerous trophies, a passel of silver cream pitchers with the Guernsey Breeders logo, and a whole herd of little plastic model Guernseys. The Black boys dominated the show ring for almost a decade. Their prize money and premiums were deposited into a joint account at the First National Bank in Fayetteville where banker John I. Smith took a personal interest in teaching them financial responsibility. This money was earmarked for college.

The Black brothers became known throughout the state for their character and integrity. They went from leadership roles in the Dutch Mills and Prairie Grove 4-H Clubs into the Lincoln and Prairie Grove Schools' Future Farmers of America (FFA) organizations, taking advantage of training programs and contests to become top leaders. Both excelled in public speaking, honing their speeches in front of Black and Kiddo, and usually placed near the top of local, district, and state contests. Their frequent wins attracted the media and soon their bright, fresh faces began to appear with regularity in newspapers and trade magazines.

Richard was elected National FFA Secretary just six months before Russell was elected Arkansas State FFA Secretary. Both boys completed the rigorous program to earn the American Farmer Degree, the highest award the FFA can bestow. Onstage, in front of 10,000 people at the National FFA Convention in Kansas City in 1962, the National Secretary and the Arkansas State Secretary jointly presented a Degree of Honorary American Farmer to their father, Keith L. Black. Because females were not allowed to be part of the FFA at that time, the boys presented their mother, Dorris McSpadden Black, a Certificate "as a token of appreciation for the encouragement, cooperation, and assistance given her son which contributed to his outstanding achievements in the Future Farmers of America."

That was a fine day.

Kiddo broke the No-Tears Rule. She wore a hat and red shoes and was presented a lei made with a hundred and twenty-nine orchids by the Hawaii delegation. That night she and Black were special guests of the American Royal Stock Show and Rodeo.

Proud to be farm boys, Richard and Russell also had other interests. Both emulated their parents' easy-going personalities. Richard's dreamy eyes gave him a romantic look, movie-star handsome, though he was also serious-minded, put-together. Russell exuded a spunky boy-next-door charm with quick, sparky eyes inherited from Kiddo. And wow, what a smile! He smiled all over his face every time you looked at him. Perhaps because the names both started with R (one each from DoRRis?), or maybe because of similar stature, Richard and Russell were often mistaken for each other. Russell was asked way too many times, much to his chagrin, "Are you the one that sings?"

At Prairie Grove High, each was elected President of his class and Captain of the six-man Tigers football team. They were a bit short to succeed at basketball. At five feet, eight inches, Russell turned out to be the tallest member of his family. But height didn't keep the honors from rolling in for both. All-district in football, Friendliest, Most Handsome, Most Likely to Succeed, Mr. Prairie Grove.

This type of recognition led to college scholarships. The University of Arkansas in Fayetteville, the state's flagship, is where their paths diverged, not just from Black and Kiddo, but from each other.

TURN! TURN! TURN!
TO EVERYTHING THERE IS A SEASON

Lyrics from the Book of Ecclesiastes, attributed to King Solomon. Title and additional lyrics by Pete Seeger, late 1950s. Recorded on albums by the Limeliters and Pete Seeger in 1962. #1 Hit recorded by The Byrds for Columbia Records, 1965.

Meanwhile, back at the ranch, as they say in old Westerns, things were changing. The boys weren't little anymore and seemed to be slipping away. They had worked like grown men since they were striplings and truly deserved all the honors. Black and Kiddo wished they could have given them more things, but as Kiddo's dear little mother said on the banks of the Concho all those years ago, things are just things. What they gave from their hearts, their sons could use for a lifetime.

After the move to Phildale, Kiddo embedded into the community quickly. With the Prairie Grove Civil War Battlefield Park less than a mile away, she joined the Auxiliary. The Park hosted a big celebration every year on Labor Day weekend called the Clothesline Fair. Local artists and craftspeople displayed their creations on clotheslines or folding tables. Square dance exhibitions and contests were getting organized. Richard square danced with one of those first groups. They performed the Virginia Reel in 1958 wearing Western outfits, pointy-yoked shirts and ties for the boys and swirly full skirts with layer upon layer of nylon net petticoats for the girls.

Square dancing stuck. It became a rite of passage for most Prairie Grove youth over the years. Richard and Russell danced every year until they graduated. Kiddo served the Auxiliary for a lifetime, often as

President. During Open Houses, she wore period outfits and bonnets to serve as hostess in the Civil War era buildings.

The Prairie Grove Women's Club asked her to join. She loved the formal meetings, conducting business per Robert's Rules of Order. The ladies wore hats and gloves, served finger sandwiches, and hot tea. Hats! Kiddo was in seventh heaven! She became close to this dear group of women and stayed friends for the rest of her life. She served as President, not only for the chapter, but for the Federation and eventually, Kiddo was elated to host the Club in her own beautiful new home.

Yes, my home. Our home. A home of our own, that we truly owned. It's time for that story.

The Phillips wouldn't sell the Big House, but instead had allowed them to lease it. Kiddo was thrilled to live in such a lovely modern home but wondered if they would ever find a place of their own. Black continued to manage Phildale, splitting farm profits with the Phillips. Then he made an agreement to slowly purchase the Phillips herd. He upgraded the dairy barn and began to work toward becoming a milk processor, the idea being to bottle and sell his own brand of milk.

In winter, when there were no farm profits, Black sometimes found work in Fayetteville as a carpenter or stone mason, building cabinets here or a fireplace there. The boys were growing, and their activities required more money. Phildale had an old one-ton flatbed truck that they commandeered for transportation. They called it Old Crunch and were lucky if it got them back from wherever they wandered.

As the boys graduated high school and went on to the University of Arkansas, things really changed for Black and Kiddo. There was less help for chores. The milk bottling idea blew up even though Black had found and purchased equipment including thousands of glass milk bottles which sat in the barn unused. Production Credit Association wouldn't finance the enterprise, ruling it a small business instead of a farm operation. And they weren't spring chickens anymore. Kiddo's aches and pains sent her to Dr. Baggett in Prairie Grove who shot her weekly with vitamin B-12. She just couldn't get as much done as she used to. Workhorse Black began to have trouble with his bad eye and his stiff neck.

In the fall of 1961, Black spent a lot of time walking the fields in his cowboy hat and boots, frown across his forehead, stogie hanging out the corner of his mouth. He walked the banks of the Illinois River claiming he was looking for arrowheads. He even found some. He had no horse to ride, no mountaintop with clear majestic vista to ride to, but Kiddo knew he was out there talking to the sky in whatever way he could, figuring out life. She waited.

"Do you want to go back to New Mexico?" She asked him at lunch one afternoon, after several days of brooding quiet. The two of them were eating in the kitchen at the Big House. A red-checked tablecloth covered the old oak table's scars. Black savored her homemade chicken soup and little ears of cornbread she had baked in her cast-iron corn molds. "Not now, but when the boys get through college and are on their own?"

"Why would you ask that?"

"Because I know you," she answered.

He considered a few minutes. "Maybe you don't know me as well as you think you do."

And there it was. That grin. Wow, how Kiddo loved that foxy grin! After all these years, he could still charm the pants off her with that grin.

"No, I don't want to go back," he went on, "Our life is here. There's nothing for us in New Mexico any more. Besides, I like these Arkansas people. They're independent as hogs on ice. No, this is home now, but I do want a place that's ours. A place to grow old in, for whatever time we have left."

"Now, Black, don't you start talking like that. We got a whole lot of life left to live. And we're going to live it. Just like we've always done. Pretty good, so far, wouldn't you say?" She tried her own sweet grin. "Do you want some pie?" She took the mincemeat pie out of the old pie safe.

"I'd feel lonesome without it," he quipped. "Yep, life's been good so far, Kiddo. A lot of hard work, but good. Not many people willing to work as hard as we have for so many years. Not many would call this success, either. Not like being a movie star." He winked at her. "But it's got its perks. Mainly you!"

As she served his pie, he grabbed her around the waist and pulled her onto his lap.

"I don't think you could have been an actor, Black. You're too real. Not enough pretense."

"I didn't want to be an actor, Kiddo, but I might have wanted to be a singer."

"You are a singer!"

"Yes, I am!"

Black kissed her and grabbed other parts. *Mercy me!*

Well, for the sake of decency, let's just say that the pie had to wait. It wasn't the first time the old oak table had been used for purposes that weren't culinary. Kiddo hoped it wouldn't be the last.

As they put themselves back together Black said, "I've got an idea I want to run past you."

"Then run it."

"I want to approach the Phillips again about buying part of this place," Black began. "There's no way we can afford all of it, but I've got my eye, my one good eye, on the piece north of the river, about a hundred and sixty acres. There's an old home site there, where that falling-down barn and cellar are, just off Highway 62. We could build us a new house there, a rock house. What do you think?"

Kiddo could see the excitement in his eyes. It buoyed her. "Well, that sounds real good, Mr. Man, but how are you going to pay for all that?"

"We're going to sell the dairy herd." Black looked pleased with himself, but that idea frightened her.

"What a crazy notion," she said. "The cows are our paycheck, Black. Little as it is. How will we live?"

"Consider the lilies of the field, how they grow; they toil not, neither do they spin." He was grinning again. Such a charmer.

"Don't go quoting the Bible to me," she said. "Lilies won't put food in your belly or clothes on your back. God helps those who help themselves. We need a plan. Be serious with me."

"I've got one," he sobered up. "Thought we might go back into the beef cattle business. That acreage would support beef cows and we wouldn't have to grow all the different feed crops like we do for dairy. Mow the pastures for grazing, rotate the fields, make a hay crop in summer. That's it. Piece of cake compared to all the froth of dairying. Richard and Russell aren't around to help much now. That's gonna get worse until they're gone completely. You and I can't do it all ourselves, nor pay for help and give the profits to the Phillips. Besides, if we tried to dairy over there at the new place, we'd have to build a barn, buy equipment. A whole lot bigger investment."

It was her turn to be quiet, studying over it all. Finally, she said, "I like it, Black. But I'm not going to get all excited and go figuring on a house until we know the land deal is done. You have to talk to Gordon Phillips first and get that part settled."

Kiddo lied. She started figuring what kind of house it would be from that very moment. *Our home. Our own home.*

"Sure thing," Black said. "I'll start trying to get hold of him this afternoon." He saw her grab a jacket and head for the door. "Hey, where are you going?"

"Over there to see our new place. I want to see the home site and walk every field. You coming?"

"You bet," said Black, catching up with her. "But there's one more thing about this deal: I want a horse. A good horse. I want to ride again while I still can."

As it turned out, another offer to purchase Phildale was made about that same time. A wild man named Danny Thomas from California had serendipitously flown his private plane over the property and declared it the most beautiful farm he had ever seen. He wanted the entire place, but the Phillips upheld their promise to Black for his years of work and sold them the land north of the river. That left the two houses, barns, and rest of the property for Mr. Thomas. At the time, Black and Kiddo had no idea how entwined their lives would become with this larger-than-life singing evangelist, their new neighbor, Daniel B. Thomas.

In February 1962, they signed the papers on their dream land in Washington County, Arkansas, about a mile east of Prairie Grove: one hundred sixty-seven acres that ran from the Illinois River north to Arkansas Highway 170, bordered on the west by U.S. Highway 62. The land rose from the river bottom to a small wooded hill on the north where they would build their home.

Kiddo didn't know all the ins and outs of the deal Black made, including selling the dairy cows and equipment, but she knew they ended up with two mortgages on their place. Federal Land Bank loaned $15,000 for twenty years. The Phillips took a second mortgage for $6,900. It seemed like a good deal, but she fretted over those annual payments, how they'd get those made. Their income was never a steady stream, more an unpredictable flood-drought cycle, and they never learned to dam up the flood, to save back for dry spells.

Plus, they still had a house to build! THE House. Tri-level, thirty-five hundred square feet, stone walls, large windows, a soaring great room with two fireplaces.

Hollywood dreams on a Cowboy budget.

Not having money never stopped Kiddo's deal-makin' man. He called another Family Council and the four of them drew house plans and stick pictures of their dream house, but the boys couldn't get caught up in it. Richard was home between national tours for the FFA. Russell was close to high school graduation and excited about his Senior Trip to Washington, D.C. Their lives were opening to a larger world. But they were willing to help with construction during the times they were at home.

An architect in Fayetteville had begun to make a name for himself with a new type of house made of stone and glass, built to look as if it grew right up out of the soil. E. Fay Jones had studied with Frank Lloyd Wright who started this movement known as organic architecture. Fay Jones used local Arkansas stone and wood in his unique designs. Among the first homes he designed, after his own, was one for Kiddo's dentist, Dr. Calvin Bain and his wife Jo. This unique house was built in Prairie Grove, their little town of a thousand people. The architect received national attention for his work when the house was featured in *House Beautiful* magazine in 1959.[11]

When Jo Bain later opened it up for a tour of homes, Kiddo toured with some of her Women's Club friends. They wore hats. Then she high-tailed it home, got Black, and took him back to see it. They were smitten with the natural materials, the feeling of being safe inside the earth itself. The ceilings were low, almost cave-like except for walls of glass, yet an open house that flowed from room to room. Ideas exploded in Black's mind.

They sought out and visited every house Fay Jones had designed in the area taking the boys with them when they were around. Black wasn't bashful when he wanted to learn something. He just walked up to the door and knocked. He charmed the homeowners and they usually invited the couple in, proud to show off their Fay Jones house. Black studied the structure and the construction. Kiddo focused on the floor plan and interior details.

Black and Kiddo weren't trying to steal his designs. They just wanted to spark their own ideas and refine what they wanted. They had waited a long time for a home of their own. It needed to be special. Still, Black didn't feel right about it, so he made an appointment and went to see the architect himself to tell him what they were trying to do on a shoestring. He found Fay Jones to be authentic, humble, and gracious—the same qualities Jones apparently saw in him. When Black told him that he would be building the house himself, inch by inch, Jones told him to call if he stalled out. Black took him up on that offer several times, and the architect visited the site to inspect Black's stone work when the fireplaces were done. Jones gave his stamp of approval.

Work started in earnest after Russ and Kiddo returned from his Senior Trip to Washington. Yep, she got to go too, as a chaperone. She had always been a home-room mother and baked more cookies than anyone else, so his classmates asked her to go. They called her Mom. The group toured the Capitol and the White House, climbed the Washington Monument, and walked along the big lawn and reflecting pool. Kiddo liked the Lincoln Memorial best. Standing at the top of the steps, looking back toward the domed Capitol, made her feel special just to be alive, maybe the way Black felt at his spot on Emery Peak.

The school chartered a bus for the trip. It was the first time out of state for many of the kids. Kiddo noticed that Russell's friend, Jim Sharp, didn't eat when the bus stopped at cafes and the kids ordered their hamburgers and French fries. He hadn't brought spending money. She told Russ to order extra food and share it with him quietly, so he wouldn't feel bad. *What kind of parents would send a kid off on a trip with no money for food?* [12]

Luckily, this was a flood time, after selling the dairy herd, so Kiddo had money to spend. Oh, you should have seen her outfits for the trip! She really dolled up. She discovered an uppy dress store in Fayetteville called Town and Country Shop. They carried brands like Pendleton and R&K Designs, beautiful fabrics. Something well-made that didn't take weeks to sew. Just make a purchase, undo the safety pin holding the tags and wallah: a dress! She made friends with the owners of the shop, Grace Vawter and her young daughter Liz. They opened a charge account for her. Black couldn't know what these clothes cost. He wouldn't understand, despite knowing how much it meant to Kiddo to dress like a lady. He'd give her a little lecture about spending too much on impractical things, so she just paid her bill a little at a time from her grocery money and hoped he didn't notice.

Besides, over the years, Kiddo had learned that Black wasn't a gift-shopper and celebrations were iffy:

1955. June 19 – Father's Day. Fixed ole Father Bear a special breakfast. Got the boys up at 5. We had ourselves a merry time fixing our big surprise and tying string on Black's toe. His hat fits real good. His pants fit good, but of course, way too long.

1957. Dec 7 – Happy 40th birthday to me from me. Guess it will have to be that way. My family don't seem to think it's necessary to ever remember. Russell went to Twirp night at school with Treka Brooks. He looked so cute. Tonight, the boys finally remembered that today was my birthday, but Black never did!

1957. Dec. 8 – Church, then to Bannons. Persis fixed Dick and I a birthday dinner. It was really nice. Enjoyed it all except the Colonel had a lot to say about my age and my gray hair. Took the fun out of it all. Russell gave me a darling little china kitty. I named her Tra-la-la.

1958. Oct 6 – Happy 18th anniversary to us. Boys judged in Chicago today. Hope they did good, will be our anniversary present. We went to Penney's in Fayetteville, bought Black a hat and I bought a hat at the Boston Store.

1958. Dec 7 – My 41st birthday. When I got up this morning, what did I find on my desk but a lovely birthday surprise! A darling pair of RED house shoes with white fur trim and a cute little birthday message from "my guys." But oh me, size 6 is too short, so shoot!

1960. Oct 6 – This is our 20th wedding anniversary. I wonder if Black thought about it.

So, in later life, when Christmas rolled around, she would pick out something special, have Town and Country wrap it up with ribbons and bows. Then she placed a tag on it that said something like "To my darling Kiddo From Black," and put it under the tree along with her gift to him. On Christmas morning, Surprise! A lovely gift from Black!

Danny Thomas gave them a year to stay in the Big House before he moved his family. He paid Black a pittance to look after things while he sold property and businesses in California and put his big plan together. Phildale Farms became the Sundowner Ranch. On Highway 62 where the dirt road turned off to the farm that he called a ranch, Danny installed a painted sign that featured a cowboy atop a rearing horse. ***THE SUNDOWNER. Daniel B. Thomas, proprietor.***

With just a year to build the house, Black bartered the use of an old International Harvester bulldozer. First, he leveled the rounded mima mounds in the bottom fields close to the river. Then he used the dozer to dig out the side of the wooded hill for the lower level of the house. He learned of a farmer near Hog Eye who wanted an old stacked rock fence removed, rocks free for the hauling. Black, Richard, and Russell took Old Crunch, the flatbed, and heaved field stones from the fence onto it, then hauled several loads to the home site.

When he ran out of those, Black located a more reliable source. The Morelocks, extended church friends, lived on a sandstone mountain south of Prairie Grove. They allowed him to come dig out whatever stone was needed, including large chunks of flat flagstone for the floor of the great room. Kiddo's three guys babied the one-ton up the dirt mountain road. Load after load, with picks, shovels, and crow bars, they dug out the rocks and weighed Old Crunch down with all he could carry, then stopped by the house where Mr. Morelock would eyeball the load and decide how much they owed, usually between ten and twenty dollars.

The digging and hauling work was too physical for Kiddo to be much help but, she found a way to be part of the team. Her men always appreciated good food so she went with them to the mountain, taking hearty picnic lunches and thermoses of liquids to replace the sweat from their strenuous digging and hefting. *Each person does what he or she can. Good support is vital to the overall success of any team. That's what I believe.*

Black started in the northeast corner of the lower level, laying a rock wall. It wasn't pretty at first, but he kept at it and got better. Kiddo complained about the rough mortar. Russell volunteered to be mud man and scraped joints way into the nights after Black had finished his day's masonry.

By the summer of 1963, the lower level of their new home was enclosed with a huge bedroom, a smaller room which served as temporary living room/kitchen, and an even smaller second bedroom/storage area, and a bathroom. It was sort of cave-like, half dug into the hill, but they moved in and kept building the upper levels.

Looking ahead, they cut long stalks of river cane bamboo from a cane-break growing around a deserted tennis court on The Sundowner. The Kiddo and the boys stripped the foliage and left the cane to dry. A few months later they varnished the canes, making them shiny. Soon after that, working on tall scaffolding, Richard and Russell maneuvered them into place on the ceiling of the soaring great room, in a herringbone pattern between the vigas. Nails couldn't go into the canes because it split them, so they were placed beside each cane to hold it in place. Grueling, meticulous work in hundred-degree heat.

"Greasy, ade-time," one of them would yell and Kiddo would scurry up the ladder with more lemonade. She was afraid one of the boys would overheat and fall as Black had when he carried the flue pipe up the ladder on his shoulder. The crazy cowboy didn't break, but they couldn't say the same for the flue.

The vigas and river cane latillas for the ceiling were Black's homage to his beloved New Mexico. Wow! What a showpiece it turned out to be. Black and the boys got a permit to cut tall pine trees at Lake Wedington. The vigas were twenty-foot-long poles and the ridge pole forty. The four of them traipsed all over the forest to find that one. The guys peeled them with drawing knives and allowed them to dry before varnishing and installation. Running diagonally, the play of light and dark of the cane latillas between the pine vigas is fascinating. *Everyone who comes into our home looks up at the shining ceiling and remarks about how beautiful and unusual it is.*

Ten years after moving to Arkansas, the family had their own place! Black was 42 years old and Kiddo, almost 46. Her hair was gray, silver really, like Grandpa Green Berry's had been. Black's hair was still thick and coal black. Sometimes, she was mistaken for his mother. *Yay.*

That year, 1963, was a rollercoaster ride. Although ecstatic to finally be living in their own digs, they were also exhausted from the labor of building and discombobulated by life's changes.

Kiddo had taken time off from the building to make a couple of trips to Texas to be with her mother after a devastating diagnosis of esophageal cancer. Then came a phone call from her sister Dot, urging her to come right away to Lubbock. Their dear little mother was losing her fight. Kiddo spent two weeks with her Texas family as they gathered in to care for their precious mother. *It felt good to be near my people. Owen, Cecil, Helen, Bernice, Dot, Jean. To feel again the special rhythm of our love for each other, as familiar as my own heartbeat.*

She told herself it was the natural order of things, for a parent to age and die, but it didn't lessen the pain and emptiness of losing her darling motherless mother. She comforted herself by imagining the two of them reunited in heaven someday where they would wear red shoes and fancy hats. She and her sisters broke Mama's No Tears Rule, as Richard sang "Asleep in Jesus" at the funeral. Then Mama lay again next to Daddy in the City of Lubbock Cemetery where Black had raked the gravesite long ago, where a piñon grows that they had brought from their mountain in New Mexico and planted there.

Not long after the family returned to Arkansas, Richard learned that his opera singing group would be going to Europe in the spring to sing for USO troops. *EUROPE! Can you imagine? Our son going abroad to see the world.* Kiddo had long ago given up her own travel dreams, contenting herself with armchair travel books from the Prairie Grove Library. But she was overjoyed that her child could have this opportunity.

In November, the coaster fell to the bottom again. Young President John F. Kennedy was shot and killed while riding in a parade in Dallas. The whole thing played out on TV: First Lady Jacqueline in her pill-box hat trying to crawl over the back seat of the convertible. Police capturing Lee Harvey Oswald, the shooter. Jack Ruby shooting Oswald. Lyndon Johnson sworn in on Air Force One with Jackie by his side in her pink blood-stained suit. Those darling little children watching their father's caisson roll by, John-John saluting.

Heart-rending. Frightening. *What has our country come to? Are we still safe?*

Nothing to do but go on. An ordinary person feels so helpless at times like these, when the world doesn't make sense.

Then Richard decided to marry. Russell moved to campus. There Black and Kiddo were, just the two of them, camped out in the basement of their large half-built empty nest, their latest flood of money trickling downstream.

ARCHY AND MAHITABEL: A BACK-ALLEY OPERA

Based on stories written by Don Marquis beginning in 1916 about a cat and a cockroach. Musical written by Joe Darion, composed by George Kleinsinger, 1954. LP recorded by Carol Channing, Eddie Bracken, and David Wayne for Columbia Records, 1954.

As National FFA Secretary, Richard was required to take a year away from college to participate in Good Will Tours. The first tour began in January 1962 in Washington, D. C. then swung through sixteen states and twenty major cities.

From the Willard Hotel in Washington, Richard reported: *Today was the day of the luncheon at the Capitol. Sat with Fulbright, Mc-Clelland, Pop's friend Trimble and a girl he brought in with him from Berryville. McClelland real nice guy.*

From the Park Shelton Hotel in Detroit he wrote about the previous day: *New York City is really a city by itself. None like it anywhere else for sure. We got to see the Broadway musical* Camelot. *U.S. Rubber Company took us to see it. Man, this was really swell! Passed by the Peppermint Lounge where the 'Twist' got started. Went to top of Empire State building and RCA building. Seeing that musical really made me the most homesick-like I have been. I really miss mostly the music, besides y'all.*

From the Morrison Hotel in Chicago: *Russ, this morning we visited the Chicago Board of Trade where the grain is bought and sold. I remember that morning we visited in 1958 and you got so sick. Ha! Just a while ago I was listening to the Bell Telephone Hour and heard part of* La traviata!

From Denver: *Probably will get to go to church at least with them* [Aunt Joyce's family]. *We have visited couple of these Episcopal jobs, sure don't amount to much.*

From the Wigwam Resort in Litchfield Park, Arizona: *Visited Goodyear Farms this morning, 14,000 acres in the valley just west of Phoenix. Picked oranges off a tree and ate them.*

Richard's singing talent was noticed at the University of Arkansas. A member of *Schola Cantorum*, the school's elite opera singing group, he was cast in a number of operas performed in the new Fine Arts Theatre on campus. He appeared in white wig, trefoil hat, and waistcoat in his first performance, *The Barber of Seville.*

In the spring of 1963, Professor Kenneth Ballenger put together a group from the U. of A.'s Opera Workshop to tour ten cities in Arkansas performing selections from the back-alley opera *archy and mahitabel.* Richard was selected for this group, as was the perky music major he was dating, Andrea McCurry of Heber Springs, Arkansas. The group, called the Uarkettes, was wildly popular, singing and acting out the catchy funny lyrics about an alley cat and a cockroach poet who hurled himself onto the keys of a typewriter to create his poetry.

In the fall, the group was selected to entertain USO troops in Europe. Swept up in the excitement and glamour of a trip to Europe, Richard and his girlfriend Andrea decided it would be more fun as a couple. Just a few days before departure, they were married in a private ceremony at the Mountain Inn in Fayetteville.

The media went wild. Statewide newspapers centered on the two of them, proclaiming "European Honeymoon" at a time when few young Arkansas couples could afford a honeymoon abroad.

Kiddo sent newspaper clippings to her family out west. Her oldest sister Helen wrote back:

> *I have <u>never</u> received any news in my life as exciting as your letter and pictures about Richard and Andrea. I just cried, too wonderful for words. They are so good looking and both so talented, is*

wonderful they are interested in the same thing. Russell, you have a sister now.

This is just about the greatest thing to happen in our family. Honeymoon in Europe! How happy and proud it would have made darling little mother. Black, you and Dorris have done a wonderful job on those boys, as we have <u>all</u> said many, many times. I can't stand to think how proud Dad would have been of them.

Except for Uncle Owen's WWII experience in France and Germany, Richard was the first in his direct family line to jump back across the "pond," since the German Schwartz family (Blacks) and the Scots-Irish McSpaddens emigrated to America in the 1700s.

A TASTE OF HONEY

 Instrumental track written by Bobby Scott and Rick Marlow for the 1960 Broadway version of a 1958 British play *A Taste of Honey*. Most popular version recorded by Herb Alpert and the Tijuana Brass for their album *Whipped Cream and other Delights*, 1965. This version won four Grammy Awards.

Black and Kiddo had acquired a 1959 Chevrolet Bel Air V-8, 4-door sedan which they dubbed "the Gray Lizard." Kiddo shared the Lizard with the boys to get them to and from college classes. By sophomore year, Russ rebelled about staying on campus late day, waiting for Richard to get through with music rehearsals. Boys from the Alpha Gamma Rho (AGR) fraternity, historically agriculture-based, spotted Russell in Ag classes. Many of them from across the state knew him from Livestock Expositions and FFA activities. Soon he was tapped for membership and moved to campus.

As a pledge, he found a home in the Mole Hole, the basement of the old red brick AGR house at 410 Arkansas Avenue across from Carnall Hall. He convinced Mother Moore, the housemother, to buy the fraternity's beef from Black, thus helping finance his new digs. He served as President of AGR during both his Junior and Senior years and spearheaded student efforts as the fraternity bought land on Razorback Road to build a new frat house across from the football stadium.

Russell's ever-smiling personality won him many friends. Among other honors, he was elected Senator from the College of Agriculture to the UA Student Senate, where he served as President Pro Tempore. His senior year, he helped a younger friend with his campaign for Student Body President. Mack McLarty won the election and wrote Russ a note of thanks, saying he owed him. Many years later, Mack became Chief of Staff at the White House for his boyhood friend, President Bill Clinton.

Russell's small white Magnavox record player was always spinning vinyl. Jazz had a special place in his heart, with Blues a close second. Herb Alpert's *Whipped Cream* album with the fast, sassy rhythms of the Tijuana Brass was his favorite. Metcalf Records next to UARK Bowl on Dickson Street and Guisinger Music Store on the square in Fayetteville were his hang-outs. Small glass-enclosed sound booths allowed customers to hear an album before buying. He spent hours there and often took a girl he was dating. Closed into the small booths, they leaned their heads together to listen to the smooth music through one set of earphones.

At the end of his senior year in 1966, Russell married that fifth-generation Arkansas girl, Brenda Clem of Branch. Yep, me—the storyteller, the author.

Russell and I had planned to wait two years before marriage, giving me a chance to complete my degree and allowing Russ to complete his military service. An officer in the Air Force ROTC on campus, he intended to train as a pilot. But the war in Vietnam had turned into a quagmire. Planes were routinely shot out of the sky, the pilots captured if not dead. Unspeakable torture stories were being told. Young men we knew were killed or came home maimed. All over the nation, people protested the war.

Recruiters from the United States Peace Corps had come to campus, offering two years of service in a third-world country in lieu of military service. Russell and I volunteered, married, and left for Peace Corps training in upstate New York. A few months after that, we flew to our assignment in Uttar Pradesh, India—a new branch of the Black family adventuring farther into the world.

CALIFORNIA DREAMIN'

♪ Written by John Phillips and his wife Michelle in 1963. Recorded in 1965 by the Mamas and the Papas (John Phillips, Michele Phillips, Denny Doherty, Cass Elliot). Dunhill Records, Hollywood.

In 1966, Black and Kiddo moved upstairs and claimed the home of stone and glass they had built with their own hands. Bright red carpet was installed on the indoor balcony and steps in the middle of the night before Russell and I were married in front of the native stone fireplace.

Furniture for the spacious great room kept Kiddo hopping. She bought matching red sofas from Roy Clinton at Lewis Brothers in Fayetteville on the installment plan. (Roy's cousin, Bill, later became Governor of Arkansas and, well, you know the rest.) She hired a man in Siloam Springs to refinish the old golden oak table, chairs, and hutch bought long ago in Chickasha, Oklahoma. They were still sturdy after all these years and, with their new finish, looked perfect by the hearth of the small rock fireplace off the kitchen. Then she hit farm sales and auctions for antiques and eventually filled every nook and cranny with her special finds.

Kiddo chose the color of her eyes for the décor palette. Her bluebonnet eyes still sparkled like the dew amid copious amounts of light blue eyeshadow accentuated by deep blue eyeliner and mascara. The kitchen sported a delft blue-patterned carpet. Blue willow china decorated the walls. A two-toned blue shag covered the master bath's floor. Blue.

Later, Black described what four years of hard work had brought them:

At the crest of the hill we turn off highway 62 into a driveway lined with native trees: oak, elm, wild cherry, and dogwood, growing just as nature planted them. The driveway, being careful not to disturb, curves gracefully among them. A plump fox squirrel scampers through the glistening brown leaves and races up a giant red oak, three feet thick and probably three centuries old! A monarch, towering above the others.

And now, we stop beside a large native stone home, as striking in its appearance as the red oak. The long massive wall is a masterful arrangement of large and small, thick and thin stone; sometimes extending to form ledges and outcrops, and in other instances receding into shadowy niches. The two-inch recession of the mortar causes each stone to stand out individually, yet the overall appearance is that of a weather-beaten bluff, eroded by the rigors of nature. At a height of about eight feet a ribbon of windows peek out under the wide overhang of the heavy, yet graceful shake roof. The whole structure blends so completely with the surroundings, it appears to have just raised up out of the hilltop!

As we reach the flagstone patio in front of the house, a swirl of pungent hickory smoke from the chimney rolls over us and out into the wide peaceful valley. Spellbound, we stand gazing at the panorama: the lazy river, winding its way through the bottoms; the highway rushing its impatient traffic to the little town across the valley; the colorful countryside, back-dropped by the renowned Ozarks: What a view!

"Come in out of the cold," a voice says.

A warm radiance engulfs us as we step through the large sliding glass door. The entire front of the house is glass except for the great stone fireplace. Here is the most delightful blending of design, feeling, and décor we have ever witnessed! Here is a wonderful contemporary balance of rugged stone walls and warm paneling, of shining flagstone floors and rich red carpeting, a spacious area made homey by well-chosen furniture, some antique, some modern.

Our eyes meet. "This is it. Our dream home."

Black got that horse he wanted, a top-quality quarter-horse stallion named Leo's Top. He sat easy in the saddle, an authentic cowboy, consummate horseman. Top was bred from racing stock, so Black hired a trainer and a jockey and entered him in regional quarter-horse races. Horse and owner stood in the winner's circle several times, but it didn't last long. Expenses far outweighed winnings. Top was retired to the farm as a stud and Black became a horse trader like his father for a few years. Below the hill, he built a small horse barn. Then for Kiddo he acquired Jubilee, a light chestnut with flaxen mane and tail and, later, Fancy, Fine Lady, Bandida, Niña.

Black enjoyed the horses but couldn't lose himself in them as he had when he was young. Passion was missing. All those building projects had fed his soul with the powerful feeling of mastery, of creating something, or seeing a project through from beginning to end. Surely there was some way to accomplish that without building more houses and barns.

He responded to a magazine ad for Bennett Cerf's Famous Writers School in Westport, Connecticut and was gullible enough to send them installments that amounted to $900 for their correspondence writing course, much more than he would have spent taking classes at the local university. A few years later, in 1970, journalist Jessica Mitford debunked the Famous Writing School in an exposé in *The Atlantic* that ignited a national scandal.

Why I Am Studying Writing
By Keith L. Black

"Work" is fast becoming a "dirty word" in our society. To work with one's hands is to be scorned as if the worker were slow or dim-witted. Some parents admonish their children to learn to get by so that they might not have to "work" for a living. Television constantly reminds the homemaker of the household drudgery involved in washing clothes and dishes and distasteful routine of caring for the family. Certainly, we need not go back to the old

and painful ways of doing things. However, there is an urgent need to put dignity and honor back into our work.

Henry Ford, when asked for his advice to young men replied, "Learn all you can about everything you can." This I have kept in mind while raising two sons who are now grown and married.

All my life I have worked with my hands: With a stone hammer and trowel I can lay a stone wall as well as any mason. With saw and hammer I can build a house or cabinet with the journeyman carpenter. With land and tractor I can raise crops as bountiful as my neighbor. With horse and saddle I can ride with the professionals. With pick and shovel I can dig ditches with any man.

These and many other things I have done; all of which are work. Hard work. Also, I have studied long and hard at the various phases of work which I have undertaken. None of these jobs have been unbearable. None bear the stigma of illiteracy or slow-wittedness. Work is honorable, and when accomplished with pride it renders great satisfaction.

The lady who says apologetically, "I'm just a housewife, that's all" seems to imply that her lot in life is a fretful mixture of dirty dishes and clothes, noisy children and pets, scanty budgets and emergencies. Actually, she is a top-flight executive bargaining in the marketplace for food and clothing, a personnel manager and counselor, the plant superintendent, and charged with the greatest of all responsibilities: to help raise a new generation which will take over the world of tomorrow! What more awesome and responsible position could a woman hold?

It is with these thoughts in mind that I now enter into a new field of work: writing. To me writing extends a challenge. I have worked hard with my hands, and now I will work equally hard with my brain.

If I can learn to express myself as I should, then I might—I just might—be able to lend a little dignity to someone who regards himself as unimportant. A ditch digger need not curse his calloused hands and tired shoulders but consider himself as an individual who has had a part in bringing fresh water to the community.

These words from Lord Byron express my fondest dream in writing:
"Words are things, and a small drop of ink,
Falling like dew upon a thought, produces
That which makes thousands, perhaps millions,
Think."

Black submitted his first story to *Reader's Digest* magazine. It was rejected. He stopped writing. The typewriter he bought worked well enough, but his two-fingered typing was not accurate, and the messes he made with carbon paper and white-out were exasperating. Kiddo couldn't type either, plus the budget was getting tight again. He could foresee that money wouldn't be rolling in from writing stories.

He contacted his architect friend, E. Fay Jones, who hired him immediately to work on the Applegate House in Bentonville, Arkansas. Constructed of native stone with rounded walls and an indoor swimming pool, the Applegate was one of Fay's largest houses and a challenge. Black worked on other Fay Jones houses around the area, including one in Joplin, Missouri, that required a daily 100-mile commute.

Along with his rock work and tending the horses, he had kept his small Hereford herd in good health, even built a weaning house for the calves. Then a cattle proposal sucked him back in full-time. This new deal came from the feral Sundowner neighbor, Daniel B. Thomas.

Black and Danny had a capricious relationship. Sometimes Black worked for him, then things blew up or a paycheck bounced, and they parted ways again. Danny bored with a big auger and had tried to start a vertically integrated beef business in Arkansas, much as Tyson Foods had done with poultry. He had purchased and leased adjacent land making the Sundowner 1,250 acres. Besides feeder cattle, he ran a herd of registered Texas Longhorns, a herd of Charolais, some Herefords and Angus as well as a small herd of buffalo and a breeding program for quarter horses. Everything Daniel B. Thomas did was over the top.

Danny moved to Arkansas from El Cajon, California, where he had run for Congress and lost by only three percent. In San Diego, he owned an apartment building, construction company, trailer park, and music publishing business. He knew how to hustle money and shuffle it around. A commercial pilot, he flew his own plane around the world to sing evangelical music and give anti-communist speeches. He had once flown five missionaries to the Amazon. As he waited for them, he got word that they had been eaten by head hunters. His story.

Danny exuded too much bluster and grandstanding to be trusted by the locals though he put a little salve on the wounds when he was quoted in *Northwest Arkansas Times* as saying that Northwest Arkansas must be a lot like Eden. "I sleep with the windows and doors open. I love the smell of the clean Ozark air. People don't appreciate it if they haven't had to breathe the air of a big city."

His vertical integration project for the beef industry didn't move fast enough. Stand-offish locals wouldn't hop on board. Danny learned that Black, besides having the community's respect, also had a lot of experience with herd improvement, genetics, artificial insemination, and other breeding practices. Just the man he needed for his newest lightbulb idea. He invited his neighbor for coffee and presented his proposal.

Black barely spoke to Kiddo for the next few days, save the niceties of getting through the day-to-day.

"Black, what's wrong with you?" Kiddo got up and turned off the TV one night, then pulled her chair to sit directly facing Black. "I can see your brain boiling. What are you figuring on? You haven't said two words since your meeting with Dan Thomas."

"Oh, that showboat! I can't decide if I want to get tangled up with him again or not."

"Black, you like everybody, but somehow you've got a burr under your saddle about Danny. What's wrong with him?"

"How much time you got? It's a long list."

"Just tell me."

"Well, to start with, he's a fake. He's not a cowboy. Just a California oozer. Wears that Tom Mix hat and alligator boots, those flashy Western-style suits. He's all hat and no cattle, like they say about some Texans."

"Now don't go disparaging my Texas boys," Kiddo interjected.

"I said *some*. What kind of cowboy do you know who stuffs his pants legs in the top of his boots and pulls his jeans up above his waist? Richard calls him the Great Wazoo."

"Well, maybe he doesn't want to get his pants dirty. Did you think of that?"

"Aw, come on, Kiddo, you know what I'm talking about."

"Yes, I do. But I also know it's not like you to be so judgmental. He's not that different from you."

"Ha! Daylight and dark."

"He's a dreamer, Black, just like you. Maybe he doesn't look like a cowboy, but he sure wants to be one. He's trying to make a success of ranching, just like you did in New Mexico and over at Salem Springs and even right there on the Sundowner. He's doing it for his kids, to get them out of the city, to give them something to hold to. Doesn't that sound like you?"

"Maybe, but . . ."

"And what about the singing? You both believe in God and sing hymns. Are you a little jealous that he flies around the world and performs in big concerts and you didn't get to do that?"

"No, I'm not jealous. All that brass clanging, I don't know how anybody hears his voice anyway." From his recliner, Black looked out across the valley, took a long slow pull off his cigar and added, "Me and God, we're good with my choices."

"Maybe he needs you to teach him how to be a real cowboy."

"I'm not sure that can be taught. That's inside. Being a cowboy is in here." Black thumped his chest.

"Well, maybe you can help Danny put some cowboy inside," Kiddo said. "Now, what is it he wants you to do?"

Black explained the premise. Danny's big idea was to import exotic breeds of cattle from Europe to cross with American breeds to improve meat production. Initially, this would be done by importing semen from championship bulls. This was a long-range plan that would require a lot of record-keeping, waiting for births, more cross-breeding, etc. It would also require large investments of capital. With the U.S. tax code allowing deductions for farming and ranch enterprises, Danny proposed selling these animals to rich people, such as doctors and lawyers, in need of tax shelters.

That's why he wanted Black. Not only did Black understand the complexity of the program, his honest sparse-words manner invited trust, whereas Danny's verbose Wazoo-ness spooked these solid-ground, middle of the country investors.

So, they hooked up. The New Mexico and California dreamers. The hymn singers. An unlikely pair who grew to understand and respect the other. Over the next decade, mid-1960s to mid-1970s, they imported semen and later the animals themselves. They were among the first in the United States to integrate these exotic breeds: Simmental, Maine Anjou, Blondie de Aquitaine, Chianina, Limousin.[13] Investment meetings were held at big hotels in Tulsa, Oklahoma City, Kansas City, Fort Worth, and Houston, as well as at the Sundowner Ranch. Danny Thomas learned to take his pants legs out of his boots. Black learned not to judge a book by its cover. Danny was shrewd but not dishonest, just trying to make his way, to find a better life.

Always a search for a better life.

Black entertained investors from Canada, Australia, and Great Britain—all pulled to the little town of Prairie Grove, Arkansas, to participate in the exotic cattle business. In South Dakota, he rounded up buffalo from a small plane with breeder Warren Melvin. At a fancy hotel in Houston, exotic bulls were paraded through the lobby and later auctioned. Black managed the sale where the top bull went over $100,000. Average price for a new import was $60,000, but rich Texas oilmen got caught up in the drama of absurd prices and waged a one-upmanship battle. Other investors bought shares, called units, if they couldn't afford the whole animal, buying perhaps a sixteenth of a bull. Profit would be made when the bull's semen was sold or when a cow's offspring was sold for breeding stock, or the animal itself was resold for an even higher price.

They made a lot of money for a lot of investors, themselves included. And somewhere along the way, a Texas Longhorn gored Black through the shoulder. Kiddo called him a showoff, said he just had to prove he was a real cowboy. He recuperated in his recliner, telling true tales of growing up on the high plains of New Mexico to the parade of well-wishers.

With this new income, Black hired carpenters, brothers Larry and Harold Bottoms of Prairie Grove, to finish the interior of their home. Kiddo bought more antiques and more clothes from Town and Country and discovered Charles of the Ritz cosmetics at Campbell-Bell's in Fayetteville. The Prairie Grove Church of Christ's collections also increased dramatically.

Then the bottom fell out.

After several years, the Internal Revenue Service closed the loophole that allowed the deduction for these types of enterprises. Investment dollars dried up. Black and Danny scrambled as they were left with $60,000 animals and no market. As Kenny Rogers sang about that time, they learned too late when to fold, when to walk away, and when to run.

That Concho-size flood of money began to drain away.

Disheartened, Danny left the Sundowner, hoping to find another Eden for himself and his family elsewhere. The two-story landmark barn burned one night, illuminating the sky for miles. The Big

House and the House on the Hill sat empty. The land was sold and sold again.

But this sumptuous valley was never loved as much as when the Blacks ran the Phildale Dairy or when, like Camelot for one brief shining moment, Keith L. Black and Daniel B. Thomas operated an international cattle business on The Sundowner, an honest-to-God big time ranch. A real-life, come-true dream for two dreamers.

Eventually, a new sign was erected: a huge native stone slab reading SUNDOWNER ESTATES. Chopped into lots, the fertile land has grown its last and most expensive crop: tall-roofed houses. But the unruly Illinois River refuses to be tamed. Spring rains often overwhelm its bottomland and send flash floods across Highway 62. The hurried vehicles are forced to stop and respect the last vestiges of wild nature in the Prairie Grove Valley. Bankside trees still hold the rookery for great blue herons. Ancient gars swim the river. Snapping turtles bury themselves in its mud. Wild coyotes run the banks, their yipping howls sending fear to the hearts of children in the tall-roofed houses.

STAND BY YOUR MAN

 Written by Tammy Wynette and Billy Sherrill. Recorded by Tammy Wynette for Epic Records, 1968.

Black was away from home more than he had ever been, wrangling those exotic cattle with Danny Thomas. Kiddo didn't mind. She was too busy to feel lonesome. Furnishing and decorating the house was fun. One time at a farm auction, she bought a lovely antique table with rope legs. As she paid out, she overheard a man ask his wife if she had won her table. The wife said, "No, that fancy woman that lives in that big rock house on the hill outbid me."

Oh, Kiddo was thrilled. Imagine, being called fancy. She knew she shouldn't be prideful, but . . . Fancy! And she wasn't even wearing a hat!

At another auction, a small spinning wheel fascinated her. She bought it. Well, things should be for use, not just decoration, so she learned to spin wool and weave small pieces. She also took embroidery lessons and made several samplers. Calligraphy caught her attention, but it was quite tedious with pen and ink. She had Women's Club work, the Battlefield Park Auxiliary, church work, and trips to the library every few days for more books to read.

One should always strive to better oneself. That's what I believe.

Middle age was working out for Kiddo. Her grandchildren brought a special joy that helped revive a sense of wonder. Richard's son, Keith, called her Nano. She became Granna to Russell's sons, Stephen and Jeffrey. Black was called Poppie. Another generation of little Black men. Watch out, world! No little women until Richard acquired a step-daughter, Cindy Weatherall, with his second marriage.

Kiddo cooked a lot of elegant family dinners that took days to prepare and more days to rest up. The recipes were elaborate though not exotic because Black was always a meat and potatoes man. She planned everything upscale (a new word for her) and used linen tablecloths and napkins, candles, and flowers. The table was set with Royal Bavarian china that she bought from her German friend at the Fayark China Shop. Gold trim on scalloped edges, delicate rosebud handles on lidded bowls. She paid for the set herself with money earned by serving on a federal jury in Fort Smith. It was an important case involving a high-up official with the Athletic Department at the University of Arkansas.[14] Made Kiddo proud to do her duty. She didn't try to get out of it like most people, though there were some harrowing days driving over Highway 59's icy mountain roads to Fort Smith.

Kiddo liked to have a lot of animals around besides the cows and horses. Once she tried raising peafowl but her big peacock, Greep, liked to go visiting. When he escaped, it took the whole community to track him down, get him out of the trees and back home again. The police knew who to call when someone reported a strange bird making a weird sound in their yard. She took her peahen Greepette along on retrieval missions.

She raised several batches of Siamese cats and English bulldogs and more than a few mutts. She was devastated when her beloved German shepherd named Schone died after many years by her side. Then her hairdresser Rosalee gave her a tiny Cairn terrier, the runt of the litter. Kiddo named her Little Alice. The kids laughed at the way her lilting little-girl's voice said "Li'l Alice," and the dog became quite the family joke. Black didn't care much for the little wiry mop-haired dog. She barked at the slightest sound or movement and snarled at visitors.

One night Li'l Alice kept jumping on and off the bed, then running to the front door barking. Kiddo would get up, go downstairs, and let her out, then she'd bark to get back in. She just wouldn't settle down. In and out. Out and in. Kiddo couldn't sleep and got upset with her. She scolded the dog, held her down on the bed and said, "Li'l Alice, you stop this foolishness and stay put."

She got a couple of hours sleep, then Little Alice started up again, barking at the front door. Kiddo put her out, told her she had to stay out this time. A bit later, she again heard Alice barking like mad.

Black woke up and said, "I'm fixin' to kill that stupid little dog."

"I'll take care of it, Black," Kiddo said. She figured it was stray cats prowling around, riling up her little dog. She rushed down the stairs and out the back door in her shorty gown.

Things got real quiet when she opened the door, no barking at all. The moon was full and bright. Kiddo called out whisper-like, so Black wouldn't hear, "Li'l Alice, Li'l Alice, where are you? Come to Mama. Come-come," but the dog was nowhere. She stepped farther into the yard. Then she spied Little Alice, just walking along nonchalant by the rock wall.

Kiddo ran over and picked her up, tucked her under her arm and gave her several swats on her behind. "Li'l Alice, what in the cat hair has gotten into you?"

The animal turned its head up and hissed, "Hiss, hissss." An ugly pink nose starred up.

Mercy! It was a possum Kiddo had grabbed up and spanked!

"Shoo," she said and flung the fool thing down. She ran one way and he lit out the other with that naked tail straight out behind him. Li'l Alice showed up and chased him into the woods, barking the whole way, then ran back, proud of herself. The troupers marched upstairs and went straight to bed. Li'l Alice didn't have anything else to say the rest of the night.

Kiddo shouldn't have told Black. He told everyone else. She never lived down the incident of Kiddo Spanking the Possum. [15]

Kiddo and "Li'l Alice."

In the 1980s Black started a church. He got sideways with another elder, Ed Broyles, at the Prairie Grove Church of Christ. Ed had been a close friend, but he supported using the church treasury to build a new church building. Black didn't think God lived inside, so he wasn't in favor of a larger, grander edifice. He thought the money should be spent helping church members and doing mission work. As arguments grew, people took sides. Eventually, Black left the church. Several members joined him, urging him to start another congregation.

This was an unhappy time in Kiddo's life. She stood by his side and walked the journey with him. But Ed's wife Mildred was her closest friend. Mildred's father's family, the Berrys, were from Warren County, Tennessee, same as her Berrys. They figured they were distant cousins somehow. Women's Club meetings became awkward.

Choices must be made. I made mine years ago when I said, "I do."

The new church met at the American Legion until they purchased an old house on East Buchanan Street. Black and others converted the two-story saltbox into a small meeting room and classrooms. The members were faithful and loyal to Black. But after a few years, there weren't enough people or contributions to sustain a congregation.

The house was sold, money returned to the members or given to missions. Black donated their share to a church in Fayetteville where they drove for Sunday services. Meanwhile, the church in Prairie Grove had erected a much larger building with a beautiful sanctuary.

"Some-some, Kiddo. Some-some." Black said one evening after studying his Bible in quiet. He crushed out his cigar, stood up and plopped his Stetson on his head.

"What are you talking about? Where are you going?"

"Where the fault lies. Some me, some him. Some-some, like everything in this life. I'm going to talk it out with Ed Broyles. Take my medicine, hope he takes his."

That easy, the feud ended. The next Sunday, they returned to their community church, the prodigal son warmly welcomed by most. Black led song service that day.

"Some-some" summed up Black's philosophy on just about everything as he aged. Not black, not white, truth lies somewhere in the gray middle. Though an egalitarian from the time he was hatched, a younger Black could be highly opinionated on certain subjects. *Yep, highly.*

During drought money spells, Black and Kiddo had sold off chunks of their land. The corner where the two highways intersect was the first to go. That sale funded building materials for the house. They were upset when the man who bought it constructed long chicken houses, the pungent smell drifting to their front door during hot summers. A small travel trailer was moved in as living quarters for the old man who cared for the chickens. They could see Charlie through the trees as he slowly went about his duties. Black walked over, introduced himself and invited the neighbor to dinner. He declined.

"I keep to myself," he said.

Black kept inviting the cantankerous old goat.

Charlie had no car, no family, and no last name. Of Italian descent, short and frail, he cussed like a sailor. They wore down a bit of his

I'm-an-island attitude. He allowed Kiddo to drive him to the grocery store now and then. Black chauffeured him to the doctor a few times. He came to supper only when he could bring a live chicken, escapee from the catching crews. Black built a chicken coop halfway between their houses. Charlie and Kiddo shared the eggs and had a few plucking, processing parties.

Eccentric folk don't bother us. People must be who they are.

Years later, the landowner abandoned the chicken houses, sold the trailer, and told Charlie to move. *Gee fuzz*, where was the old buzzard supposed to go? No family, no Social Security because his employer had paid him in cash, no homeless shelters.

Black figured and came up with a plan. On Richard's farm stood an unused concrete-block dairy barn. Black stopped his doings and converted that space into two livable rooms for Charlie. They provided a bed and a comfy chair and kept him in groceries and visits. Not the Ritz, but cozy.

Charlie lived in the dairy barn until he died in his sleep.

Black didn't wear his religion on his sleeve. He lived it. Seems like the lonely, the oddballs, the down-in-the-mouth folks, flocked to him. He put smiles on faces with his easy-going ways and his story-telling. Kiddo did her part, too. She cooked a nice meal for whoever he dragged home. Visited with them. Treated them with dignity. *The least of these my brethren.*

Black and Kiddo hadn't returned to New Mexico since moving to Arkansas except for one quick trip in the 1960s to show off their first grandbaby, Keith. In 1985, Russell and I bought a recreational vehicle (RV). Our sons, Stephen and Jeffrey, were young teenagers. They had grown up hearing Poppie stories and wanted to see his West. The six of us made the journey in our version of a covered wagon, the RV.

Out through the panhandle of Oklahoma and into New Mexico along the Dry Cimarron, following the Loving-Goodnight trail, the same path of the wooden-wheeled covered wagon that carried Corwin and Albert (A. B.) Black—these youngsters' great and great-great grandfathers—into the Territory before statehood. The high-desert plains were still sparsely settled, an almost-deserted and inhospitable land. Hard to imagine thousands of heads of cattle being herded through there. The RV clanked and rattled over the sandy washboard road. Dry dust sifted in, coating everything and everybody.

Red Black had moved from the home place to a comfortable house in Des Moines. In his fifties, he had married a schoolteacher named Willie Pearl Adams, the first marriage for both. He gave up ranching, leased the land to others, and took a job as rural mail carrier, a job he dutifully performed for over thirty years.

Razz, long divorced from his third wife, still ran cows on his portion of the family ranch but had also moved to town.

At the old home place, the Black Family Ranch, the house and outbuildings stood deserted, looking the same as the day Red had moved out. Buildings stand forever in this dry land. Rot isn't a problem. Furniture, old papers, pictures, and other domestic debris were strewn about. A dilapidated ¾-ton 1941 Chevy, the ranch truck that long-ago had brought baby Russell home from Miners' Hospital in Raton, sat abandoned beside the house, camouflaged in tall grass.

Black claimed an old wooden pendulum clock from the mantle to give to Richard. Russell dug a rusty wagon wheel and horseshoe from the equipment yard. Then Red gave him the saddle that A. B. Black had ridden in the Oklahoma Land Run. When I admired an antique Remington Standard typewriter, Red smiled.

"That belonged to my dad, Albert Black," he said. "He was an educated man. Brought it out in the covered wagon with us from Kansas in 1913. I can still see him pecking on it." He passed the typewriter into my hands. "It's yours now. They tell me you're a writer. That would have pleased him."

Later, Razz joined the family at Red and Willie Pearl's house.

The spark and wittiness of his youth were missing. He now wore A. B.'s solemn demeanor. Maybe three failed marriages and no children will do that to a man. Russell parked the RV nearby and serious visiting ensued over the next few days. As the Arkansawyers were leaving, Razz handed Russell, his namesake, an envelope with a hundred-dollar bill inside.

"To help with expenses. Thanks for bringing Black and Kiddo to see us. Best days I've had in a long time. Your dad is like a brother to me."

On the backside of Emery Peak near Tollgate Canyon, Black and Kiddo returned to their own place. It had been more than thirty years since they drove away. The fields had been fenced with barbed wire, the road grown over with bear grass and sideoats grama. Chaparrals skittered as Russell parked the RV on the shoulder of NM456. Six Blacks crawled through the fence, forded the Cimarron, and hiked to the old house on the side of the draw, the first of many such pilgrimages for Black sons, grandsons, and great-grandchildren.

As we walked, Black recited a poem *(I think he wrote it)* for the umpteenth time. The grandsons joined in on the last lines, making mock-horror faces:

The old Gray Mare lay on the ground.
Ten Thousand Buzzards gathered around.
One said, "Ain't this a Pie?"
Another reached over and plucked out an Eye!

Then he noticed that the wind charger on the hill was gone. That prompted a story he had been too embarrassed to tell:

Many years earlier, he had worked for weeks, cutting timber to build a tower for the wind charger. It had been constructed on the ground, then pulled into position using an elaborate cable system incorporating a few tractors and trucks. Several neighbors plus Red, Razz, and Corwin had helped with the project. After a grueling day, the tower was finally in place. Kiddo cooked vittles for everybody. Then the others went home, and Black fell asleep exhausted. The next morning, he woke late and remembered he was expected at a job site in Folsom. Rushing, he ran to his truck, jumped in, and floored it.

Creak! Bang! Plop! The tower crashed, barely missing his truck. He had forgotten to unhook the cables and pulled it down as he sped away.

We laughed at his story, but Kiddo recalled how angry she was that day. "I was so mad. Days of work down the drain. For all Black's creativity and work ethic, he has an uncanny knack for carelessly making things harder on himself and on those around him. Good thing he married a forgiving person who tolerates his erstwhile foolishness, don't you think? Tee-hee."

Arriving at the draw, we toured their old abandoned home, admonishing the youngsters to keep an eye out for "shake-tails." No one had lived in the sturdy house since the family left thirty years earlier. Kiddo turned the Lazy-Susan in the kitchen cupboard and opened the wood chute, searching for a Germit.

Outside, Black pointed out dozens of deer antlers still attached to the windmill tower where he had mounted them so long ago.

Russell showed Stephen and Jeffrey the petroglyphs on Indian Rock. They scrambled to the top, their imaginations searching for Indians just as Kiddo's boys had done.

On the first bench, Russell and I held hands and walked in silence, tracing the stone circles where teepees once stood. We found a small petrified horn from a buffalo calf among the stones.

The family climbed to the third bench and higher yet, to get to Black's majestic viewpoint. Nothing had moved since he last stood there. Capulin Volcano, Sierra Grande, Rabbit Ears, the vast grasslands, Laughlin Peak, the Sangre de Cristos on the western horizon: steadfast as ever.

Black's love of this ancient land seeped through the generations and permeated us all.

"I used to ride my horse up here when I was your age," he told his grandsons, "just to feel this place. See that tiny wooden windmill way down there? That's the home place. That's where I rode from."

Kiddo saw the tears coming. Black rubbed his eyes with the cuff of his sleeve.

"Her name was Ginger."

A few years later, Red phoned Black from New Mexico. "Razz had a heart attack. They've taken him to the hospital in Trinidad. Better come quick if you want to see him."

Black and Kiddo packed furiously, hopped in their little Dodge Colt, and sped away.

Razz had improved by the time they arrived twelve hours later. They sat by his bedside, Black telling stories, saying his little sayings, making Razz smile. His voice was weak, so he beckoned Black to lean in.

Razz asked for paper. "Don't have a will. I want my land to go to you and Russell. Write that down. I'll sign it."

Black was stunned. "Don't worry about that, Razz," he said. "Doc says you're better. Let's wait till you're up and around again, see how you feel then."

"Never know. Promises not kept toward you." Razz's voice was raspy. He spoke in short bursts, but that wasn't new. Thin and frail, he looked like a small child in that white hospital bed. "You and Russell been calling, writing me all these years. Got his boys' pictures in my wallet. Fine boys. You're my family, Black. Get the paper. I'll sign it. Or get Red in here, so I can tell him."

"Red's not here."

"Some other witness, then."

"Tomorrow's soon enough," Black said.

A second heart attack in the night took Razz home as Black and Kiddo slept in a Trinidad motel.

Black never told Red about Razz's request. The land was sold. Proceeds were divided according to New Mexico law between his surviving brothers (Red and Norman) and various nieces and nephews. Black's part as nephew was $30,000. He gave $10,000 each to Richard and Russell and bought himself a used pickup.

A decade later, with Red suffering from Alzheimer's, his wife Willie Pearl sold the remaining Black land to a great-nephew of hers shortly before she died. Russell learned of the sale a year later when Red passed. He tried to buy a parcel of the land to hold onto for the family. The great-nephew wouldn't sell.

The ninety-year-old Black Family Ranch near Des Moines, New Mexico—over 2,000 acres of paradise at its peak—also passed away.

AMAZING GRACE

Words written in 1748 by John Newton, after his ship survived a violent storm off County Donegal, Ireland. First published in 1779 in John Newton and William Cowper's Olney Hymns. Sung to various melodies until 1835, when it was joined with a tune named "New Britain."

Thro' many dangers, toils, and snares
I have already come;
'Tis grace hath brought me safe thus far,
And grace will lead me home.

After the exotic cattle business exploded in the mid-1970s, Black settled back at home with his Chianina herd and his well-dressed Kiddo. Then his fingers began to hurt. A rare visit to the doctor revealed arthritis in his 55-year-old hands.

"What do I do, doc?" Black asked.

"Find something to keep your fingers moving," the doc said. "I recommend you get a tennis ball and squeeze it every chance you get."

Black wasn't a tennis-ball squeezing kind of guy. Too bad there were no cows to milk. He came up with a better idea. Wood-carving. He had carved little creamy-colored horses from orange crate slats when he was a youngster and carved toys for his boys back in New Mexico. Maybe try that again.

Russell and I were erecting greenhouses on our farm to supply our fledgling plant business. A building project. Black helped, of course, and Kiddo supplied frequent lunches and picnics for the work crew. One evening Black took home the ends that had been cut from six-inch-square redwood posts being used for greenhouse support. He dug out his pocket knife and started whittling. Telling Kiddo that he would clean it up later, he sat in his recliner with his stogie in his mouth and let the cuttings drop into his lap and onto the flagstone floor.

A few nights later he had carved two realistic busts, Apache Brave and Apache Maiden. Effuse praise came from everyone who saw them.

Black started figuring on a new dream. Not too late to chase success again. No half-way measures. *If you're going to do something, do it!* Using Kiddo's library card, he checked out every book in the Prairie Grove Library on woodcarving and sculpting. Chunks of cherry and walnut were procured from the local Nations Hardwood. Subject matter came from the Western spirits that lived in his soul. Horses, cowboys, native Americans, mules, mountain lions, and bulls emerged from those wood chunks. Entire scenes were carved in relief: a buffalo wallow, a cowboy burial, a herd of horses.

When he eyed a fallen tree and envisioned *Smoke Dream*, a scene with Apaches dancing around a fire, each limb a different warrior, Kiddo drew the line.

"Now, Black, you're not bringing that old stump into my beautiful living room. It's bad enough with shavings and cigar ashes all over everything. We're not going to live like heathens. Let's make you a place to work downstairs."

They cleaned out the accumulated junk from their old living quarters. The lower level of their home became Black's sculpture studio. His own space. He could be as messy as he needed.

As Black's art progressed, he sought out masters. He found the famous Cherokee wood sculptor, Willard Stone, across the Oklahoma border at the Cherokee Heritage Center in Tahlequah. He made many trips to carve alongside Willard at his studio in Locust Grove. As they carved, the two spiritually-minded men discussed the flow of life. Sometimes they used words.

Later, Black enrolled in sculpting courses at the University of

Arkansas, the oldest student in his classes by far. His instructor, internationally-known sculptor Subrata Lihiri, taught him both the lost wax process and cold cast methods of creating sculptures. A native of India, Professor Lihiri shared Black's mystic inclinations. He helped Black to envision the whole, to see the parts he couldn't see, to embed the completed piece in his mind before he began, thereby circumventing the problem of Black's depth perception due to having only one good eye.

Black's sculptures drew attention. State and local newspapers ran stories. Ernie Deane, journalist for *Arkansas Gazette* and *The Morning News*, featured Black's work in his column and a book, *Ozarks Country*.[16] Asked to teach others, Black taught woodcarving for several years in Fayetteville's community adult education classes. A cadre of followers came for carving lessons and stayed for his wit and wisdom. Tales of his scrapes as a child on the high plains of New Mexico was a favorite topic.

Black began to show his work, locally at first at the Prairie Grove Clothesline Fair and the War Eagle Arts and Crafts show. Then he and Kiddo loaded the back of their Dodge Colt hatchback and drove to art shows and sales in other states. The Trail of Tears show at Tsa-La-Gi in Tahlequah, the Cowboy Hall of Fame's Prix de West in Oklahoma City, as far west as Prescott, Arizona, for the Phippen Museum's Art Show and as far north as Minneapolis, Minnesota to the National Wildlife and Western Art Show where "Visions," his bronze casting of a Native American with three eagles, won Best of Show.

As he moved into creating cold cast and bronze sculptures, commissions were offered: a cast eagle with spread wings for the new First National Bank building on the east side of the Fayetteville Square, a four-foot tall bronze rooster for A. Q. Chicken House in Springdale, a black walnut carving of J. B. Hunt's prized Santa Gertrudis bull, a raven for Billie Jo Starr's Ravenwood, amid many others. To commemorate *The Blue and The Gray*, a TV mini-series filmed in Northwest

Arkansas in the 1980s, he sculpted a limited-edition bronze of two mounted soldiers in combat. The musculature of the horses, the tension of the soldiers, and the accuracy of the details is reminiscent of, and on par with, similar Remington and Russell bronzes.

Black's work was sold in art galleries in Santa Fe and Taos, Oklahoma City and Tulsa, as well as in Ozarks Arts & Crafts stores in Fayetteville and Little Rock. He learned about trust and human nature when he didn't receive payment for pieces sold in the Little Rock gallery. Then it closed. The remaining sculptures disappeared, never returned to him.

In the 1990s, Black's commissions grew to include large pieces of public art. He created a life-size bronze statue of a coal miner for the city of McAlester, Oklahoma. The miner stands on a pedestal in a small park created to honor those who perished in the mines, their names inscribed on a nearby granite wall. His bronze bust of a Vietnam Soldier with gun outstretched was installed at the Veteran's Hospital in North Little Rock. "Antonio," a life-size Italian immigrant, stands on a pedestal in front of City Hall in Tontitown, Arkansas. His last sculpture, created when Black was 84, was placed in a cemetery. Parishoners requested a life-size statue of St. Joseph holding a child for the grave of a young priest who committed suicide and could not be buried in the Catholic cemetery. It is the only religious work that Black created, though spirituality flows through most of his pieces.

Perhaps Black's most spiritual sculptures were the ones he donated to his places of the heart: the small museum in the former Doherty Mercantile building in Folsom, New Mexico, and the Choctaw Nation of Oklahoma, the tribe of his aunt Maybel, who had nursed him as a child.

Black with his wood carvings, "Showdown" and "Sacred Rite."

Black and Kiddo with his eagle sculpture, "The Provider,"
at First National Bank, Fayetteville, Arkansas.

Black and Kiddo at dedication of his sculpture, "Pioneer Coal Miner,"
for the City of McAlester, Oklahoma.

WHEN IRISH EYES ARE SMILING

Lyrics by Chauncey Olcott and George Graff, Jr. Music by Ernest Ball. Published in 1912. Recorded during World War I by Irish Tenor John McCormack.

When Irish Eyes are Smiling, sure 'tis like a morn in spring.
In the lilt of Irish laughter, you can hear the angels sing.
When Irish hearts are happy, all the world seems bright and gay.
And When Irish Eyes are Smiling, sure, they steal your heart away.

To honor her 80th birthday in 1997, Kiddo received an extraordinary gift, a trip to Ireland. We hoped it was enough to make up for all the uncelebrated birthdays.

I arranged a five-week home exchange in Kesh, County Fermanagh, Northern Ireland. Black, Kiddo, Richard, Russell, and I stayed in the home of Mervyn and Adele Walker. Richard's wife, Louise Alexander (an Arkansas native from Conway), was unable to join us. The Walker home made a wonderful base, with attentive neighbors and Mervyn's mom looking out for us. Daily sightseeing excursions in the Walker's car ended with the oldies home in the same beds and with familiar food each night. For farther trips, we stayed in B&Bs a night or two.

Donegal, Killybegs, and Glencolumbkille on the West Coast was our first jaunt. Aren't the names fun? The Atlantic Ocean was ice cold, but the hardy Irish were swimming in it.

The Belleek factory on the shores of the River Erne was a highlight for Kiddo, a member of the Belleek Collector's Society since 1980, when she first discovered the fine parian at Perry's Fine Gifts in Fayetteville. Exquisite tiny green shamrocks decorate the delicate creamy china, so thin you can almost see through it. Kiddo treasured her Belleek teapot. We watched specimens being made, toured the museum, ate in the tearoom and then, *tah-dah*, the gift shop. Kiddo and I fretted, trying to decide which special piece to buy. She finally chose an Irish Harp. With its musical implications, it became a precious token of our Irish adventure.

North to Bushmills, McDonald Castle, the Giant's Causeway, and Carrick-a-Rede Rope Bridge. The cold wind was hateful. It blew like mad. Kiddo had taken lovely clothes for her first and only trip abroad. Liz Fulton at Town and Country Shop had helped her choose beautiful linen suits and summer dresses. She even took a hat thinking we would be dining in elegant places. Unfortunately, traveling abroad wasn't quite the way she had read about in the novels of her youth. Rain poured every day, and even though it was mid-summer, the wet cold penetrated her old bones. I had bought navy blue sweatpants and sweatshirts for me and for her just before we left home. She thought they were ugly and resented the space they took in her luggage. But, *boy oh boy*, we were both glad to have their warmth for our outings.

Southwest to Connemara, Clifden, Galway. Lunch at Ashford Castle. The car was stopped at the border between Northern Ireland and the Republic of Ireland and we were questioned by R.U.C. (Royal Ulster Constabulary) armed guards. Razor wire fences and tall guard towers made us skittish, but soldiers waved us through after checking passports. We middle-of-the-nation Americans had not encountered such borders in our own country.

In Galway, Richard, Russell, and I walked to a pub from the B&B for a magic night of Irish music. More singers and players arrived until the pub was jammed wall to wall with people. Turns out the star musician was a member of the band U2, home for a break between concerts. Lucky us!

A ferry took our band of adventurers to the Aran Islands,

Black's and Kiddo's first time on a large boat. Black turned green, sea-sick. Open heart surgery had leveled him six weeks earlier, leaving a long scar on his chest to match the one Kiddo had from the same surgery two years earlier. When he had his attack, Kiddo thought her Ireland trip was a goner. But he cowboyed up and there they were, gray-headed world travelers, Kiddo with her cane, Black with a little blue oxygen pack dangling from his shoulder. They kept calm and carried on.

While we younger ones explored the sea cliffs and the old stone fort, Dun Aengus, they waited on a bench in a small garden. Then Black spotted an Irish pony-trap for hire. "Kiddo, want to go for a ride and see the sights?"

Somehow those old bodies clambered into the high cart. A courteous Irishman in a wool tweed vest and paddy cap ferried the American tourists about the island, sharing its history and culture and his own family stories in his charming brogue, the sound of it making

Kiddo's heart sing. It was a magical ride that she didn't want to end, so they sat in the cart having an Irish gab until we joined them again. Richard took their picture.

President Bill Clinton had put Arkansas on the map. When we told people we were from Arkansas, they invariably asked if we knew Bill Clinton. We were proud that someone from our little state could be elected President. It felt like kin had won the lottery and passed some along. We held our heads a bit higher with this proof that dreams do come true when you come from a place called Hope. Bill had done an outstanding job as Governor and, as far as we could tell, an even better job as President. The U.S. economy was humming right along. Russell and I had visited with Bill when he came to Prairie Grove as Governor to dedicate a new industrial plant. Another time, I had helped host a reception for Hillary, but tornado warnings canceled the event. So, no, none of us Blacks knew them personally, but the Clintons were friendly and open and felt like kindred citizens. *If only Hillary would cut that long hair!*

In Belfast, we visited the shipyards where many Scots-Irish emigrants had left for America and the Botanic Gardens near Queen's University.

Later, on another outing to the National Stud in County Kildare, Black eyed the thoroughbreds. "Sure wish I could climb up on one of those stallions and take off riding again. Wouldn't that be fine?"

"It would," Kiddo answered. "And I wish I could hop on stage with the Irish step-dancers. Kick up my knees like *Riverdance* in those lovely high steps, keeping pace with the merry jigs. The fiddlers are intoxicating, aren't they? I can just see Grandpa Green Berry clicking his heels in the air."

Kiddo finally got to wear her hat and linen suit to afternoon tea at the Shelbourne in Dublin. Oh, so elegant. Luscious buttery scones, dainty finger sandwiches, rich little desserts, fruit and cheese, and more types of tea than she knew existed. *Oh, if my dear little mother could see me now.*

The most exciting adventure was the one to County Down in Ulster province, where Kiddo met her McSpadden kin. Her daddy John had told the story of his ancestors coming to County Down from Scotland during the Plantation around 1640 and staying for a hundred years before immigrating to America. Kiddo looked in the phone book and called every McSpadden listed. The last one, Barbara McSpadden, said, "My son has been digging into this genealogy stuff. He would be interested in talking to you. He's on a trip to Portugal right now, but back soon. He works in Belfast, an Aeronautical Engineer."

A week later, we traveled to a B&B in Rathfriland, where Clifford McSpadden came to meet us that evening. As soon as Kiddo saw him, she proclaimed him kin. A tad over thirty, tall and handsome, he looked like the McSpaddens in the picture of her dad and his six brothers. She burst into tears and embraced this image of her father. After a short visit, he invited us to be guests in his home the following night. We protested. After all, we were five complete strangers from a foreign land, but he insisted.

The next morning we drove to Clifford and Joanne McSpadden's home in the lush Irish countryside near Banbridge. Clifford was standing out front with his wee daughter Holly hanging onto his leg. Later we learned that she had just asked him, "How will we know, Daddy, if they are really kin?"

"Well," Clifford had answered, "it is really difficult to be sure, Holly, but there are two things to look out for. First of all, that beautiful clear blue, pool-like eye colour that runs through the family is a good start. The second is if they are Presbyterians."

As Kiddo walked toward them, both of them looked into her eyes and smiled at each other. When she then confirmed her Presbyterian/Methodist roots, wee Holly seemed to have all the proof she needed.

Clifford had taken the day off work. In his blue SUV, he drove us across the mystic Mountains of Mourne with their graceful sweeps to the Irish sea. Emerald green pastures divided by stacked rock fences reminded us of Arkansas.

"I've hiked these mountains since I was a boy," Clifford said. "I like it best when I climb alone. The gradual ascension makes me feel closer to God."

Black grinned. "I know what that feels like," he said. "Only, my mountains weren't green."

Clifford treated us to a lovely fish lunch at the seaside in Annalong, then directed us to a small beach where the Irish Sea rolls granite into delightful hard baseballs, souvenirs to make our suitcases heavier. Back in Rathfriland, we stopped on top of the hill for its famous ice cream cones. Then to Drumballyroney Church where the Bronte sisters' father had preached before the family moved to England. In the cemetery beside the church, Clifford showed us the grave of Alexander McSpadden, his great-great grandfather. His detective work had produced records back to the 1600s, with the family names of William, John, and Thomas resonating along Kiddo's American family lines. In a different cemetery, he had found an old grave of Thomas McSpeden. Records showed that some of Thomas's offspring had migrated to America. There were still many dots to connect.[17]

Next, Clifford stopped the car in front of huge iron gates connecting six-foot high stone and stucco walls. Beside the gate the dancing blooms of a tree-size cherry-red fuchsia and the sweet smell of honeysuckle welcomed the visitors. Inside the compound, the house and barn were one unit, its red paint faded into splotches. Several slate-covered outbuildings held various farm implements from decades past. We stepped back in time.

"This is the old McSpadden home place, where my grandfather grew up," he said. My second cousins, Sydney and Laureen, still live here, brother and sister. Their father and my grandfather were brothers. They are dear to me, the last of that generation."

Sydney and Laureen were a delight but their Irish brogue was hard on our ears, more difficult to understand than Clifford's worldly-tuned words. Sydney showed us the old guns and the secret door in the barn loft where, long ago, Orangemen held meetings and hid to escape the Irish Republican Army (IRA). Laureen offered tea and showed us the small living quarters where McSpaddens had raised their children for generations. Farmers. Pretty much the same, no matter the country. How warm their welcome.

From the mantle, Laureen took a small silver bell with a leprechaun on top. She handed it to Kiddo. "For you," she said, "it has been here as long as I remember."

For Irish luck, Sydney gave Black a rusty horseshoe from the barn. "Hang it by your door with the ends up, so your luck doesn't run out," he said.

Before we left Kiddo had a request, "Can we go see the land, walk in the fields?"

"Of course. Of course." This seemed to please them, but not as much as it pleased her. Everyone walked down a small hill, through rows of potatoes, the Kelly-green foliage shin high. Kiddo talked about her daddy and all the vegetables he grew in the hot West Texas wind in someone else's soil, how he would have loved this verdant rainy McSpadden land.

Clifford took Kiddo's hand and walked her to the hawthorn hedge at the edge of the field. "Let me show you something that has been waiting here for your return." He pointed to some large, thick stones beneath the thorny green branches.

"These stones will be from a cottage that stood here back in the 1600s and 1700s. They were too big for the farmers of old to move when they farmed the land, so they were simply rolled into the hedge. You could now be standing on the very spot where your ancestor gave his Mummy a final kiss as he left these shores for a new life in America; and you are the first descendant to return to the same spot."

Kiddo's tears were the only replies she could muster, tears of sadness for that Mummy and tears of joy for this homecoming.

She sent Russell to the car to get the camera and the rolls of extra film. When he got back, we took pictures. Then she asked him to take the film out of the small canisters.

"Let's fill them with soil," she said. "I want to take some homeland back with me, some to keep, some to put on Daddy's grave."

There must not be a No-Tears Rule in Ireland because there we all were, crying with no shame while filling little plastic film canisters with rich Irish soil. Then we stood in a circle holding hands, while Clifford said a prayer.

Family. People of the heart. I doubt a paper trail can be found to connect Kiddo's McSpaddens to these gracious people. No matter. Family is where you find them. She found these an ocean away during the sunset of her life.

That night we went home with Clifford and spent time with his wife Joanne and their young children: Scott, Glenn, and Holly. Clifford's mother, Barbara, and his sisters Debbie and Paula joined the party also. Joanne had spent the day cooking all sorts of vegetables and meats and had piled the table high. "I was so afraid I wouldn't have enough," she said. "On the American TV programs, they always show so much food on the tables. People over here talk about it all the time. Just how much do the Americans eat?"

Clifford led a tour of their new timber-style home, beautiful and unique. Kiddo's favorite was the Irish low room, a step down from the main floor, reserved for music and gab. A small poteen jug adorned the mantle. Too bad Black's breathing problems from his recent illness prevented a songfest.

Clifford and Joanne presented Kiddo with a shillelagh made by Joanne's father, Mervyn. The Blackthorn walking stick was perfect for her weak knees, and the thorns could do serious damage to an attacker. Another perfect gift from these generous people.

As the night wore down, the young Irish lads, fascinated by the

American Cowboy in their midst, became brave. Glenn shyly asked if he could wear Black's hat. Black took off his Stetson and plopped it on Glenn's head. Then he slipped out of his pointy-toed boots. Scott wasted no time thrusting his feet inside. Two happy munchkins took turns, sloshing up and down the kitchen in oversized cowboy gear, drawing fast and shooting each other with their fingers. Kiddo said the scene reminded her of little women playing dress-up beside Mother's trunk.

Black blew the smoke from his finger gun after a good shot. Then he quickly sketched a cowboy for them, using Holly's colored pencils nearby.

"So, the kids know about cowboys, huh?" Russell asked.

"Oh yes," Joanne answered. "Those old American shows about the wild west are on TV, mostly Saturday mornings. They didn't know they were going to meet a *real* cowboy, though, did you boys?"

Young Scott shot his brother one last time, then placed the Stetson back on Black's head and fell into him with a loose hug.

"Are you Roy Rogers?" he asked.

I glanced at my father-in-law.

Black looked like a movie star with those piercing eyes, that wavy gray hair combed back and that grin. What a charming grin, like he knew a secret.

Black winked at Kiddo as he answered.

"No, but I almost was."

HAPPY TRAILS

Written by Dale Evans, 1950. Recorded by Roy Rogers and Dale Evans, released in 1952 on RCA Victor Records. Theme song for the 1950s radio and television programs starring Roy Rogers, "King of the Cowboys," and Dale Evans, "Queen of the West."

Black & Kiddo, 2004.

NOTES

PROLOGUE
1. Charles Marion Russell quote from his 1917 poem, penned alongside his painting of a longhorn skull:

The west is dead, my Friend.
But writers hold the seed,
And what they saw
Will live and grow
Again to those who Read.

RED SHOES
2. Different versions of "Red Shoes" won first place awards for creative nonfiction at both Ozarks Creative Writers (OCW) Conference in Eureka Springs, Arkansas, and Oklahoma Writers Federation Inc. (OWFI) Conference in Oklahoma City, Oklahoma.

GANDY-DANCERS BALL
3. McSpadden, Marguerite (Graham). *Papa Built a Railroad.* Amarillo, Texas, 1992.

T IS FOR TEXAS
4. Westbrook, Ray. "The A-J Remembers." *Lubbock Avalanche-Journal, lubbockonline.com.* January 10, 2011.

Burkholder, Joyce Halsey. Odessa, Texas. Telephone interview. 2012. "Nine-cent malts were our specialty." Joyce's brother, Marcus "Hop" Halsey served in the Texas state legislature. After Blackie, Hop took over the radio broadcasts, singing from Mark Halsey Drug store. "That really took off after he returned from the war. 'Drug Store Cowboys' was the name of Hop's band."

PUTTIN' ON THE RITZ
5. Postcard signature: Jno is an abbreviation of the Latin Johannes. In medieval Latin, this could be written as Jhohannes, abbreviated Jho. Over the years, the second letter (h) lost its ascender and came to be written as n. Hence, Jno, short for John.

THIS LAND IS MY LAND
6. Black family history: The Black family was of German heritage, from the Palatinate of the Rhine in the Baden-Wurttemberg area. Seeking freedom of religion, the first of the family to America landed in the 1700s in Pennsylvania. This immigrant changed his name from Johannes Schwartz to John Black. The family migrated to Ohio in 1810, then west to Iowa in 1860 and on to Kansas in 1871, following the American frontier as it opened for settlement.

In the latter part of the 1800s, three generations of Black men (John, his son Henry, and his grandson Albert "A. B.") owned dry goods stores in Severy, Kansas. A. B. also bought and sold real estate and worked as an insurance agent. He rode in the Oklahoma Land Rush in 1889, treasuring the new saddle acquired for the event.

At age 21, A. B. married Zera Belle Davidson, the only child of a wealthy widow. After seven years of marriage, Zera died during the birth of their first child, Floyd. Zera's mother took over care of the baby.

Two years later, A. B. married Minnie Dwyer. She birthed three sons, but only one survived infancy: Corwin Ercel Black. When Minnie became ill with consumption, a doctor suggested higher altitude. A. B. took her and young Corwin to Pikes Peak, Colorado in a covered wagon, using his rifle to confront ranchers who threatened them, calling them squatters. With no improvement in Minnie's health, they returned to Kansas. As a last resort, the doctor suggested drier air, so A. B. moved his family to Albuquerque in New Mexico Territory. He bought two sandy lots on South Walter Street and erected a tent house on each of them, living in one and renting the other. Aided by Minnie's younger sister Josephine (Jo), A. B. cared for his family as best he could. In 1909 Minnie died. Her body was shipped on the train and buried next to her two sons and A. B.'s first wife in the Twin Grove Cemetery near Severy, Kansas. A. B., Jo, and his son Corwin, eleven at the time, returned to Severy by wagon.

Within a year, A. B. married Josephine Dwyer, Minnie's sister. He was 46 years old, had buried two wives and two of his four sons. Jo was 26 and ready to begin her own family. A daughter, Hermona, was born, then a son, Lynn, later called Red. With this new family, A. B. decided a fresh start was needed. In 1913, he sold two houses in Severy, then loaded his family and belongings into a covered wagon and headed southwest. His first-born, Floyd, didn't make the trip. With money left in trust from his mother, Floyd had enrolled at the University of Kansas and later completed a law degree at Stanford University.

The family traveled through Oklahoma, then west along an old cattle trail into New Mexico, which had become a state the previous year and offered free land. The family settled on a homestead claim northeast of Des Moines about ten miles, built a small house, bought cattle, and became ranchers. The "claim place," a half-section (320 acres) of native grassland, lay at the head of Traversiere Canyon. Another son was born, Norman, and then the last, the runt, Russell, called Razz. They proved up their claim and obtained the land patent in 1917, signed by President Woodrow Wilson. Eventually, A. B. bought more land just north of the little town of Des Moines, the "home place," where they built a true home and thriving ranch—the Black Family Ranch, C Lazy K brand.

When the widow of A. B. Black, Josephine, died in 1943, her will legally deeded a portion of the Black land to the Des Moines Cemetery.

GIT ALONG LITTLE DOGIES

7. For more stories of the colorful history of northeastern New Mexico see:

Click, Mrs. N. H. (Cora). *Us Nesters in the Land of Enchantment.* Des Moines, New Mexico, 1968.

Centennial Book Committee. *Folsom 1888-1988, Then and Now.* Folsom, New Mexico, 1988.

8. Max Evans. Several years after the young cowboys' adventure, Black's cousin, Afton Thornton, known to the locals as Filthy McNasty, married Max's ex-wife, Helene Caterlin, and helped raise Max's daughter. That was way before Max Evans named that part of New Mexico the "Hi Lo country" and made it famous in his books and movies. Black's and Max's rancher friend with the fine horses, Wiley Hittson, Jr., became "Big Boy" Mattson, lead character in Max's book and film, *The Hi Lo Country*.

ARKANSAS TRAVELER

9. Arkansas was the "Land of Opportunity" from 1953 until 1995, when legislation was passed changing the nickname to "The Natural State," to reflect the growing tourism industry. Act 1352 cited "unsurpassed scenery, clear lakes, free-flowing streams, magnificent rivers, meandering bayous, delta bottomlands, forested mountains and abundant fish and wildlife." *Encyclopedia of Arkansas History and Culture* (online).

10. James R. (Dick) and Delphia Murray were still living on their dairy farm in Cincinnati, almost sixty years after moving from New Mexico to Arkansas when, in 2010, Dick was killed by a tornado while milking cows.

TURN! TURN! TURN!

11. "Your Heritage from Frank Lloyd Wright." *House Beautiful*, October, 1959.
Nichols, Cheryl and Barry, Helen. "The Arkansas Designs of E. Fay Jones 1956–1997." Arkansas Historic Preservation Program, Department of Arkansas Heritage. Little Rock, Arkansas:

"In October of 1959, *House Beautiful* was the first national magazine to publish Jones's work. In that issue, the magazine featured a house Jones had designed in 1958 for Dr. and Mrs. Calvin Bain in Prairie Grove, Arkansas. The article focused on the home's "open plan" as well as on the architect's exquisite use of simple natural materials, concluding with a statement that could apply to a majority of Fay Jones designs: "This ability to get the most out of the simplest materials, combined with the magnificent development of interior space, resulted in true refinement at modest cost." According to Gus (Mrs. Fay) Jones, the magazine article about the Bain residence brought more than 600 unsolicited requests for house plans and it was just the first of several House Beautiful articles during the late 1950s and early 1960s that featured Fay Jones houses."

12. Many years later, after Jim Sharp had become James Sharp, MD, an eye surgeon, his daughter Kimberly Vale was paired with Russell's son Jeffrey in a physics lab at the University of Arkansas. They dated for a long while before discovering that their fathers were friends. Later, Jeffrey and Vale gifted Black and Kiddo with triplet great-grandchildren.

CALIFORNIA DREAMIN'

13. Brown, Connell J. *Cattle on a Thousand Hills: A History of the Cattle Industry in Arkansas*. University of Arkansas Press, Fayetteville, 1996.

p.111: "Four purebred Maine-Anjou heifers arrived at the Sundowner Ranch, Prairie Grove. These were part of the first import by air from England." 1974.

p.112: "Sundowner Ranch's Maine-Anjou sale averaged $5,051 on 150.5 lots. Sundowner's first Simmental sale averaged $3,771 on 129 lots. Their Chianina sale averaged $1,272 on 90.5 lots, at Prairie Grove, on September 19, 1974. Two purebred embryo transplants sold for $40,000."

STAND BY YOUR MAN

14. *Northwest Arkansas Times*, Fayetteville, Arkansas. November 29, 1973.
Robert D. (Bob) Cheyne, 46, former Sports Information Director for the University of Arkansas, was found innocent of income tax evasion. He had been charged with receiving funds from a New York advertising agency for sports shows, money that should have gone to the University. He had held his UA position for twenty-two years before resigning in 1969, when charges were made.

15. "Li'l Alice," a first-person version of Kiddo spanking the possum, was broadcast on *Tales from the South*, a show affiliated with National Public Radio, produced by Paula Martin Morell. Little Rock, Arkansas. May, 2011.

AMAZING GRACE

16. Deane, Ernie. *Ozarks Country*. The Ozarks Mountaineer, Branson, Missouri, 1988.

Excerpts from pgs.112–13, "Former Cowboy Now an Ozarks Sculptor":

". . . Keith in the past eight years has quickly developed into one of the most skilled and imaginative wood sculptors in this part of the country. . . In many ways his sculptures, mostly in wood but some cast in bronze, remind the viewer of the western works of Charles Russell and Frederic Remington.

. . . So far, possibly the greatest recognition has come from members of the motion picture industry who filmed much of the TV show, "The Blue and the Gray," within a mile of his riverside ranch. Keith captured in his sketchbook the violent action of Union and Confederate cavalrymen. Then, in walnut, he locked two opposing soldiers and their horses in mortal combat with sabers. From this original, a limit of 25 castings was made, 13.5 inches high, tagged each for $3,500.

. . . Every piece of wood is carefully selected with an eye to use of grain, colors, knots, etc. An example is a portrait in cherry of his wife's favorite riding horse. The animal's mane was of lighter color than its skin hair. After a long search, Keith found a chunk of wood with just the shade of lighter colored streak he needed for the mane.

. . . moved to the Ozarks 20 years ago in search of water and green grass for their milk cows. Both now laugh about their half- load of 'skinny milk cows that never tasted green grass until coming to Arkansas.' . . . You'll not meet a more modest man, even so, or in my opinion one with a greater feel for the beauty of wood in art."

WHEN IRISH EYES ARE SMILING

17. McSpadden, Clifford. *The McSpadden Family History 1600– 2016 (And still counting, thank God!)*. Banbridge, Northern Ireland, 2016.

CMS Global Limited is Clifford's consulting company, specializing in the renewable energy market. Banbridge, Northern Ireland.

ACKNOWLEDGMENTS

The journey that led to the publication of this book began over twenty years ago in Ireland, with Black's answer when asked if he were Roy Rogers, "No, but I almost was." I then realized there were hidden family stories, in addition to the ones I already knew by heart, and began to ferret them out. After their deaths I found his writings and her journals. Though I lived close and in concert with them for decades, I never knew Mom kept journals, nor that Pop wrote stories. I am forever grateful to my beloved in-laws for taking me on this journey and to their sons for trusting me with these primary sources which have provided the soul of this book.

Eight years ago, as I lessened my involvement with our family nursery business, I wandered into a writing class offered by the Osher Lifelong Learning Institute (OLLI), through the continuing education department of the University of Arkansas. In this class, taught by memoir guru Marilyn H. Collins, I wrote the first Black & Kiddo stories. Marilyn became my writing mentor and friend. Two other writers in that class, Lavania Fritts and Melba Payne, became ardent supporters of my work. The four of us joined regional writing groups and attended conferences, traveling together to other states. Who knew I would find such wonderful gal pals at this stage of life? A big thanks for constant cheerleading and bucket loads of fun to these women, especially to Lavania for keeping my chakras balanced and to Melba for the original subtitle (though cut by the publisher): "A True Story of Extraordinary, Ordinary People."

My first critique group was Northwest Arkansas Writers Workshop, led by western author Dusty Richards and romance author

Velda Brotherton. I am grateful to these veterans for sharing their extensive knowledge. In this group, I became friends with a phenomenal group of women writers, "Sisterhood of the Traveling Pen"—Linda Apple, Pamela Foster, Jan Morrill Vanek, Patti Stith, and Ruth Burkett Weeks. Always ready to go the extra mile, they have given me great advice, support, and friendship. Thank you.

After publication, I joined and still meet with the literary Writers Guild of Arkansas, anchored by Maeve Maddox, Barbara Youree, and Marilyn Collins. Heartfelt gratitude to them and other members who took time to read my work and offer suggestions—Raymona Anderson, Lorraine Heartfeld, Pat Prinsloo, Vic Fountain, Robin Mero, Denton and Kay Gay.

I am also grateful for the superb critiques received from members of the Ozarks Mountain Guild Writers (OMG!)—Duke and Kimberly Pennell, Lori Ericson, Mike Miller, Russell Gayer, Jim Davis, Meg Dendler, Julie James, and Alice White.

And in her own lane, Nancy Hartney has been a trusted friend in all three of the above groups. I can always count on her honest feedback. For taking a personal interest in my project, I am grateful to Missourians Diane Yates and Karen Nelson.

Thanks to my beta readers not mentioned elsewhere who read the manuscript and offered valuable critiques—Richard C. Black, Dr. Gerald Klingaman, Hubert Ferguson of Boxley Valley, Chris and Glenna Lyon of Oklahoma City and Rudy, Arkansas. For vetting specific sections, thanks to Keith A. Black and his wife, Lisa Horowitz, of Los Angeles, Dino Cornay of Folsom, New Mexico, and to Clifford McSpadden of Banbridge, Northern Ireland.

For early advice and encouragement, I am grateful to the graceful Mary Joyce Young. To Lorraine Cathro of Calgary, thanks for years of heartening emails from Canada. To Wyoming publisher (High Plains Press) Nancy Curtis, thanks for your openness, honesty, and hand-holding. Special thanks to Ollie Reed Jr. of Albuquerque for the introduction to Max Evans and to Max himself for the wonderful blurb and for revealing the true identity of Filthy McNasty.

Heartfelt thanks to Anne Hillerman of Santa Fe who took time away from writing her best sellers to read my entire manuscript and for giving me such gracious comments. She is a true woman of the West, a writer helping other writers.

Thanks to all the Black and McSpadden cousins who shared family memories, especially Dr. Bobbie Jean Snodgrass of Lubbock and Amy Helen Gilliland of Amarillo. Amy Helen died before the project was completed, but I am sure she is gabbing with Black & Kiddo about it now. I am grateful to Mrs. Truva McSpadden of Little Rock for sharing her memories.

Thanks to the professionals who made my book better: Dr. Terry Ropp of Bugscuffle, Arkansas, for two rounds of proofreading; Linda M. Hasselstrom of Hermosa, South Dakota, for "Writing Conversations" and the developmental editing which gave my book its structure; Amy Ashford of Baton Rouge, Louisiana, for an outstanding interior layout which incorporates the many elements of this text. Huge kudos to Erin Wood, my wonderful editor at Et Alia Press, and her staff. Erin's excellent editing skills have made the storyline hum. I have found my "Nan Graham" and am forever grateful.

To my professional granddaughter who is so much like her Gi-Gi (Kiddo)—Rebecca Black, graphic designer—thank you for the beautiful cover which truly reflects the story. The vivid color and trendy design showcase your awesome skills. Special thanks, also, to my youngest granddaughter, Jasmine Black, for many hours of exacting digital photo restoration. You did an outstanding job of preparing the pictures for publication. I loved working with both of you on this family story of your great-grandparents. I am glad you both inherited G-Poppie's artistic talents.

I am grateful to my sweet, generous brother-in-law, Richard Corwin Black, for his excellent photography, for letting me mine his memories, and for sharing the family archives. Thanks also to his wife, Louise Alexander.

And to my own family, John Stephen Black and Lana Lyon, Jeffrey Richard Black and Vale Sharp, and grandchildren Michael, Rebecca, Jasmine, Theodore, and Jackson: huge bouquets for years of understanding and moral support as this project took so much of my time. You are loved. Remember.

Finally, down to this part, the best part, the part that gives me life. There aren't enough words to thank the one who still calls me "the goodest of girls," the man who listens, laughs, and cries as I read my writing to him, who never wavers in his support of me, who brings me humor, joy, solidness, and a grounded life—Black & Kiddo's youngest, Russell Owen Black.

Brenda Clem Black is a fifth-generation Arkansawyer, holds degrees from the University of Arkansas, and still lives in the Ozarks. A nursery entrepreneur and former family and children's therapist, she continues to labor beside her husband in the family business, Westwood Gardens, Inc., now powered by their grown sons. Though a life-long award-winning writer with shorter works published in anthologies and read on NPR, *Black & Kiddo* is her first book—the product of eight years of researching, writing, and twenty years of thinking. Connect with Brenda on Facebook or find her at www.BrendaClemBlack.com.

Brenda the storyteller with grandchildren. 2004.
(L to R) Rebecca and Michael and triplets: Jackson, Theodore, and Jasmine.
Photograph by Andrew Kilgore.

CPSIA information can be obtained
at www.ICGtesting.com
Printed in the USA
FFHW02n0552070818
47668433-51283FF

9 781944 528959